THE LANGUAGE OF POLITICS
in the Age of
WILKES AND BURKE

STUDIES IN POLITICAL HISTORY

Editor: Michael Hurst
Fellow of St John's College, Oxford

THE LANGUAGE
OF POLITICS
in the Age
of Wilkes and Burke

by

JAMES T. BOULTON

Reader in English Literature
in the University of Nottingham

LONDON: Routledge & Kegan Paul
TORONTO: University of Toronto Press
1963

First published 1963
in Great Britain by
Routledge & Kegan Paul Ltd
and in Canada by
University of Toronto Press

Printed in Great Britain by
Richard Clay & Co. Ltd

Edited by James T. Boulton
A PHILOSOPHICAL ENQUIRY INTO THE ORIGIN
OF OUR IDEAS OF THE SUBLIME
AND BEAUTIFUL
by Edmund Burke

FOR
H.B.
AND
A.M.P.B.

EDITOR'S NOTE

UNLIKE so many history series this one will not attempt a complete coverage of a specific span of time, with a division of labour for the contributors based on a neat parcelling out of centuries. Nor will it, in the main, be a collection of political monographs. Rather, the aim is to bring out books based on new, or thoroughly reinterpreted material ranging over quite a wide field of chronology and geography. Some will be more general than others, as is to be expected when biography is included alongside of detailed treatment of some comparatively short period of crisis like the appeasement of the Axis Powers. Nevertheless, whatever mode of presentation may have been appropriate, each work should provide an exposition of its subject in context and thus enable the reader to acquire new knowledge amidst things he knows, or could have known.

MICHAEL HURST

St. John's College,
Oxford.

CONTENTS

ix

PREFACE

Two convictions prompted the writing of this book: first, that the political literature of the later part of the eighteenth century has been undeservedly neglected in works of literary criticism; and second, that the insights obtained from a literary-critical examination of these—and any other—political writings should be considered by historians and political theorists as significant to their own special enquiries. The former conviction needs no verification: it is a fact. The latter is more contentious, and for that reason it is briefly argued in the introductory essay and provides the theme for the concluding chapter.

The choice of the two periods of political controversy—1769–71, centring on Wilkes's election, and 1790–93, with the debate on Burke's *Reflections* as its focal point—was determined both by their historical importance and by the stature of the writers involved in them. They did not, however, warrant investigation with the same degree of thoroughness, hence the unequal size of the two parts of this book. The first period lacks the cohesion which the publication of the *Reflections* provided for the second, and it did not engage a comparable number of talented contributors whose work merits critical assessment; nevertheless, the participation of three such writers as Junius, Samuel Johnson, and Edmund Burke is reason enough for discussing it, even though its byways are not explored. The historical 'survey' with which each part opens is—especially in the case of the earlier controversy—intended to remind the non-professional historian of some essential facts; the second survey is necessarily more extensive, and it also offered more scope for originality.

The publication of this book enables me to acknowledge many debts. The award by the Durham Colleges in the University of Durham of a research studentship, made tenable at

xi

Oxford fourteen years ago, brought me into contact with that most stimulating of scholars, the late Humphry House. Some of the work begun under his guidance is incorporated in the chapters which follow. To others I owe valuable critical appraisals of various sections of the book; among these are the General Editor of the series, Mr. M. C. Hurst, Professor Irvin Ehrenpreis, Mr. Charles Parkin, Dr. A. E. Rodway, Professor John C. Weston, Jr., and, in particular, Mr. W. R. Fryer, whose expert knowledge I have never consulted in vain. I am also grateful to Dr. Rodway for checking the proofs and to Mrs. Sheila Dryden for excellent secretarial assistance. For any errors which remain I am, of course, solely responsible.

My indebtedness to my wife is beyond measure, as it is to my parents, to whom the book is dedicated.

J. T. B.

University of Nottingham.

ACKNOWLEDGMENTS

I GRATEFULLY acknowledge the permission given by the Earl Fitzwilliam to quote from his collection of Burke manuscripts deposited in the Northamptonshire Record Office, Delapre Abbey. I acknowledge too his Lordship's permission, together with that of the Trustees of the Wentworth Woodhouse Settled Estates, to quote from the Burke manuscripts and the Papers, Correspondence, etc., of 2nd Earl Fitzwilliam in the custody of the City Librarian of Sheffield.

I also wish to acknowledge permission to reprint material originally published in article form. Chapters II, VII, and VIII are revised versions of articles published in the *Durham University Journal*, *University of Nottingham Renaissance and Modern Studies*, and *Essays in Criticism* respectively.

INTRODUCTION

EW periods of history have raised such passion among
professional historians as the reign of George III; the non-
professional who ventures into the field does so with some misgivings. He feels like an intruder in a battle between the old
pretenders and the young, between the Whig historians and
those stigmatised by Professor Butterfield as the new Tories, 'the
Presbyterian literalists and counters of heads'.[1] Yet something
remains to be said and from a new angle—that of the literary
critic.

The truth of this claim is borne out by the fact that none of
the writings which I propose to discuss, from two of the most
significant political controversies of the eighteenth century, has
been subjected to thorough literary-critical analysis. In other
words, the fundamental verbal examination of writings which,
in varying degrees, have influenced thought and action from
their own day to ours has been neglected by both literary critics
and historians (in their published work at any rate). To take the
example of Junius's *Letters*, which are occasionally touched on:
Mr. Steven Watson, in his recent book *The Reign of George III*,
speaks of the 'balanced but hysterical prose' in which Junius
'savaged those in authority'.[2] It is an astute remark—though it
may not be immediately apparent that prose can be at once
balanced and hysterical—but more literary analysis than Mr.
Watson had room for was needed to support it and to demonstrate *how* Junius 'helped to convince the literate classes that
Grafton's administration really constituted a threat to English

---

[1] *George III and the Historians* (1957), p. 274. (The place of publication of
all works quoted is London unless stated otherwise.)
[2] Op. cit. (Oxford, 1960), p. 145.

liberty'. Again, while Donald Greene's excellent study, *The Politics of Samuel Johnson* (1960), has rectified many misconceptions about Johnson's political attitudes, it has not fully satisfied the need for a close examination of his use of persuasive language in a political cause. As for Burke, no one since John Morley has attempted anything approaching a thoroughgoing scrutiny of the *Thoughts on the Cause of the Present Discontents*, the work which historians use almost as a touchstone for determining the folly of their predecessors' interpretation of the first part of George III's reign and for displaying their own percipience. The *Reflections on the Revolution in France*, Paine's *Rights of Man*, and the others have remained similarly unexamined.

The assumptions which underlie such neglect appear to be chiefly two: firstly, that from a literary standpoint the political writings examined in this book offer little that is aesthetically rewarding, or perhaps that such writings do not come within the traditional field of *belles lettres* and are therefore not worthy of serious critical attention; and secondly, that from the historian's standpoint literary criticism has little to do with matters of historical investigation. I do not challenge the first here—the analyses which follow aim to reveal the special qualities of the writings in question—but the second is worth some consideration. For my own basic premise is that while the purpose of the literary critic is not consciously to act as an accessory to the historian, historical knowledge is necessarily incomplete and handicapped without the contribution he can make.

His distinctive function is to elucidate the features of a piece of writing which produce permanent interest, pleasure, or attention, and the literary techniques employed to achieve this result. He will ask of a political pamphlet—as of any other kind of literature—questions such as whether human passions of a permanent or merely of a transient nature are involved, whether the quality of the writing provides the reader of any age with an exciting aesthetic experience, or whether the writer's attitude to his immediate problem is of continuing relevance to the human condition. This is admittedly an oversimplified view, but it is on grounds such as these that the literary critic will make his strictly literary judgment. He is not, then, interested in the past merely for its 'pastness' but there are nevertheless—in addition to the features already mentioned—matters which he must take account of that are obviously significant for the historian. He may wish to enquire into the conditions under which the work was written, the impetus that brought it into being and the writer's response to that impetus, the audience being addressed and the extent to which the chosen idiom, imagery, or prose style would affect it, or the precise meaning the writer's language would carry for the original readers. An enquiry of this complexity will provide valuable insights into the temper of a particular age, the patterns of words and ideas to which men responded most readily, or the kind of literary sensibility which was generally accessible to a writer appealing to a certain body of readers. Especially, then, with literature of a persuasive character, the critic is faced with the whole question of the methods of communication between men with ideas and those to whom the ideas are directed; when he examines and assesses these methods—because they involve a consideration of the intellectual, moral, cultural, and above all, emotional resources of the writer and his audience—he is dealing with evidence as important to the historian as any naked event or bare idea.

Briefly to support such claims we may start from Collingwood's assertion in *The Idea of History* that the historian is concerned with both 'the outside and the inside of an event', with the facts relating to physical activity and with those elements 'which can only be described in terms of thought'.[1] Historical knowledge, he asserts, consists both in possessing the first kind of facts and in 'discerning the thought which is the inner side of the event'.[2] If, then, an event is to be 'historically known' it must be apprehended in its entirety by a mind capable of informing itself of the thought-processes which led up to and were involved in it. (The term 'event' here must, of course, be taken to include not simply the happenings we call the Middlesex elections of 1768–69 or the French Revolution but also their repercussions on the thought and action of the literate population in this country. In short, both the occurrence and its consequences in which political writers were implicated—and which they in part directed—must be understood.) It surely follows from this that the process by which a man—particularly one eminent in practical politics like Burke—formulated his thought

[1] Op. cit. (Oxford, 1946), p. 213.   [2] Ibid., p. 222.

in writing, the reasons that led him to select a particular idiom, to adopt a certain attitude to his material and to his readers, to employ a peculiar tone of voice—in brief to use a specific style: it follows that this process is properly a matter of concern to the historian. Why Burke did not adopt the style of, say, Junius or Godwin, to give a crude example, should be an issue of first importance. The means by which such an issue is decided are those of literary criticism; they reveal much about Burke's mental processes, about the character of his thought (through analysis of his mode of expression), and thus about Burke himself. It is self-evident that such understanding is essential.

What the literary critic does is to bring his own expertise to bear on the nature of the thought embodied in a written statement and, among other things, to estimate by means of comparison the success with which that thought is communicated. He is interested—as the historian should be—in giving an answer, in terms of the manipulation of language, to the question why and how Burke rather than Junius or Johnson was the most influential writer of the 1770s, or why and how Paine's *Rights of Man* was more effective than the sixty or more other replies to the *Reflections*. Here again, by setting himself to analyse techniques of communication, he can help to enrich historical awareness.

At this point, however, Collingwood may be thought to enter a caveat with his remark:

> the mere fact that someone has expressed his thoughts in writing, and that we possess his works, does not enable us to understand his thoughts. In order that we may be able to do so, we must come to the reading of them prepared with an experience sufficiently like his own to make those thoughts organic to it.[1]

While this is indeed a warning to the literary critic not to claim too much for his insights by themselves, it should also make the historian aware that part of his essential equipment is some understanding of a writer's attitude to language and of his literary training, since such things are vitally present in the total personality engaged in writing a political pamphlet. (Particularly should one remember this in the eighteenth century: to

---

[1] *The Idea of History*, p. 300.

recall that before Burke had entered into any political controversy he had published a work of aesthetic criticism, and that behind Johnson's pamphlets of the 1770s lay vast literary experience is merely one way of underlining this obvious assertion.) We should recognise, in fact, just how extensive are the demands made by Collingwood on the historian. The knowledge of literature that a writer draws on to invigorate both his own expression and the reader's response; the awareness he reveals of the resources of language; the kind of material he uses in imagery or symbolism; the methods he employs to translate ideas into vivid and meaningful experiences for his audience: these are only some of the manifestations of the 'experience' a writer brings to the articulation of his thought. The historian who is aware of such complexities cannot dispense with the findings of literary criticism.

Furthermore, though it is clearly the job of the historian to determine to what extent a political pamphlet truthfully reflects the facts of the situation it claims to comment on, it is also necessary for him to recognise—if he has the original audience in mind—that in one important sense this kind of factual accuracy is of secondary importance; the beliefs which the pamphleteer tried to persuade his readers to accept assume supreme significance. In this sense it is immaterial whether, in the *Present Discontents*, Burke is imagining the situation he writes about, whether or not the Court Party or the 'King's friends' ever existed in the first years of George III's reign, or whether he is perpetrating what Mr. Romney Sedgwick has called an 'elaborate fiction'.[1] Equally is it in this sense irrelevant whether Junius is accurate in his assessment of the English situation or Paine in his of the French. For it is a truism that people respond to a given situation because of what they *believe* to be the truth about it rather than what necessarily is the truth. Thus, if Burke, Junius, or Johnson persuade their readers to accept their interpretation of the circumstances in 1770 subsequent actions will be effectively determined by literary as well as by factual considerations. The problem implicit here is one that offers further scope for the literary critic to try to define the character of the persuasion exercised by the political writers and to estimate their effect on the prevailing climate of opinion. His function in this respect

[1] *Letters from George III to Lord Bute* (1939), p. xviii.

5

is important because he is concerning himself with factors which mould the response of the reading public to subsequent events.

It is also an issue of some consequence to decide whether a writer who is occupied with an actual (or even an imaginary) situation of the moment is addressing himself solely to his contemporaries or writing for posterity as well. In either case both the style and the perspective the man has of his material are directly affected, and they provide clues to his intentions. Consequently, unless a fundamentally literary approach is made to a piece of writing, the author's purpose may be misunderstood because of an inaccurate response to his style, tone, and perspective. Burke's view in the *Present Discontents*, for example, is as much to the future as to the past, and it is possible to argue that Mr. Sedgwick's description of this pamphlet as 'literary afterthoughts'[1] (in the sense that Burke was justifying past conduct) is a result of the inaccuracy just mentioned. Literary analysis reveals many stylistic features which suggest that immediate and contemporary issues were not the sum of Burke's objectives.

What follows is an attempt to apply literary-critical techniques to pamphlets which, for the importance of their political ideas, their energy, their distinctive use of language, or their value for comparative criticism deserve attention from students of both history and literature. No attempt will be made to cater for what might be supposed to be the different needs of these two groups of readers; it is assumed that, at the level of fundamental analysis, they are broadly identical. Neither will any conscious attempt be made to underpin separately the claims already advanced, as if individually they were of cardinal importance; they are intended to provide one general frame of reference which may increase the value of the ensuing chapters for some readers. If Collingwood is near the mark in claiming that 'historical knowledge has for its proper object thought . . . the act of thinking itself',[2] then the approach made here requires no further justification, since it concerns itself entirely with examining the written evidence of thought and various attempts to influence thinking. And, finally, Samuel Butler

[1] *Letters from George III to Lord Bute*, p. xliii.
[2] *The Idea of History*, p. 305.

6

(writing about Darwin) may be allowed to furnish a salutary reminder:

> It is not he who first conceives an idea, nor he who sets it on its legs and makes it go on all fours, but he who makes other people accept the main conclusion, whether on right grounds or on wrong ones, who has done the greatest work as regards the promulgation of an opinion.[1]

[1] *Life and Habit* (1916 edn.), p. 276.

PART ONE

Political Controversy
1769–1771

I

WILKES AND THE MIDDLESEX
ELECTION: A BRIEF SURVEY

'THAT devil Wilkes' (to quote George III) was notorious from 1763 onwards. In that year, because of the outspoken attacks on the Court and Government in his journal, *The North Briton*, he was arrested. Wilkes took his stand, however, on the illegality of general warrants and on his privilege as the Member for Aylesbury, and was liberated; he also took his opportunity to present himself to the public as a symbol of the individual battling for liberty against the tyranny of the Crown. Later in the same year the Government retrieved the position to some extent when the Commons voted the famous *North Briton No. 45* a seditious libel and removed the protection of privilege from Wilkes. Whereupon he fled to France and remained there until 1768. In his absence (in February 1764) he was tried for seditious libel and for publishing the pornographic *Essay on Women*; since he was contumacious, his punishment was outlawry.

Almost at once on his return to England Wilkes stood as a candidate in the Middlesex parliamentary election and topped the poll.[1] However, the convictions for seditious libel, publishing pornographic literature, and contumacy still stood against him; he was arrested and sentenced to imprisonment. But he was now

---

[1] For an informative analysis of the political repercussions of Wilkes's return and subsequent career, see Lucy S. Sutherland, *The City of London and the Opposition to Government, 1768–1774* (1959). See also George Rudé, *Wilkes and Liberty* (Oxford, 1962).

a Member of Parliament and claimed privilege; moreover, economic distress in and around London was widespread, strikes were numerous, and there were disorderly, potentially violent crowds who regarded Wilkes as a symbol of revolt against injustice. Nevertheless, the Government stood firm and, on the grounds that he was still an outlaw when he was elected, the Commons expelled Wilkes from his seat in February 1769. He was at once returned unopposed by his constituency; again he was expelled; a third time he was returned and a third time expelled. At the fourth election candidates were found to stand against him, but out of a total poll of just over 1,400 Wilkes received more than 1,100 votes and his three opponents the rest. The Commons were now faced with the most serious challenge to their authority; they resolved the problem, in May 1769, by declaring that Wilkes was ineligible as a candidate because he was in prison when nominated; his nearest rival, Colonel Luttrell (who received 296 votes), they deemed to have been elected.

It is clear that out of a situation which delighted the Opposition because of the embarrassment caused to the Government, a constitutional issue of real moment had been raised. Were the Commons right to declare Luttrell elected on a minority vote, a fifth of the votes cast? As Mr. Steven Watson observes, the issue turns on the degree of coercion, whether from the executive or from popular pressures, that is thought to be legitimate.[1] Some contemporaries felt that the pressure exerted by the mobs and organised Wilkites to secure Wilkes's election was unconstitutional and that therefore the administration's action was justified. Others believed that this action revealed an executive, backed by court influence, wielding too great a power for the healthy functioning of the legislature, and consequently that the administration had wrongfully arrogated to itself the power to nominate a member of the Commons. Broadly speaking, these are the questions debated by the pamphleteers whose writings will be discussed.

There can be no doubt but that the furore over the election was a godsend for the Opposition, despite their reluctance to be associated with the disreputable Wilkes; as Burke told Rockingham in September 1770:

[1] *The Reign of George III*, p. 138.

We have never had, and we never shall have a matter every way so well calculated to engage [the people]; and if the spirit that was excited upon this occasion were sufferd to flatten and evaporate, you would find it difficult to collect it again, when you might have the greatest occasion for it.[1]

Moreover, the energy (modified in the case of the Rockingham group) with which Opposition parties engaged in the business of promoting petitions to Parliament for redress and to the King for dissolution, is evidence of their opportunism. Wilkes as an individual proved a liability in some respects. Burke, for example, was relieved by the presence, at a meeting to consider the Yorkshire petition, of 'a considerable Number of the Clergy ... because some people were willing to cast a stain of prophaneness upon our Conduct, from our supposed Patronage of Wilkes'.[2] But the principles involved were larger than the fortunes of one man; the Rockingham view of them is contained in part of a proposal for the terms of a petition included in a letter from the Marquess to Burke, 29 June 1769:

> *Might it not set forth*—that the great and continual increase of the power and influence of the Crown in the course of this century (if the Crown should unfortunately be led by weak—wicked and arbitrary ministers and surrounded by evil counsellors) would operate most dangerously to the Constitution.[3]

This is the theme which, in some shape or other, constantly reappears in the letters of the Rockingham Whigs, who seem to have been thoroughly convinced, even if without much foundation, that in this 'great Crisis'[4] they were the only opposition group acting on principles which were other than self-centred. Undoubtedly part of the intention of the *Present Discontents* was self-justification; it was to show

> the ground upon which the Party stands; and how different its constitution, as well as the persons who compose it are from the Bedfords, and Grenvilles, and other knots, who are combined for no publick purpose; but only as a means of furthering with joint strength, their private and individual advantage.[5]

[1] Ed. Lucy S. Sutherland, *The Correspondence of Edmund Burke* (Cambridge, 1960), II, 155. (Burke's *Correspondence* is used as the main evidence for this 'outline' because of the leading part he played in the pamphlet debate.)

[2] Ibid., II, 96.   [3] Ibid., II, 38

[4] Ibid., II, 54.   [5] Ibid., II, 101.

At least it cannot be denied that the Rockingham group had one objective to which they consistently directed their efforts: the destruction of what they chose to think was a Court Party or, as Burke called it, 'the Bute faction'.[1] Whatever may be the truth about the reality of such a party, the frequency with which the Rockingham Whigs refer to it is at least proof that it existed for them if only as an impetus to united effort. Bute for them was 'the Thane',[2] and moves to quieten the Opposition by bringing men from various groups into the administration were seen as attempts to make yet another government dependent on 'the Court System'.[3] Burke writes to the Marquess in October 1769:

> nor can it be thought that by sending for Lord Chatham they mean anything else than to patch a Shred or two, of one, or more of the other parties, upon the old Bute garment; since their last piecing is worn out.[4]

The Rockingham Whigs believed themselves able to provide the Government with a new set of clothes. They looked for a union of Opposition groups, 'of all the Parties into one'; it was to be a union based on principles and the 'great principle' Burke had outlined to Temple: 'that the King's men should be utterly destroyed as a Corps'.[5] We can be certain that the letter (written in November 1769) in which this remark is recorded reflects Burke's fascination with the arguments he was then expounding in the *Present Discontents*; the 'king's men' had become an obsession with him. Rockingham is more balanced in his comment on the importance of the forthcoming pamphlet:

> I wish it read by all the members of Parliament—and by all the politicians in town and country prior to the meeting of Parliament. I think it would take universally, and tend to form and to unite a party upon real and well founded principles—which would in the end prevail and re-establish order and Government in this country.[6]

There is greater balance here, but the claim for the urgent importance of Burke's pamphlet is also great. Both Burke and the Marquess recognised that fundamental principles—of lasting

---

[1] Ed. Lucy S. Sutherland, *The Correspondence of Edmund Burke* II, 43.
[2] Ibid., II, 59n.   [3] Ibid., II, 105.   [4] Ibid., II, 101.
[5] Ibid., II, 113.   [6] Ibid., II, 92.

value as we can now see—were involved; it was not a publication 'animated by a direct controversy'[1] but a statement of a 'political Creed'[2] given extra relevance and a particular focus by the furore over Wilkes. And there is some irony in the way it was received: the 'Courtiers' admitted 'it to be a piece of Gentlemanlike Hostility'[3]; the fiercest denunciation came from the extreme radical members of the Society for the Defence of the Bill of Rights, a body founded (in February 1769) to secure Wilkes's election to Parliament.

Wilkes in 1770 was interested primarily in John Wilkes; it was left to others to debate the issues and principles raised by his earlier activities. The writings of Junius, Johnson, and Burke provide ample evidence of the differing levels of literary achievement called forth by the debate.

[1] Ed. Lucy S. Sutherland, *The Correspondence of Edmund Burke* II, 109.
[2] Ibid., II, 136.   [3] Ibid., II, 139.

II

THE LETTERS OF JUNIUS

I T has invariably been assumed that, among the polemical
writers connected with the Wilkes furore, Burke was pre-
eminent, but the validity of the assumption has never been
satisfactorily tested. The principal difficulty hitherto has been
to see his achievement in perspective, as a passage from Coleridge's *Friend* makes abundantly clear.

> The fact was, that Burke in his public character found himself,
> as it were, in a Noah's ark, with a very few men and a great
> many beasts. He felt how much his immediate power was lessened
> by the very circumstance of his measureless superiority to those
> about him: he acted, therefore, under a perpetual system of
> compromise—a compromise of greatness with meanness; a
> compromise of the philosopher (who, armed with the twofold
> knowledge of history and the laws of spirit, as with a telescope,
> looked far around and into the remote distance) with the mere
> men of business, or with yet coarser intellects, who handled a
> truth, which they were required to receive, as they would handle
> an ox, which they were desired to purchase.[1]

While Coleridge's remarks go far beyond our present purpose,
they serve to focus attention on the problem which has be-
devilled most attempts at a literary assessment of Burke's performance: the belief that there was no controversialist of the day
with whom it is profitable to compare him. Coleridge's remarks
also suggest a possible corollary to this first problem—that other
political writers may have been unjustly depreciated in order to
demonstrate Burke's 'measureless superiority to those about

[1] Ed. K. Coburn, *Inquiring Spirit* (1951), p. 268.

him'. John Morley, for example, dismisses Junius as 'never more
than a railer and very often . . . third-rate even as a railer';[1] he
does not give so much as a mention to Samuel Johnson's political writings; indeed, he looks back to Swift's *Conduct of the Allies*
(1711) as the pamphlet which, nearest in time, most merits
comparison with the best of the early Burke, *Thoughts on the
Cause of the Present Discontents* (1770). And even of Swift's pamphlet Morley remarks that, with few exceptions, 'nobody need
read it today'. Morley, then, largely exposes himself to the risks
of the non-comparative method of criticism; he also acts on the
assumption that no other late-eighteenth-century political writer
can usefully be examined in order to set off Burke's peculiar
excellence. This is simply not true. And while no extravagant
claims are to be advanced for Junius or Johnson, this study presupposes that Burke's undoubted superiority—it is foolish to
conceal the obvious overall judgment—can be satisfactorily
established only by comparative analysis.

To quote from Coleridge again is to cite one authority who
was in no doubt about the quality of *The Letters of Junius*: 'It is
impossible to detract from the merit of these letters; they are
suited to their purpose, and perfect in their kind.'[2] It is proper,
of course, adapting Burke's question about Bolingbroke, to ask,
'who now reads Junius?' and the answer is certainly one pointer
to the literary 'kind' Coleridge was referring to. The *Letters* are
ephemeral—nevertheless, they were probably read in their day
by a larger audience than read Burke; their appearance in *The
Public Advertiser* seems to have been anticipated with an excitement similar to that which later attended the publication of a
new part of a Dickens novel; and to reveal the literary causes of
their success is at the same time to go some way towards isolating
the nature of Burke's achievement. Johnson, much closer in
style to Burke and yet sharing to some extent the object of immediacy which is a hallmark of Junius, provides a further comparative standard.

*   *   *

Of Junius it cannot be said, as of Ulysses, that he scatters ambiguous expressions among the vulgar; for he cries havock without

[1] J. Morley, *Edmund Burke* (1879), p. 48.
[2] Ed. T. M. Raysor, *Coleridge's Miscellaneous Criticism* (1936), p. 314.

reserve, and endeavours to let slip the dogs of foreign or of civil war, ignorant whither they are going, and careless what may be their prey.

Junius has sometimes made his satire felt, but let not injudicious admiration mistake the venom of the shaft for the vigour of the bow. . . . Novelty captivates the superficial and thoughtless; vehemence delights the discontented and turbulent.[1]

Though confessedly partisan Johnson's charges compel attention to some fundamental questions about the art of political writing as well as to various salient features of Junius's *Letters*. Is Junius (or any political pamphleteer) merely delighting in his own power to excite his readers, or has he something of importance to say? Is this 'something' of permanent as well as of immediate value, or does it apply only to the existing situation? Is it merely addressed to the superficial reader or would 'the judicious', to use the Augustan term, also find it satisfying? Is the writing memorable as well as immediately stimulating, thought-provoking as well as urging to an active response? Such tests can rightly be applied, as Johnson applied them, to Junius —but also to Burke and to Johnson himself.

One, at any rate, of Johnson's charges can be disposed of at once: that it was merely the novelty and vehemence of Junius which accounted for his popularity. Seen as an isolated phenomenon, the letters might appear to bear out the accusation; seen in their historical context as part of the vast newspaper war of the late 1760s and the next decade, when anonymous correspondents were innumerable and their vehemence often startling to a modern reader, then the letters can be viewed in perspective and Junius's achievement more accurately measured. The letters should not be read simply in isolation but in a compilation such as *The Repository or Treasury of Politics and Literature . . . Being a Complete Collection of the best Letters and Essays from the Daily Papers*. Only then can one see Junius emerging from among correspondents calling themselves 'Cato', 'Seranus', 'Tullius', 'Old Slyboots', 'George II' (writing from 'Elysian Fields'), or 'Elizabeth' (presumably writing from the same place but giving no address). It is significant that from that babel of voices denouncing the deficiencies of the mini-

---

[1] Johnson, *Works* (Oxford, 1825), VI, 204–5.

sterial party or the decrepitude of the Opposition, only Junius's is now even faintly heard.

The reasons for this are chiefly three: Junius had something to say and said it consistently; he was superior in literary talents; and his anonymity allowed him to attack not measures but men.

As is made abundantly clear in the Dedication and Preface to the *Letters*, as well as elsewhere, the first principle of Junius's political philosophy was that 'the power of the King, Lords and Commons is not an arbitrary power. They are the trustees, not the owners of the estate. The fee-simple is in us.'[1] From this conviction stemmed his violent opposition to any invasion of popular rights, such as the expulsion and attempted exclusion of Wilkes, and his concern lest septennial parliaments should mean that popular opinion was consulted only once in about every six years—'your representatives have six years for offence, and but one for atonement. A death-bed repentance seldom reaches to restitution.'[2] From the same principle sprang his hatred of general warrants, indeed of anything savouring of arbitrary power. And since in the nine years 1763–72 (from the publication of Wilkes's famous *North Briton No. 45* to the cessation of Junius's letters) there seemed in the view of many contemporaries, of whom Junius was one, to be unmistakable signs of absolutism in George III, Junius did not hesitate to attack the person of the King himself. Again, and necessarily, the freedom of the Press was jealously regarded by Junius—it is 'the *palladium* of all the civil, political, and religious rights of an Englishmen'[3]— as was the right of juries to pronounce on the law as well as on the facts in cases of seditious libel.[4] But he was no leveller; he was sceptical, for example, of a proposal to defranchise rotten boroughs and challenged Wilkes on this issue:

> When you propose to cut away the *rotten* parts, can you tell us us what parts are perfectly *sound*? Are there any certain limits in fact or theory, to inform you at what point you must stop, at what point the mortification ends?[5]

[1] Ed. J. Wade, *The Letters of Junius* (1910), I, 88. cf. Burke, *Present Discontents*: King, Lords, Judges, and Commons 'all are trustees for the people' (*Works*, Bohn edn., 1886, I, 348).
[2] *Letters*, I, 89. [3] Ibid., I, 88.
[4] Ibid., I, 93–9. [5] Ibid., I, 469.

Whig constitutionalist, then, and no republican, reformer but no democrat, Junius knew where he stood. Not to be compared with Burke for profundity of political thought, Junius's views, addressed to 'the plain understanding of the people',[1] had the advantage for a pamphleteer of simplicity; more akin to Swift in this respect, he saw issues in terms of right and wrong, friend and foe, freedom and tyranny, opposition and ministry, and this simple form of dualism gives an incisive edge to his writing which a more profound view might have blunted. There is substance in what Junius had to say, but it is not, as it is in Burke, made weighty by any significant depth of thought or philosophical originality. It is true—and here Johnson scores a point in his *Falkland's Islands* pamphlet quoted earlier—that in his hatred for what he conceived as a tyrannical and corrupt government Junius was willing, apparently to any degree, to exacerbate and prolong the strife between Ministry and Opposition. Yet here again the dualism operated: the Ministry is arbitrary; therefore the Opposition must unite to defeat it at any cost. When the Opposition was more and more split by factious disputes (as between Horne Tooke and Wilkes, or Junius and Tooke), when 'there are not ten men who will unite and stand together upon any one question',[2] only then does the situation seem to Junius 'vile and contemptible'; despair follows and his disappearance is inevitable.

> The great art of Junius is never to say too much, and to avoid with equal anxiety a commonplace manner, and matter that is not commonplace. If ever he deviates into any originality of thought, he takes care that it shall be such as excited surprise for its acuteness, rather than admiration for its profundity. He takes care? say rather that Nature took care for him.[3]

This perceptive comment from Coleridge makes plain the advantage to Junius of the simple dualism and the lack of philosophical profundity noted above. It also helps to place Junius among those pamphleteers whose concern is principally with the immediate issues and who have little in the way of thought to offer succeeding generations. Junius was not interested, any more than Swift, in adapting his writing 'for the closet of a

[1] *Letters*, I, 92. Cf. I, 197. [2] Ibid., II, 60.
[3] Ed. T. M. Raysor, *Coleridge's Miscellaneous Criticism*, p. 314.

Sidney, or for a House of Lords such as it was in the time of Lord Bacon';[1] his writing was calculated to create excitement, as Coleridge observes, in the coffee-house, the lobby of the House of Commons, or a public meeting. It was also intended to create a *persona* for himself: that of a shrewd, well-informed man who could use the language of witty conversation with sufficient finesse to command the attention of the judicious, and yet without so great a subtlety as to put the common reader at any disadvantage. The whole audience is indeed flattered—as Pope flattered his readers to a far greater degree—by the assumption that they can comprehend irony, and that they have intelligence and sensibility enough to appreciate literary skill. Junius does not distinguish, as did the Augustan satirists, between the judicious and the 'mob', between those who have and those who have not that intelligence and sensibility; his readers are treated alike because, all alike (whether enfranchised or not) they enjoy political rights, and these in his opinion are threatened. There is, in fact, a close correlation between his political views and his literary manner.

A passage which is worthy of a rapid glance occurs in the Preface to Woodfall's edition of the *Letters*, published in the late months of 1771 when Junius was known to the public by over sixty letters. It is a paragraph towards the close which is described by Coleridge as 'a masterpiece of rhetorical ratiocination'; it deserves a brief mention for this reason, but also because the Preface represents Junius in the unusual rôle of a man making a general statement to justify his approach and epistolary manner. The occasion was, for him, unusual in that it called for careful composition not prompted, like the letters themselves, by a particular person or event of the moment. Nevertheless, here, as in the letters, Junius's standpoint is the traditional one for the satirist and reformer, that expressed by Pope in his *Epistle to Dr. Arbuthnot*:

> A lash like mine no honest man shall dread
> But all such babbling blockheads in his stead.

Junius reserves the 'babbling blockheads' more particularly for the letters; here he is concerned with general issues such as the use he has made of the freedom of the press, the duties of juries

---

[1] Ed. T. M. Raysor, *Coleridge's Miscellaneous Criticism*, p. 314.

in cases of libel, and the responsibility of the King for the present political situation. The paragraph praised by Coleridge deals with the last of these topics.[1]

After the hint to his readers expressed through the cautious remark, 'when the character of the chief magistrate is in question, more must be understood, than may safely be expressed', Junius introduces the constitutional issue of *the king can do no wrong*. He does not analyse it; he simply observes that this 'is not the only instance . . . where theory is at variance with practice' and adds that 'exemption from punishment . . . [in] no way excludes the possibility of deserving it'. The heart of the paragraph is quickly reached with the warning to the 'King of England' (not George III by name) not to violate the spirit of the constitution, 'a mistake' that 'proved fatal to Charles and his son', and the remainder of the passage is occupied with a sustained rush of fierce rhetorical questions which, as Junius had remarked earlier, 'carry a decisive answer along with them'.[2] These questions are again not addressed directly to George but are examples of what Junius would ask if he had the 'misfortune' to live 'under the inauspicious reign of a prince whose whole life was employed in one base, contemptible struggle with the free spirit of his people'. The ironic veil is too thin to obscure his meaning from any reader, but it allows Junius to increase the pace and virulence of his writing to match the movement from the general issue with which the paragraph opens to the specific matters of immediate and urgent moment carried in the questions:

> With a great military, and the greatest naval power in the known world, have not foreign nations repeatedly insulted you with impunity? . . . Are you a prince of the House of Hanover, and do you exclude all the leading Whig families from your councils? . . . Are you so infatuated as to take sense of your people from the representation of ministers, or from the shouts of a mob, notoriously hired to surround your coach, or stationed at a theatre?

Such questions point to a second notable feature of this writing: the way Junius manipulates rumours and suppositions (many of them still unconfirmed by historical research) as if they were facts. He asserts, for example, that despite the royal wealth,

---

[1] *Letters*, I, 100–2.   [2] Ibid., I, 99.

George has been reduced to 'vile and sordid distresses', that this wealth is used to corrupt the people's representatives, or that royal advisers favour 'arbitrary principles of government'. This use of 'facts' also coheres with a third feature—the concentration on a single individual to give the whole paragraph a specific focus. The guilt of George III is illustrated from both his public and his private life, in a way that anticipates Byron in *The Vision of Judgment*—

> is it any answer to your people, to say that among your domestics you are good-humoured?—that to one lady you are faithful?— that to your children you are indulgent?

and it provides the focal point for the whole passage. In using material such as this Junius was drawing on 'information' available to any reader of the Opposition newspapers. Consequently, the common reader would never be out of his depth, his intelligence would not be stretched, but his interest would be held by the energy and resource displayed in Junius's literary manner. The tone of his writing is conversational but not the easy, cultivated conversation of an Addison; it is defiant, hard-hitting, shrewd, and invariably on the mark. And the target is a contemporary one; the general nature of the issue in question is only once in this paragraph, and then briefly, allowed to come through; for the rest Junius is concerned with the situation in 1771 and that only.

Herein, of course, lies one major factor in his success: he did not aim at originality of thought—all the material in the paragraph just discussed consists of the commonplaces of Opposition charges against the Government—but he kept his reader's attention on matters of immediate relevance. In the letters, moreover, these matters are generally given a focus by linking them with prominent individuals of the day. And in the 1760s—with the renown of Lord Bute, the brief administration of the Rockingham Whigs, the eclipse of Chatham, the manoeuvring of Grafton, Bedford, North, and the rest, and the dominant interest of the populace, Jack Wilkes—issues were inevitably associated with the names of individuals. Hence pamphleteers tended much more than during the final years of George II when, other than Pitt the men were largely uninteresting, to concentrate on men rather than on measures. This was nothing basically new:

23

pamphleteers and satirists have traditionally centred their attacks on persons either real or imaginary. It is, however, significant that the two major Augustan satirists, Pope and Swift, had moved increasingly in the direction of attacking leading individuals by name. Pope is the more explicit on this subject in his famous letter to Arbuthnot, 26 July 1734 (as well as in the *Epilogue to the Satires*, Dialogue II):

> To reform and not to chastise, I am afraid is impossible; and that the best precepts, as well as the best laws, would prove of small use if there were no examples to enforce them. To attack vices in the abstract, without touching persons, may be safe fighting indeed, but it is fighting with shadows. My greatest comfort and encouragement to proceed has been to see that those who have no shame, and no fear of anything else, have appeared touched by my satires.[1]

It is of the greatest interest that Junius appends this passage as a note to one of his own letters. He clearly shared Pope's view completely as this remark makes plain:

> *Measures and not men*, is the common cant of affected moderation; a base, counterfeit language, fabricated by knaves, and made current among fools . . . gentle censure is not fitted to the present degenerate state of society.

Such a statement might cover merely the hypocritical slanderer who delights in savage railing; for both Pope and Junius, it expresses firm conviction.

It is a happy coincidence that Junius's best literary talents— like Pope's—are active when an individual is the object of attack. At times these attacks degenerate into malicious sneering as, for example, in the letter to the Duke of Bedford, 19 September 1769. Bedford is described as 'ridiculous and contemptible even to the few by whom he was not detested'; Junius rejoices in the occasion when his victim was horsewhipped, in 'the public infamy and [Bedford's] own sufferings'; he finds it 'a pleasure to reflect that there is hardly a corner of any of His Majesty's dominions, except France, in which, at one time or another, your valuable life has not been in danger';[2] and he pictures George III as besieged by Bedford's influence—it will remain so 'until your Grace's death or some less fortunate event shall

---

[1] *Letters of Junius*, I, 224n.   [2] *Letters*, I, 214.

raise the siege'.[1] There is nothing to be said in defence of such ill-shaped malice; it is the work of a man who feels himself so much the superior of his victim as to lose his sense of proportion. Yet even this letter is not without its moments of distinction. The device of creating an imaginary Duke of Bedford in order to demonstrate how incompatible he is with the reality is masterly. 'Consider the character of an independent, virtuous Duke of Bedford; imagine what he might be in this country, then reflect one moment upon what you are.'[2] It is the satiric mode, displaying the difference between what is and what might be, and despite the undeniable blemishes in the tone, Junius carries it through with sustained irony. The concluding paragraphs, which cumulatively depict the whole country from London and Plymouth to Woburn and Scotland as united in detesting the Duke, are a triumph of passionate malignity. There is indeed something in the assertion that 'in invective which is uninformed by any generosity of feeling [Junius] stands unequalled'.[3]

It would, however, be stupid to expect 'generosity of feeling' to be of the essence of satire; it is only when the satirist feels some respect for the man he is attacking that he can afford to display this quality. We find it in Dryden's portrait of Shaftesbury in *Absalom and Achitophel*; it is present to some degree in Pope's 'Atticus' portrait of Addison; but only a sentimentalist would condemn the 'Sporus' portrait, Pope's brilliant statement of hatred for Lord Hervey's detestable qualities, because it lacks 'generous feeling'. It is the satirist's ability to give order and shape to his disgust, to produce from it a satisfying literary experience, that we should look for. Junius should not be condemned for detesting Bedford so much as for failing both to discipline his hatred and to translate his insights into effective literary terms.

When, on the other hand, in his first letter Junius surveys the 'character of the ministry' and opens one paragraph—'It has lately been a fashion to pay a compliment to the bravery and generosity of the commander-in-chief, at the expense of his understanding'[4]—the control of language evidenced by his

[1] *Letters*, I, 217.   [2] Ibid., I, 212.
[3] *Cambridge History of English Literature* (Cambridge 1913), X, 406.
[4] *Letters*, I, 109.

holding back the 'punch-line' suggests an equivalent control of emotion. There is an essential detachment about the writing; Junius has distanced his personal feelings to the extent that he can concentrate on the most effective expression of them. This impression is sustained as he goes on to describe the Marquess of Granby's generosity—in providing for his family at the public expense; as he remarks that 'Nature has been sparing of her gifts to this noble lord'; and as he labels Granby a man who has 'degraded the office of commander-in-chief into a broker of commissions'. Junius then turns to the Navy: 'I shall only say, that this country is so highly indebted to Sir Edward Hawke, that no expense should be spared to secure to him an honourable and affluent retreat.' Again the control so necessary to the ironist is demonstrated by the placing of the final words.

The treatment of the Duke of Grafton in Letter XII exhibits a similar mastery of tone and diction. Junius's detestation for Grafton equalled the distaste he felt for Bedford, but this letter is superior to the one discussed earlier principally because the detachment is greater here.

> . . . let me be permitted to consider your character and conduct merely as a subject of curious speculation. There is something in both, which distinguishes you not only from all other ministers, but all other men.[1]

The statements are direct, but the tone of superior politeness and the deliberate slowing up of the style to sharpen our curiosity in that 'something', heighten the impact of the sentence which follows:

> It is not that you do wrong by design, but that you should never do right by mistake.

The antithesis which causes amusement is not merely verbal; it is a moral unbalance to which Junius calls attention, and the opposition of 'wrong' to 'right', of 'design' to 'mistake', as well as the controlling negatives suggest not only a dangerous character but one which is constitutionally incapable of right action. It is comparable with Dryden's brilliant comment (in *MacFlecknoe*) that Shadwell 'never deviates into sense'. The air of astonishment in both cases increases the pungency of the statements. The

---

[1] *Letters*, I, 154.

portrait of Grafton, as it develops, is not without savagery, but it is not the sneering malignity of the Bedford portrait:

> The character of the reputed ancestors of some men has made it possible for their descendants to be vicious in the extreme without being degenerate. Those of your Grace, for instance, left no distressing examples of virtue even to their legitimate posterity, and you may look back with pleasure to an illustrious pedigree in which heraldry has not left a single good quality upon record to insult or upbraid you.

Here it is a caustic wit which does its diminishing work; the irony is embittered by the unremitting application of a perverse logic; and the reader derives pleasure from the resource as well as the control Junius displays. When it is recognised that Grafton was illegitimately descended from Charles II the ironic edge becomes sharper and the decorous use of language more deadly. It is indeed a savage attack, but the occasion must not be overlooked. According to Junius's lights, Grafton was an inconstant, untrustworthy man in a position of great authority (as George's chief Minister); his conduct 'comprehends every thing that a wise or honest minister should avoid';[1] and whether Junius's view was right or wrong, it was certainly widely held among Opposition writers to the Press.[2]

Grafton was frequently the target of Junius's letters. Of one of them (10 April 1769) Coleridge was prompted to remark:

> Perhaps the fair way of considering these Letters would be as a kind of satirical poems—the short, and for ever balanced sentences constitute a true metre; and the connection is that of satiric poetry, a witty logic, an association of ideas by amusing semblances of cause and effect—the sophistry of which the reader has an interest in not stopping to detect—for it flatters his love of mischief, and makes the sport.[3]

There is, as earlier remarks may have suggested, considerable truth in Coleridge's description; the opening paragraph of this letter will illustrate it still further. Junius refers to a pamphlet vindicating Grafton's career, supposedly by Edward Weston;

---

[1] *Letters*, I, 162.
[2] Cf. *The Repository or Treasury of Politics and Literature for 1770* (1771), I, 204, 205.
[3] *Miscellaneous Criticism*, p. 317.

he says that he would accept Weston's claim that the Duke had had no hand in the pamphlet were it not for one thing—its failure to hit the mark. This, Junius observes, is the distinguishing characteristic of all Grafton's activities. In illustration of his assertion he says:

> Your first attempt to support Sir William Proctor ended in the election of Mr. Wilkes; the second ensured success to Mr. Glynn.[1]

The list of failures continues, and then:

> With this uniform experience before us, we are authorized to suspect that when a pretended vindication of your principles and conduct in reality contains the bitterest reflections upon both, it could not have been written without your immediate direction and assistance. The author, indeed, calls God to witness for him, with all the sincerity, and in the very terms of an Irish evidence, *to the best of his knowledge and belief.* My Lord, you should not encourage these appeals to heaven. The pious prince, from whom you are supposed to descend, made such frequent use of them in his public declarations, that at last the people also found it necessary to appeal to heaven in their turn. Your administration has driven us into circumstances of equal distress;—beware at least how you remind us of the remedy.

The success of this writing derives from two main features: the choice of a central idea and the nimbleness of the writer's mind in developing a train of associations. The controlling idea—as in Letter XII mentioned earlier—is Grafton's success in achieving the opposite of his intentions, and around that idea Junius lets his mind have free, but disciplined, play in a manner reminiscent of Swift in his *Short Character of Wharton.* The irony is sustained throughout, and the reader experiences a delight in watching the manipulation of language which, for its consistent aim and its wit, would not disgrace a Swift:

> The House List of Directors was cursed with the concurrence of government; and even the miserable Dingley,[2] could not escape the misfortune of your Grace's protection.

The logic of the argument, proving the derivation of the pamphlet by its failure, is intelligent, if perversely so, and the ironic play with Weston's plea to Heaven, recalling the behaviour and

[1] *Letters*, I, 142.
[2] Whom Grafton persuaded to stand for Middlesex without success.

fate of Charles I, is superbly managed. There is, of course, beneath the wit a serious undertone which comes through in the final threat, but the reader's attention is initially caught and then maintained by a lively use of language. One cannot mistake the indignation which informs Junius's writing, but there is no virulence about it; this is not the kind of abuse in which John Dennis or Edmund Curll indulged against Pope, where violence does duty for intelligence; nor is it the honest bluster of Sir William Draper, who misguidedly challenged Junius to verbal combat.

> Junius delights to mangle carcases with a hatchet, [protests Draper] his language and instrument have a great connection with Clare-market, and, to do him justice, he handles his weapon most admirably. One would imagine he had been taught to throw it by the savages of America.[1]

Draper obviously felt strongly, and with good reason, but his abuse is relatively clumsy; it lacks the sportive play of the mind that distinguishes Junius at his best.

When writing below his best Junius is more scoundrelly than those he attacked. On these occasions—as in the letter to Bedford—he becomes a Draper; his control over emotion vanishes, and as a consequence the language carries the raw material of feeling rather than the refined essence of it; the indignation is crude, the violence lacks shape, and the controlling intelligence is absent. Long, flabby sentences are often a sign of Junius's second-best; the short, crisp jab is his most effective punch. Like Paine, he falters badly when he tries to be high-sounding; he succeeds only in being pretentiously wordy. Letter XX, for example, begins promisingly with an ironic assault on an adversary who had 'honoured' him with 'six quarto pages' of attention:

> The advocates of the ministry seem to me to write for fame, and to flatter themselves that the size of their works will make them immortal. They pile up reluctant quarto upon solid folio, as if their labours, because they are gigantic, could contend with truth and heaven.[2]

but it ends with an inflated rhapsody:

---

[1] *Letters*, I, 122.   [2] Ibid., I, 197.

We owe it to our ancestors to preserve entire those rights which they have delivered to our care—we owe it to our posterity not to suffer their dearest inheritance to be destroyed. But if it were possible for us to be insensible of these sacred claims, there is yet an obligation binding upon ourselves, from which nothing can acquit us,—a personal interest, which we cannot surrender. To alienate even our own rights would be a crime as much more enormous than suicide as a life of civil security and freedom is superior to a bare existence; and, if life be the bounty of heaven, we scornfully reject the noblest part of the gift if we consent to surrender that certain rule of living without which the condition of human nature is not only miserable, but contemptible.

There is no distinction about such writing; any of a score of writers to the Press could have done as well. Few, on the other hand, could rival the sinister balance of his calculated rhythms—

as you [Grafton] became minister by accident, were adopted without choice, trusted without confidence, and continued without favour, be assured that, when an occasion presses, you will be discarded without even the forms of regret.[1]

or match the cumulative weight of his sharp, cogent sentences:

[Edward and Richard II] had as many false friends as our present gracious sovereign, and infinitely greater temptations to seduce them. They were neither sober, religious, nor demure. Intoxicated with pleasure, they wasted their inheritance in pursuit of it. Their lives were like a rapid torrent, brilliant in prospect, though useless or dangerous in its course. In the dull, unanimated existence of other princes, we see nothing but a sickly, stagnant water, which taints the atmosphere without fertilizing the soil. The morality of a king is not to be measured by vulgar rules. His situation is singular.[2]

This was the writing shaped, not 'to instruct the learned, but simply to inform the body of the people', and proper to 'that channel of conveyance [the Press] which is likely to spread farthest amongst them'.[3]

At his best, then, Junius is more than an excellent railer; he is the master of the language of factious politics. It would be unwise to maintain that he was devoid of political faith; he held beliefs with powerful conviction, but it was not germane to his purpose to elaborate on them or expound their validity. He

---

[1] *Letters*, I, 174.   [2] Ibid., I, 301.   [3] Ibid., I, 197.

takes their rightness largely for granted and works by assertion, not by proof; as a result, his letters are positive, onward-moving, and robust. For his purpose—an immediate one aimed at producing action rather than thought—it was enough to demonstrate his intellectual superiority over his opponents by means of literary skill. To this end irony, wit (which presupposes intellectual astuteness), antithetical balance, the logical development of an idea, together with a shrewd exploitation of language, metaphor, and allusion—these are Junius's weapons. This armoury, strengthened by his use of the satiric 'character' which is such a notable feature of the writings of Dryden, Pope, and Charles Churchill among others, places Junius quite securely in the Augustan tradition of satire. There was, as Johnson remarked of Junius, venom in the shafts; there was also great vigour in the bow.

III

SAMUEL JOHNSON:
THE FALSE ALARM

THE period covered by the Junius *Letters*—1769–72—was one of the most turbulent in eighteenth-century Britain, and it is as well to emphasise the reality of 'the present discontents' as they were called. It was in Junius's interest to sustain and inflame the discontents in order to drive the Opposition into unity, the better to counteract what he saw as ministerial tyranny. Johnson, on the other hand, tried to minimise and explain them away, Burke to account for them and suggest a remedy. Johnson's was the most thankless task, for there was no doubt among a large section of the population that a crisis in national affairs existed. As Burke remarked in the *Present Discontents*:

> Nobody, I believe, will consider it merely as the language of spleen or disappointment, if I say, that there is something particularly alarming in the present conjuncture. There is hardly a man, in or out of power, who holds any other language.[1]

Junius never let the crisis be forgotten, but the tone adopted by the completely ephemeral writers is instructive. For example, a correspondent writing to the *Morning Chronicle*, 16 April 1770, under the pseudonym 'Tanaquil', declaims after detailed grievances:

> Thus have the present ministry gone on progressively in destroying the rights of the nation in Westminster, and in trampling on

[1] *Works* (Bohn edn., 1886), I, 307–8.

the rights of the citizens by their tools in the metropolis. Like common liars they have been obliged to commit a hundred crimes to palliate and support the first. They have stimulated an oppressed people to rage; let them stop before they descend the precipice and open their eyes before they find themselves drowning.

Or 'A Loyal Subject' begins his letter to *Lloyd's Evening Post*, 14 May 1770: 'The times are critical; discontents every where prevail.' He goes on:

the spirit of government, and the spirit of the people, have been in opposition; and the contest, at present, seems to be which shall prevail. By the people, I do not mean the rabble, the scum of the earth; I mean, the respectable members of both houses of parliament, the unplaced, unpensioned, independent members; the *real representatives* of a free people.

These two extracts have the incidental merit of illustrating the average level of writing to the newspapers against which we should measure Junius's, but their main purpose here is to reinforce a comment in another letter—from 'Old Slyboots' to the *Public Advertiser*, 7 May 1770: 'It is impossible to conceive a more difficult employment than that of a political writer engaged on the side of government.' It was this 'difficult employment' that Samuel Johnson took up in 1770 and to which we must now turn.

The False Alarm, Johnson's favourite pamphlet, was written, according to Mrs. Thrale (Piozzi), in just over twenty-four hours.[1] It does not give this impression. It has the characteristic Johnsonian assurance and weightiness, and is obviously not the product, as were Junius's letters, of the day-to-day journalistic controversy. There is also a firmness and methodical arrangement present in the pamphlet which one associates with Johnson. Where Junius allowed his thought and perverse logic to develop in the very act of writing, Johnson's style is studied and the result of mature deliberation; Junius's follows the movement of an alert and lively mind in the act of composition, whereas Johnson knows precisely where he is going and exactly how he is going to get there. As his contemporary Arthur Murphy observed, Johnson 'never took his pen in hand till he

---

[1] Ed. Birkbeck Hill, *Johnsonian Miscellanies* (1907), I, 173.

had weighed well his subject, and grasped in his mind the sentiments, the train of argument, and the arrangement of the
whole'.[1]

Two further differences of approach between Junius and
Johnson should be noticed. In the first place the length of a
pamphlet allowed Johnson the freedom to develop an argument
and indulge a phrase where the length of a letter denied Junius
the same latitude. Secondly, Junius addressed himself to an
audience of greater width and variety than Johnson's; while he
knew intimately the passions and prejudices of that audience,
and played on both, the limited literary training and background on which he could rely, together with the urgency of
the immediate issues, made it impossible for him to use anything
like a Johnsonian style. Johnson makes his appeal unreservedly
to wavering supporters of the administration and counts on the
traditional literary training of educated and cultured men. The
very audience he addressed, then, made it inevitable that his
style would give to an ephemeral subject some qualities of
permanence; his readers looked for and appreciated subtleties
of tone, modulations of rhythm, skilled choice of words, and so
forth; they were indeed capable of aesthetic pleasure as well as
of political thinking. Where Johnson goes astray is when he has
little to say but struggles to say it impressively, when his humour
becomes heavy-handed, or when his contempt for the Opposition is expressed with such weight as to appear arrogant.

Johnson's intention—for which he was accused by correspondents in the newspapers of being hired by the Government[2]—
was to minimise the seriousness of the Wilkes issue. He put the
administration's case that because Wilkes had been expelled
from the Commons he could not be a legal candidate for re-
election, that any votes cast for him were automatically invalid,
and that therefore Luttrell was legally elected as the candidate
with the highest number of lawful votes. Johnson also wanted
to stigmatise the Opposition as weak and contemptible, claiming that the furore they had raised was mere sound and fury.
The Wilkes furore was, in other words, 'a false alarm'. Making
this his object, then, Johnson could not hope to conciliate the
Opposition; it was not to be an effort to unite the country

[1] Ed. Birkbeck Hill, *Johnsonian Miscellanies* 1907, I, 426.
[2] *Treasury or Impartial Compendium for 1770*, II, 185.

behind the Government, but rather to stiffen the resolve of nominal government supporters and to diminish the effect of Opposition propaganda. His purpose was, therefore, as much anti-Opposition as pro-Administration.

To minimise the significance of the Wilkes question Johnson's main technique is to play down the particulars of the case and concentrate attention on its general features. He was doubly wise: first, the particulars of Wilkes's trial and expulsion, with their multitudinous consequences, had been thoroughly exploited by the Opposition, making a counter-attack over the same terrain almost impossible; second, Johnson's style and whole cast of mind were pre-eminently suited to the general, the abstract, and the philosophical aspects of any issue. Paine's method later in the century provides a sharp contrast. When he came to reply to Burke's *Reflections* he based his argument solidly on a basis of evidence, he met fact with fact and supplied others. Johnson, on the other hand—as his criticism of Swift's pamphleteering style makes clear[1]—was constitutionally uninterested in such a procedure. He relates his view of the Wilkes case to the general moral law; he invokes what he calls 'the great and pregnant principle of political necessity' as his standard of value.[2] As a corollary, he treats the Opposition as people who are primarily concerned with a material existence, who are incapable of philosophical thinking or of handling general truths, and who are largely unintelligent and uneducated. On the contrary, his appeal is directed to 'the wise', to those who are intelligent and cultured, and these turn out to be men of the upper classes. Johnson's literary manner and his political theory, therefore, fuse completely: his 'aristocratic' style and philosophical approach suggest the mental and social calibre both of his own audience and of the Opposition; unequivocally they make a division between his audience and his opponents which is at once moral, social, and intellectual.

The opening paragraph of the pamphlet fixes the discussion on a philosophical level and gives a clear indication of the readers Johnson had in mind. How far he was from Junius is immediately evident.

One of the chief advantages derived by the present generation from the improvement and diffusion of philosophy, is deliverance

---

[1] *Works*, VIII, 203.   [2] Ibid., VI, 161.

from unnecessary terrors, and exemption from false alarms. The unusual appearances, whether regular or accidental, which once spread consternation over ages of ignorance, are now the recreations of inquisitive security. The sun is no more lamented when it is eclipsed, than when it sets; and meteors play their coruscations without prognostic or prediction.[1]

This is the Johnson of whom Boswell remarked—'Mr. Johnson has gigantic thoughts, and therefore he must be allowed gigantic words'.[2] It is the writing of a man whose authority to speak derives from his ability to detect general truths behind an array of specific facts. His words are carefully chosen: 'unnecessary' and 'false' as applied to the current furore provide the key to Johnson's whole approach. And nothing here is specific or concrete—indeed no such aspects appear in the first six pages. He does not speak of certain people in particular 'ages of ignorance' —the whole concept is generalised; in the final sentence he becomes specific to the extent of mentioning 'sun' and 'meteors', but the language, by its distance from everyday speech and its scientific flavour, emphasises the general significance of the events mentioned. This is exactly where Johnson wants his emphasis to be. One can sympathise with the newspaper comment on the meteors and 'their coruscations without prognostic or prediction'—'intolerable fustian'[3]—and with Wilkes, in his reply to *The False Alarm*, for exploiting the opportunity for irony and burlesque:

> Believe me, Sir, the *intellectual sight* of ordinary freeholders is liable to be *offusqued* by a *superfluous glare* of erudition. The dimension of OUR understanding is not of the proper magnitude to admit of *sesquipedalian documents*. OUR undisciplined taste is apt to be nauseated by the reduplicated *evomition* of unknown idioms.[4]

The newspaper correspondent also counter-attacks by translating Johnson's sentence, 'The sun is no more lamented when it is eclipsed, than when it sets', into, 'The people are as little terrified at an eclipse, as at the setting of the sun.' This critical method of

[1] *Works*, VI, 155.
[2] Ed. Scott and Pottle, *Private Papers of James Boswell from Malahide Castle* (New York, 1928–34), VII, 174.
[3] *Treasury or Impartial Compendium for 1770*, I, 218. (Quotation is from the *London Packet*, 22 January 1770.)
[4] [Anon], *A Letter to Samuel Johnson, L.L.D.* (1770), pp. 6–7.

translating into common speech the language of a writer who habitually uses a heightened and 'literary' diction is precisely that used elsewhere by Wilkes, and by Paine in his reply to Burke's *Reflections*. The object is, by reducing the level of the language, to reduce the authority of the man using it, to suggest that it is merely an apparent authority residing in the pompous quality of the words rather than in any profundity or rightness of thought. Wilkes remarks:

> It shall be my humble, but laborious province, to endeavour to reduce your lofty speculations to the level of vulgar apprehension . . . to develope [*sic*] what little meaning you may have wished to impart, by dissipating the *cloud of words* in which it is at present involved, and by exhibiting it in the form in which it must destroy itself, the language of common sense.[1]

The splendour of Johnson's general concept certainly disappears in the newspaper writer's 'translation'; his inherent claim to authority as a man writing above the common reader's intelligence retreats almost to vanishing point. It might be added, too, that only the committed reader would proceed beyond the 'coruscations', 'prognostic and prediction' which sound almost like a Johnsonian parody. Johnson is obviously not in the same world as Junius: it is as if Junius were on the boards of the hustings and he in some spectators' gallery.

With only few, though significant, exceptions Johnson's concentration on general, philosophic aspects continues throughout his pamphlet. In his third paragraph he assumes that his audience is interested in the contrast between the willing reception of new ideas in natural science and the hostility which greets them in the world of political science. In the paragraph which follows he invites us to consider how unacquainted we are with 'our own state' (i.e. the general human condition) and how unskilful in our 'pursuit of happiness'; this must be so when the country can be disturbed by a clamour which has prevailed, he claims, only on 'ignorance and timidity'. The introduction of abstract issues as well as his use of the abstractions 'ignorance' and 'timidity' again make plain the presupposition that universal truths alone are of interest to intelligent men. Right from the outset, indeed, Johnson makes a distinction Junius never made,

---

[1] [Anon], *A Letter to Samuel Johnson, L.L.D.*, p. 8.

between the educated and intelligent, on the one hand, and the ignorant and vulgar, on the other. It is the distinction characteristically adopted by the major Augustan writers.

Again he is unlike Junius in the position he adopts *vis-à-vis* the whole controversy. Johnson describes the Opposition, for example, as both 'wicked' and 'weak'. By the first term he invokes a moral judgment; the Opposition is being judged by universal standards of right behaviour and not relative to the political behaviour of the day. In the second, 'weak', is implied the standpoint of a man who claims to see further than ordinary men and can afford to look down on his opponents from his lofty detachment. Where Junius is in the midst of the furore, participating in and exacerbating it, Johnson sits above in philosophic calm.

It is the generalised, abstract nature of his language, in fact, that most clearly marks the difference between himself and Junius. Where Junius speaks of, or addresses himself to, real men with a distinct identity and personal attributes, Johnson refuses for the first six pages even to name the man at the centre of the furore he is discussing. Wilkes is referred to as 'the man', even as 'a man'; Johnson explicitly declines to delineate his character, adding: 'Lampoon itself would disdain to speak ill of him, of whom no man speaks well.'[1] To such an extent can generalisation be taken: the writer himself disdains to condemn, an abstraction ('lampoon') is made the agent, and then the abstract agent refuses to act. Of course, the generalised mode allows Johnson at the same time to distort the truth: he attracts notice to his verbal mastery and limits attention to Wilkes's moral character, which virtually no one would defend; he conceals Wilkes's essential importance as a rallying-point against potential tyranny. In this sense many people spoke well of Wilkes.[2]

As one would expect, the argument over the Commons' right to expel one of its members and then to exclude him, or over their right to make their own rules of procedure, is conducted in general terms—but once more no concession is made to particularity. This enables Johnson to maintain the philosophical level of his discussion; it also enables him to gloss over difficulties and

---

[1] *Works*, VI, 156.

[2] A few years later Johnson himself was to speak of him as 'a scholar' with 'the manners of a gentleman' (ed. Hill and Powell, Boswell's *Life of Johnson* (Oxford, 1934–50), III, 183).

make claims which need the support of concrete evidence. No man, he rightly states, can be an M.P. who is convicted of felony; he then goes on to claim that 'a man, so like a felon that he could not easily be distinguished, ought to be expelled'.[1] Now here Wilkes is obviously the man, but he is not named; furthermore, the claim advanced needs analysis of detailed evidence to support it if it is to be honestly maintained. The House of Commons could use this kind of language and formulate a ruling in these terms on its own responsibility; a private commentator is in no position to arrogate such authority to himself. Johnson gets away with it by using the language appropriate for enunciating general truths—he could claim that this is what he is doing here, since Wilkes is not named—but the refusal to descend to facts saves him a great deal of trouble.

In his desire to minimise the seriousness of the Wilkes case the generalised language and viewpoint are of enormous advantage to Johnson: he simply removes the issue from the context of immediate events and passions and places it in a universal pattern.

> Yet, though all this has been done, and though, at every new parliament, much of this is expected to be done again, it has never produced, in any former time, such an alarming crisis. We have found, by experience, that though a squire has given ale and venison in vain, and a borough has been compelled to see its dearest interest in the hands of him whom it did not trust, yet the general state of the nation has continued the same. The sun has risen, and the corn has grown, and whatever talk has been of the danger of property, yet he that ploughed the field commonly reaped it; and he that built a house was master of the door; the vexation excited by injustice suffered, or supposed to be suffered, by any private man, or single community, was local and temporary, it neither spread far nor lasted long.[2]

Moving beyond his wry humour directed at one kind of common practice—the corruption usual at elections—Johnson introduces a pattern of unchanging life and nature; his language in mid-paragraph, where he speaks of the sun, growing corn, the ploughing and reaping of the field, and so forth, takes on almost the character of the *Book of Proverbs*; it certainly carries something of the authority of the Old Testament. The viewpoint invited is, indeed, *sub specie aeternitatis*: against such a background

[1] *Works*, VI, 159.   [2] Ibid., VI, 170.

the Wilkes affair is effectively diminished, the reader's attention is diverted from the particular event and its reverberations.

Before turning to the exceptions to Johnson's use of a generalised diction it is instructive to look at one or two examples of his extended imagery. He argues at one point that all government implies subjects and obedience, and that to suppose in the state the right to command what the subject has the right to refuse, is absurd; he then goes on:

> A state, so constituted, must rest for ever in motionless equipoise, with equal attractions of contrary tendency, with equal weights of power balancing each other.[1]

The diction of the opening phrase ('motionless equipoise') carries the authority of a general, scientific law; that of the second ('equal attractions of contrary tendency') extends the application of the thought to the field of magnetism; and the final phrase ('equal weights balancing each other') involves the world of physics. Each phase of the image, then, draws in new illustrative material, but the central idea remains static; it is shown to be related to greater areas of knowledge, but is not itself enlarged. Nevertheless, because each elaboration reinforces the controlling idea with unquestionable scientific truth, its wisdom *seems* to be increased. Johnson's method is multiplication for the sake of weight and emphasis; as in this image, so generally in the style of the pamphlet (and for that matter in most of his writings) this is his principal persuasive technique—the reader is to be overwhelmed with the weight of his utterance. And, it should be noticed, the appeal in the passage is wholly intellectual; there is no sensory appeal whatever: a reader cannot be sensibly aroused by 'equipoise', 'contrary attractions', or 'weights of power'.

Later, when Johnson asserts that governments formed by chance and evolved through accidental circumstance and expedient cannot be tried by a regular theory, he remarks:

> They are fabrics of dissimilar materials, raised by different architects, upon different plans. We must be content with them, as they are; should we attempt to mend their disproportions, we might easily demolish, and difficultly rebuild them.[2]

The centrepoint of this image is the word 'fabrics', which is admittedly concrete but is also generic and consequently vague;

[1] *Works*, VI, 161-2.   [2] Ibid., VI, 164.

Johnson is putting no control on our response, allowing each reader to interpret the image as he wishes. Are these 'fabrics' castles, houses, churches, public buildings?—we are not told; they are simply objects involving architects and builders. They are, in other words, objects suggesting something specific but generalised almost to vanishing point. It is again on the general idea that Johnson wishes to concentrate, and his method once more is elaboration, for emphasis not clarity; again, too, no sensory appeal is made.

If we put this last image alongside one from Burke, essentially making the same point, the nature—and the limitations—of Johnson's method become clearer. In the *Present Discontents* Burke writes:

> Our constitution stands on a nice equipoise, with steep precipices and deep waters upon all sides of it. In removing it from a dangerous leaning towards one side, there may be a risk of over-setting it on the other.[1]

Now Burke, like Johnson, is not precisely confining our response; while we recognise that some physical structure is involved—it stands, it may lean, and, if adjusted, may topple in the other direction—we are not specifically told that it is a building. But the whole image comes alive, remains memorable, and is given a sensory reality by virtue of the 'steep precipices' and 'deep waters' which surround the political structure. These details put one in touch with a reality and a world we recognise as our own; there is little in Johnson's imagery that can claim to do the same. Or, to take a second example, in the *Reflections* Burke contemplates the situation in which, as it were, Johnson's 'fabrics' have been demolished and have to be rebuilt; he tells his French correspondent:

> Your constitution, it is true, whilst you were out of possession, suffered waste and dilapidation; but you possessed in some parts the walls, and, in all, the foundations, of a noble and venerable castle. You might have repaired those walls; you might have built on those old foundations.[2]

[1] *Works*, I, 368.
[2] Ibid., II, 308 (cf. Dryden, *Absalom and Achitophel*, I, 801 ff: 'If ancient Fabrics nod, and threat to fall,/To Patch the Flaws, and Buttress up the Wall,/Thus far 'tis Duty').

Here, even more than in the previous example, Burke keeps his reader in touch with the real world; the dilapidated French constitution becomes completely identified with the ruined castle, and the way the latter would be restored is identical with the manner in which the former should have been restored. The two principal elements in the image become fused, they generate a life of their own and yet actively forward Burke's thesis.

Burke's method, then, is to establish a general truth which his reader cannot fail to associate with a concrete image making a vivid sensory appeal. To speak comparatively, Johnson fails to make a strong imaginative impact because of his determination to sustain his thought on a philosophic level. There is little doubt which kind of writing is the more politically effective.

Johnson, however, could make use of concrete details and be specific when he considered it desirable: the occasions when he did so are highly significant. They lead us back to the question of his audience, for it is precisely when he wishes to characterise the Opposition that concrete terms suddenly appear in his language. Early in the pamphlet we are told that only 'the wise' have escaped infection from the Opposition's clamour, and it is, of course, to the wise that the philosophical discussion has been directed. Later, after an ironic passage, Johnson turns to the unwise, who have been infected:

> Fired with this fever of epidemic patriotism, the tailor slips his thimble, the draper drops his yard, and the blacksmith lays down his hammer; they meet at an honest alehouse, consider the state of the nation, read or hear the last petition, lament the miseries of the time, are alarmed at the dreadful crisis, and subscribe to the support of the bill of rights.[1]

As soon as the behaviour of the unwise is to be sketched, men with specific trades appear—tailor, draper, blacksmith—each is given a symbol of his trade—a thimble, a yard, and a hammer; these tools are indeed only symbolic, but they are concrete objects and to that extent denote a language quite different from what has gone before. It should be noted that 'the wise' are not identified with any active occupations, they are not associated with any objects from the material world. They are those who, like Johnson himself, are deemed to make an intellectual and

[1] *Works*, VI, 171.

philosophical response to the situation; the ignorant and foolish, on the other hand, down the tools of their trades, meet in an honest alehouse, and refuse to listen to the general wisdom of the benevolent but imprudent gentleman who intrudes upon their deliberations there.

Similar observations are prompted by what is, perhaps, the best passage in the whole pamphlet, the lengthy ironic description of the progress of a petition (in reference to the many petitions urging the King to dissolve Parliament after the expulsion of Wilkes). Johnson wishes to create a picture of deluded low-class, uneducated boors, drunkards, and tradesmen: once more the diction immediately becomes increasingly specific and concrete. We hear of meat and drink, ale, turtle, and venison; we see the low-class individual patronised by 'Sir Francis, Sir Joseph, or Sir George', and 'the poor loiterer, whose shop had confined him, or whose wife had locked him up';[1] we are told of the man who signs the petition because 'he has vowed the destruction of the turn-pike', another 'because it will vex the parson', and so forth. In other words, the scene suddenly comes alive, it comes close to real existence; it is an animal kind of existence and is completely devoid of any concern with the life of the mind; it is in fact the life of the ignorant poor when flattered by the irresponsible rich. Significantly the man who rebukes the petitioners—like the intruder in the alehouse—is one of 'higher rank and more enlightened mind'.[2] Here indeed are the two modes of distinction—'rank' and 'mind'. Throughout, the wise are of superior rank and intelligence, the Opposition appear as of lower rank, education, and intelligence; the former are those who can appreciate abstract and philosophical discussion, the latter are associated with the material world, which is evoked by concrete and specific language. And the implication that these last are unable to rise to the level of the wise in any respect is too obvious to require insistence. What happens when levelling occurs is quite clear in Johnson's mind: a year of election he sees as 'a year of equality', and to the lower classes this means drunkennness, venality, indolence, and impertinent behaviour.

There is no doubt, then, that Johnson's was a deliberate appeal to the cultured and intelligent among the reading public.

[1] *Works*, VI, 172.　　　　　　　　[2] Ibid., VI, 173.

The generalised diction and philosophical discussion, the Latin quotations, the contemptuous description of a popular orator as 'the *Cicero* of the day',[1] and the disdain of the vulgar, the 'rabble', with their 'plebeian grossness'[2]—all were calculated to appeal to a class-conscious and educated audience. Add to this evidence Johnson's contempt, in the final paragraphs, for religious nonconformists, and the character of his intended audience becomes even more certain. For such readers the pamphlet would be effective—it flattered their prejudices and their superior education, and appealed to their vested interests. To others, particularly those accustomed to reading Junius, those who would later read Paine or who had earlier read Defoe, Johnson would have little to offer. To such readers Johnson was —to use the words of a newspaper commentator—'a Butean sycophant and ministerial defender of usurpation'.[3] Both by political theory and by literary manner he seemed to be of the 'establishment'.

[1] *Works*, VI, 172.   [2] Ibid., VI, 176.
[3] *Treasury or Impartial Compendium for 1770*, I, 218 n.

IV

JUNIUS AND JOHNSON: THE FALKLAND ISLANDS DISPUTE

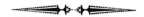

A CLOSER critical comparison between Junius and John-son is possible because they were both contributors to the controversy over the English retreat from the Falkland Islands. This had followed a rather complex pattern of action and negotiation. In 1764 England had stationed a small garrison in Port Egmont and in 1769 informed the Spanish forces that they should withdraw from what was a British possession. Spain was not so easily to be deprived of what she considered her own sovereign rights. In December 1769 the Spanish Captain General of Buenos Aires sent ships to expel the British forces, but the captain of a British warship refused them entry. Six months later, however, the Spaniards compelled the garrison to surrender, disabled the frigate, *Favourite*, by removing her rudder, and then allowed the British forces to leave unharmed. Negotiations between the two governments ensued. Britain threatened war, but eventually came to terms, Spain agreeing to make restitution without prejudice to her right to possession of the territory. George III informed Parliament of the settlement on 22 January 1771. Junius, on 30 January, denounced what he saw as a humiliating agreement and the betrayal of national rights; Johnson, in his *Falkland's Islands* pamphlet of the same year, vindicated the Government's action.[1]

[1] For further details see J. Goebel, *The Struggle for the Falkland Islands: a study in legal and diplomatic history* (New Haven, 1927).

The principal differences between their two publications stem not only from diversity of political opinions but also from difference of audience and circumstance. Johnson's is a pamphlet of some forty-five pages, Junius's a letter only about a third as long, addressed to a newspaper. Johnson takes for granted an audience willing to follow a leisurely argument based on the philosophical proposition that peace is more desirable than war, interested in an historical survey of the general situation reaching back to Columbus and Elizabeth, and contemptuous of the cits and boors who were, they felt, deluded by Junius. Junius, for his part, has to move much more quickly to his points; he does not assume an interest in anything beyond what might seem to affect the relationship between the English people and their Government; and as a result of his intention to sharpen the conflict between Government and Opposition, he works solely by unqualified assertion and conjecture. One finds in Johnson an apparent willingness to consider qualifications to his thesis (even though one is sure he knows exactly what conclusion he will reach); no such tolerant ease of manner was likely or would have been wise in Junius's letter. This last would probably have the greater immediate effect, it would incite emotion and was at any rate calculated to lead to action[1]—but it sacrified permanent interest in order to achieve immediate objectives. Johnson, on the other hand, did not seek to arouse a fervent response or positive action—acceptance of the *status quo* was what he sought to encourage—and the result of reading his piece is intellectual stimulus to a degree greater than was strictly necessary to secure his first object. The effect of his pamphlet in 1771 would be less violent and activating than Junius's, but because it directs attention to issues which have remained relevant, the pamphlet is more permanently interesting.

Johnson opens with nearly twenty pages of historical introduction, surveying Hispano-British relations, emphasising the barrenness of the islands in question, and describing the recent dispute and negotiations with Spain. These pages are punctuated

---

[1] Unfortunately no details of the sale of this letter are available. Public demand for the previous letter (14 November 1770) led to the printing of 600 extra copies of the *Public Advertiser*, and the subsequent letter (22 April 1771) necessitated 500 extra copies. (*Letters*, I, 18 n.)

with statements of general wisdom that automatically enlist the agreement of intelligent men:

> war is not the whole business of life; it happens but seldom, and every man, either good or wise, wishes that its frequency were still less.[1]

> as the world is more enlightened, policy and morality will, at last, be reconciled, and . . . nations will learn not to do what they would not suffer.[2]

> 'nil mortalibus arduum est.' there is nothing which human courage will not undertake, and little that human patience will not endure.[3]

Such statements add weight to the writing as well as giving it the character of temperate thoughtfulness and conviction; they make it possible to read the pamphlet with interest nearly two hundred years after the events which provoked it; and they presuppose readers who, in addition to having a direct concern in affairs of the day, were not limited by such concerns. The quality of the prose, the invocation of Horace's authority, and the stimulus to abstract thinking all point to an educated and intelligent audience.

Junius's letter begins in a totally different manner:

> If we recollect in what manner the *King's friends* have been constantly employed, we shall have no reason to be surprised at any condition of disgrace to which the once respected name of Englishmen may be degraded.[4]

This brief sentence introduces the central topics of the letter—'the *King's friends*' and 'disgrace'; it opens up an ironic tone in which a great part of the letter is written; and by the first words —'If we recollect'—it confirms what we know, that Junius was aware of an audience to whom he had already addressed forty-one letters and with whom he had established some community of interest and values. When he goes on to make his main charge against the administration—'violence and oppression at home can only be supported by treachery and submission abroad'— there is a thrust and a savagery about the antithesis which are not to be found in Johnson's pamphlet. The urgency of the situation, as well as restricted space, demand these qualities;

[1] *Works*, VI, 183. [2] Ibid., VI, 184.
[3] Ibid., VI, 187. [4] *Letters*, I, 316–17.

47

furthermore, the antithesis is not merely verbal as some of Johnson's tend to be—Junius is, from his own viewpoint, making a valid charge economically and cogently.

Junius's survey of the events in the Falkland Islands which led to the British expulsion takes him eight lines, whereas it occupies five pages for Johnson. Junius's purpose is to give what he calls the 'facts' in such a way as to suggest calculation and a deliberate desire, on the part of Spain, to expel the British forces. Johnson, in his relatively leisurely fashion, gives a more objective account of events and allows the reader greater freedom to estimate the merits of the actions of both Spanish and British forces; he certainly makes it clear that all the right was not on the British side.

By comparison, then, Junius is jingoistic where Johnson is intelligent and sober in his argument over the international dispute. Junius argues from grounds of political expediency; he claims that England could have dictated the terms of a settlement with Spain, and if war had come it might have broken the Hispano-French alliance, so that by refusing to take stern measures and by making peace the British Government may well have fostered this alliance so dangerous to itself. Johnson, by contrast, does not argue from expediency; while he is content to accept the settlement by which Britain gained all she asked—'satisfaction' for an injury done, and reparations—he is also concerned with the general question of war or peace.

> As war is the last of remedies, 'cuncta prius tentanda', all lawful expedients must be used to avoid it. As war is the extremity of evil, it is, surely, the duty of those, whose station intrusts them with the care of nations, to avert it from their charge.[1]

Johnson goes on to give a picture of war, admittedly in generalised terms but vivid for all that, stressing the slaughter as well as the deaths from causes other than combat; he asserts that only parasites and contractors gain from it; and he tries to destroy the 'dream of idle speculation' which seems to promise notable gains from war with Spain. For Johnson the action of making peace is that of a government 'who know the value of life',[2] and he very astutely introduces his attack on Junius (partly quoted above[3]) by accusing him of contemplating the wanton sacrifice

[1] *Works*, VI, 199.   [2] Ibid., VI, 204.   [3] See pp. 17–18.

of human lives in the selfish hope that war would bring down the Government.

To set a brief passage from Johnson alongside one from his adversary is to clarify the contrast between them even further. Commenting on the King's speech of 13 November 1770, Junius claims that although the Administration had taken pains to minimise the indignity suffered by Britain, the people should be prepared for the total abandonment of our possession of, and right to, the disputed territory. He goes on:

> The event shows us that to depart, in the minutest article, from the nicety and strictness of punctilio, is as dangerous to national honour as to female virtue. The woman who admits of one familiarity seldom knows where to stop, or what to refuse; and when the counsels of a great country give way in a single instance, when once they are inclined to submission, every step accelerates the rapidity of the descent.[1]

Compare with this passage Johnson's handling of the Spaniards' action in removing the rudder from the British naval ship *Favourite*, in order to prevent her sailing from Port Egmont (in the Falklands) without their permission.

> If the English intended to keep their stipulation, how were they injured by the detention of the rudder? If the rudder be to a ship, what his tail is in fables to a fox, the part in which honour is placed, and of which the violation is never to be endured, I am sorry that the Favourite suffered an indignity, but cannot yet think it a cause for which nations should slaughter one another.[2]

In both cases the nature of the analogy largely establishes the character of the writing. Junius introduces into a political argument the lively but nevertheless rather vulgar simile of the loose woman; the point he wishes to make about the Government's action is sharpened at the cost of some coarseness, but the very coarseness adds an acerbity of tone that an analogy of greater propriety would not have achieved. The earthy kind of humour degrades the Government, but in a manner Johnson would never use. He may remark of Junius:

> What, says Pope, must be the priest, where a monkey is the god? What must be the drudge of a party, of which the heads are Wilkes and Crosby, Sawbridge and Townsend?[3]

---

[1] *Letters*, I, 319–20.   [2] *Works*, VI, 208–9.   [3] Ibid., VI, 206.

but the diminishing effect works by quite different means from those employed by Junius. It is based on what may broadly be called a religio-philosophical speculation and carries with it the authority of Pope, whereas Junius's illustration comes right out of life itself and marks the writer as one who habitually thinks in terms of actual living. There is an immediacy about Junius's writing born from his being immersed in the business of life and the effect of politics on it.

The impact made by the Johnsonian passage on the removal of the ship's rudder is quite otherwise. As with the Pope reference, the source of his analogy is literary; the choice of an allusion to a fable further removes the event from contemporary life and gives it a timeless significance; and associating the rudder (over which a great deal of 'patriot' fervour had been spilled) to a fox's tail not only serves an ironic purpose but also enforces the impression of a writer loftily able to detach himself from the rough and tumble of politics. Furthermore, Johnson makes greater mockery of the alleged insult to national pride by confining his pity to an inanimate object—'I am sorry that the Favourite suffered an indignity'—thereby making appear more foolish the clamour for revenge over the incident. Johnson's technique, then, is like Junius's to the extent that it is diminishing—the fate of the ship's rudder engrosses our attention and it is not to be construed as a *casus belli*—but it establishes him as a person able to speculate on the issues behind a trivial event, to redress the disproportionate reaction to that event, and then, by drawing on his intellectual resources, to put the intelligent reader in his own position of vantage. Both Johnson and his reader are elevated above the sorry world of politics; Junius and his reader are more firmly involved in it.

In a comparison of the two publications, therefore, Johnson scores heavily for statesmanlike and sober argument; there is no doubt who is morally superior. Moreover, his style is highly appropriate: the cultured, balanced, restrained style, using a philosophic and generalised diction, is as it were an outward sign of inward virtue—it perfectly embodies an argument for the civilised condition of peace. His classical references, his allusions to Pope and Milton, his general appeal to a cultivated audience, again all suggest that he speaks with the authority of learning and intelligence, that he can see beyond the immediate facts as isolated phenomena and can see them in a large context where universal moral truths—principally that peace is the most desirable human condition—are of pre-eminent importance.

Junius comes out of the comparison as having a relatively restricted vision and writing the more ephemeral piece. Yet his own astuteness cannot be overlooked. His irony is bitterly effective; so is his method of gradually isolating the King as his principal target and then creating what he calls a 'fable' of an imaginary king who is profoundly humiliated. And the final image to clinch the idea that the honour of the Crown and the rights of the people are identical, and if the former is debased the latter is jeopardised—this image is masterly.

> Private credit is wealth, public honour is security, the feather that adorns the royal bird, supports its flight; strip him of his plumage and you fix him to the earth.

It is one of the few images in popular political controversy fitted to be compared with Paine's famous jibe at Burke—'he pities the plumage but forgets the dying bird'—which it so nearly resembles.

V

EDMUND BURKE:
THOUGHTS ON THE CAUSE OF THE PRESENT DISCONTENTS

J UNIUS's letters, according to Coleridge, 'impel to action
and not thought'; Johnson's pamphlets, as we have seen,
provoke thought but were not intended to urge men to act and
indeed would have been inappropriate for that purpose; Burke's
Present Discontents impels both to thought and action. From
first to last he is concerned with action. He stresses the urgent
need for the people to ensure that Parliament remains dependent on them so as to avoid its becoming dependent on some
other power (the Crown and 'king's men'); the need, too, for
Parliament to recapture its original *raison d'être*, control over the
administration; and the need for good men to combine in
effective opposition. Towards the end of the pamphlet, indeed,
he insists, on the necessity

> To be fully persuaded, that all virtue which is impracticable is
> spurious; and rather to run the risk of falling into faults in a
> course which leads us to act with effect and energy, than to
> loiter out our days without blame and without use.[1]

Action both thoughtful, purposeful, and energetic, then, is the
keynote; attention to it reveals much about the nature of Burke's
argument and the methods he chose to make the argument
effective.

In terms which recall Newman's later distinction between the

---

[1] *Works*, I, 379.

Church of England and that of Rome, Burke distinguishes between a commonwealth which is 'no better than a scheme upon paper' and 'a living, active, effective constitution'.[1] The life, energy, and activity to which he refers do not, of course, reside in the constitution as a body of laws and precedents, but in the men who govern and the people who elect and should in a sense control their governors. What Burke calls 'the vivifying energy of good government'[2] can emerge, in fact, only when the people assert their right, through Parliament, to refuse support to an administration which is not acceptable to them or which is dominated by a faction that lacks their confidence. In other words, both the people and their representatives must act in the defence of unalienable rights and in support of measures designed to forward their common interests and welfare. As a direct corollary, therefore:

> The ignorance of the people is a bottom but for a temporary system; the interest of active men in the state is a foundation perpetual and infallible.[3]

In consequence, the quality of these 'active men' becomes a matter of profound importance. Burke's judgment in this respect is governed by experience. We must, he says, 'be tainted with a malignity truly diabolical, to believe all the world to be equally wicked and corrupt';[4] on the other hand, he does not expect human perfection nor '*perfect* satisfaction in government'.[5] 'Abstract, universal, perfect harmony'[6] is not to be looked for, but there are 'means of ordinary tranquillity' which will ensure the greatest possible political good, and these should be used. The whole question eventually settles into a moral issue: the moral quality of the men who govern and who are governed. The criteria of judgment in both cases are the same: what makes for goodness in private life provides the basis for it also in public.

> We are born only to be men. We shall do enough if we form ourselves to be good ones. It is therefore our business carefully to cultivate in our minds, to rear to the most perfect vigour and maturity, every sort of generous and honest feeling that belongs

[1] *Works*, I, 332. [2] Ibid., I, 333.
[3] Ibid., I, 313. [4] Ibid., I, 332.
[5] Ibid., I, 336. [6] Ibid., I, 337.

to our nature. To bring the dispositions that are lovely in private life into the service and conduct of the commonwealth; so to be patriots, as not to forget we are gentlemen.[1]

The authority of the Romans is invoked to support this view. 'This wise people'

> believed private honour to be the great foundation of public trust; that friendship was no mean step towards patriotism; that he who, in the common intercourse of life, showed he regarded somebody besides himself, when he came to act in a public situation, might probably consult some other interests than his own.[2]

Even though one knows that behind this kind of statement lay the implicit claim that the Rockingham Whigs were the only group who acted on the principles outlined and even though the passage is followed by the explicit assertion that 'the great connexion of Whigs in the reign of Queen Anne' also acted on them[3]—in other words, even though Burke is flying in the face of historical fact here—the reader could scarcely fail to respond to the emotive force carried in the accumulated phrases of this style. Burke's own passionate belief in the ideas expressed is clear; his moral fervour helps to establish himself as one of a line of 'good men' dedicated to the well-being of their community and convinced that 'the only proper method of rising to power [is] through hard essays of practised friendship and experimented fidelity'. The key words are 'practised' and 'experimented': friendship is a good in itself, but it needs to be tested in action for it to form the basis of public trust. Thus, though the principles are given a dignified (and, in part, a false) historical ancestry, they would make a forceful appeal to normal moral sensibilities.

Burke's vision of the importance of the combination of good men dedicated to the well-being of the community and active in its pursuit, through practical political effort—this directs his writing throughout. It lends to his pamphlet a wholeness and largeness of view beyond the capacities of Junius or of Johnson in his rôle as political writer. Junius was not capable of an equal degree of abstract thought; Johnson, while Burke's equal as a

[1] *Works*, I, 378–9.   [2] Ibid., I, 374.
[3] Ibid, I, 374–5.

moral philosopher, lacked a comparable experience of practical politics, of the means whereby theory could be translated into day-to-day practice. That the Opposition needed such a unifying vision as Burke provided is clear enough; his letters to various members of the Rockingham Whigs at the time of the Wilkes furore and later make it evident. And the absence of the unity he desired was, of course, a principal cause of Junius's despair. Burke's intention was to stimulate thought about 'the necessity of honest combination'[1] and to induce men to act as a result of it.

He was clear, too, about the factors he considered inimical to the country's good; here again they concern men in action—the actions of evil men. Burke's principal charges against 'the king's men', the Court Party of George III, are that they owe their power not to popular election or acclaim but to royal favouritism; that they deliberately foster disunity among other parties to forward their own ends; and that they are turning Parliament into an ally of the Executive instead of a control upon it. It is a propaganda point with them—which Burke strenuously counters—that the allegiance implicit in a party system destroys an individual's freedom of thought and action. Burke asserts that this view is not only calculated to destroy the Opposition's political effectiveness, it is also morally evil in that it encourages distrust, lack of political integrity, and self-seeking.

> All this is done upon their favourite principle of disunion, of sowing jealousies amongst the different orders of the state, and of disjointing the natural strength of the kingdom; that it may be rendered incapable of resisting the sinister designs of wicked men, who have engrossed the royal power.[2]

Again he is concerned with men in action. Their principles are evil; they rely 'on distrust, on disconnexion, on mutability by principle, on systematic weakness in every particular member'; and though the result of their efforts will lack 'substantial strength of any kind', nevertheless these men are active.[3] 'Their restless and crooked spirit drives them to rake in the dirt of every kind of expedient';[4] they raise divisions in the populace because they cannot control it and reward individuals on their ability to

---

[1] *Works*, I, 379. [2] Ibid., I, 324.
[3] Ibid., I, 324–5. [4] Ibid., I, 342.

create confusion. Good men, powerless to act owing to the weakness of Parliament, 'look upon this distracted scene with sorrow and indignation'.

> Everything partakes of the original disorder. Anarchy predominates without freedom, and servitude without submission or subordination.

Chaos is come again. There is little doubt that this is what Burke implies here; 'original disorder', 'anarchy', and the strong suggestion of the overthrow of a traditional social order (especially in the final phrase) all confirm it. This, he implies, is what results from evil in action, and the satanic image contained in the crooked spirit which rakes among the dirt would not be lost on his contemporaries. Burke indeed sees an active principle in evil as well as in good. The achievements of the latter are preferable because they produce a state of unity, trust, and civilised behaviour in public and private affairs, but they require energetic effort to secure them. They must, furthermore, be secured against men who have no relish for 'peace and prosperity', whose power rests on national discontents, and who are 'a species of men to whom a state of order would become a sentence of obscurity'.[1] It is towards this 'state of order' that Burke endeavours to persuade his audience.

Such an argument as is briefly sketched here could be conducted on the Johnsonian philosophical level, using a generalised diction; it could also conceivably be translated—though not without the loss of grandeur and universality—into the particulars and invested with the violent acerbity to be found in Junius. Burke uses neither alternative, but devises his own combination of both. He expressly refuses to malign Lord Bute—'I have carefully avoided the introduction of personal reflections of any kind';[2] the Wilkes affair appears only in the second half of this 125-page pamphlet, and then not in any detail; and George III does not emerge as an individual but rather as an influence, a source of power or of majesty. Individuals are not of prime significance; they are parts of a larger whole, manifestations of active and permanent principles. These last are Burke's main concern. Generalised, philosophic diction was, then, inevitable, but since these principles were active in a real world of men, it was essential

---

[1] *Works*, I, 341.   [2] Ibid., I, 330.

to show their relevance to such a world: as Sir George Savile remarked when he saw the pamphlet in draft form, 'People in general skip over mere truths.'[1] And the dual requirement produced the distinctive character of Burke's literary manner.

The principal appeal of the *Present Discontents* is rational and argumentative; Burke apparently desired what he called in his *Observations on 'The Present State of the Nation'*, 'the coolness of philosophical inquiry'[2] but with the temperature slightly raised. It is true, of course, that he does not want to follow the example of the writer to whom he replies in that earlier work, twisting 'into frightful shapes' transitory passions, 'in order first to terrify and then to govern the populace';[3] this comes nearer to Junius's intention. Nevertheless, as Burke well knew, if the reader's judgment was to be shaken, then there had to be something 'to refresh the imagination'.[4] In the case of the *Present Discontents* if 'the system' was to be submitted to the scrutiny of philosophical enquiry and judged according to principles of morality and political effectiveness, for which a generalised diction is almost inevitably the medium, then the reader had imaginatively to be kept in touch with the real world in which the system operated. Metaphor, simile, allusion, analogies, all drawing their material from a recognisable and concrete world—these then became indispensable. What is distinctive about Burke's use of an apparently commonplace technique is the way in which imagery becomes not merely additional ornament but the vehicle for conducting the argument itself. Though there are a few exceptions, for the most part the imagery cannot be separated from the thesis Burke is urging: it *is* the argument in a way quite beyond Junius or Johnson. 'How closely that fellow reasons in metaphor', as one correspondent reported to Hannah More of Burke's performance in the Commons[5]—and it is to this reasoning in metaphor that attention must be given.

One preliminary point should be made about it. Burke's purpose in the *Present Discontents* is quite different from that, say, in the *Reflections*. That work is intended to arouse intense emotional fervour; the reader's mind is bombarded with highly emotive material so as to excite his fear of complete moral and

[1] *Correspondence* (1960), II, 120.　　[2] *Works*, I, 271.
[3] Ibid., I, 225.　　[4] Ibid., I, 263.
[5] *Johnsonian Miscellanies*, I, 174 n.

political upheaval; and the style carries overt evidence of strong feelings the significance of which, in Burke's view, distinguished his philosophy from the Revolutionists'. Consequently, Burke could permit himself a set-piece such as the 'apostrophe' to the Queen, the almost horrific account of the attack on Versailles (with its 'blood', 'massacre', 'scattered limbs and mutilated carcases'), and the generally heightened style. No such technique was appropriate in the *Present Discontents*. Imagery is certainly present, but it does not draw attention to itself, or if it does, in my opinion it fails; it is normally used to sharpen the validity and make concrete the application of the politico-philosophical argument; and it does its best work unobtrusively.

One example—and there are few—of Burke's failure to show the kind of decorum appropriate to his purpose appears in the following passage:

> When the people conceive that laws, and tribunals, and even popular assemblies, are perverted from the ends of their institution, they find in those names of degenerated establishments only new motives to discontent. Those bodies, which, when full of life and beauty, lay in their arms and were their joy and comfort, when dead and putrid, become but the more loathsome from remembrance of former endearments. A sullen gloom and furious disorder prevail by fits: the nation loses its relish for peace and prosperity. . . .[1]

The first point to notice is that Burke holds up the progress of his argument while he develops his image; the argument does not advance through the image, but is only illustrated by it; indeed, if the second sentence were removed entirely the argument would scarcely be impaired. Moreover, the macabre material of the image draws the reader's attention to itself and away from the thesis being presented, and Burke explores the details in such a way as to compel one to examine them. It then becomes evident that the details are not wholly pertinent: laws, tribunals, and assemblies do not lie in the people's arms in anything approaching the way suggested by the image; it is also difficult to imagine the situation in which a lover would so fondly contemplate a putrefying body, however beloved it had been when alive. Burke, then, fails here in various respects, and

---

[1] *Works*, I, 341.

some aspects of his failure are brought to the reader's notice because the image itself becomes the focus of attention instead of being embedded in the argument.

In sharp contrast there is a passage describing the way in which (as Burke believed) the court junta induces eminent men of various parties to take office in an administration, assuring them of their support, gradually withdrawing it, and finally leaving the Ministers powerless and disgraced in the party from which they came.

> In the beginning of each arrangement no professions of confidence and support are wanting, to induce the leading men to engage. But while the ministers of the day appear in all the pomp and pride of power, while they have all their canvass spread out to the wind, and every sail filled with the fair and prosperous gale of royal favour, in a short time they find, they know not how, a current, which sets directly against them; which prevents all progress; and even drives them backwards. They grow ashamed and mortified in a situation, which, by its vicinity to power, only serves to remind them the more strongly of their insignificance.[1]

Here the image is completely successful. The argument progresses *by means of* the image, which gradually and almost imperceptibly takes it over; it is not merely held up while an imaginative illustration is provided. In the course of the image we learn a great deal about the confident behaviour of success-ful men, their enjoyment of royal favour, their puzzlement on discovering obstacles to their success, and their final despairing retreat. The argument then goes directly on and no thematic hiatus has occurred. But the argument has undoubtedly gained in vividness, in its being related to a concrete, recognisable world, and in being translated into terms of human activity. Moreover, the eighteenth-century reader was made vitally aware of the way in which the active principle of evil went to work; in view of the earlier remarks on Burke's thesis, this is of great importance.

As a further example we may take the brief passage referring to the ill-fated Rockingham administration (1765–66); the fact that Burke was himself a minister in that government shows how carefully he has his emotions under control here. In a passage of

---

[1] *Works*, I, 325.

this kind we might have expected Burke, who was always sensitive to political failure, to allow feeling to emerge to the detriment of the argument, but it does not happen.

> It is true, that about four years ago, during the administration of the Marquis of Rockingham, an attempt was made to carry on government without [the Court Party's] concurrence. However, this was only a transient cloud; they were hid but for a moment; and their constellation blazed out with greater brightness, and a far more vigorous influence, some time after it was blown over. An attempt was at that time made . . . to break their corps, to discountenance their doctrines, . . .[1]

Here, too, the argument is not interrupted by the image, but flows through it and is vitalised at the same time. The success of the active men—the 'king's friends' who, according to Burke, defeated the Rockingham Whigs—is given the inevitability of a natural phenomenon. Political strength, enhanced by triumph over a temporary setback, is effectively suggested by the 'greater brightness' with which a group of stars seems to shine after being dimmed by passing clouds.

This mode of imaginative reasoning appears to develop under Burke's hand while in the act of writing, and its onward, inevitable movement seems to support this view. Burke's style maintains a nice balance between what Professor Sutherland calls 'the foreseen and the fortuitous';[2] unlike Johnson, in whose prose 'the foreseen triumphs continually over the fortuitous', Burke does not give the impression that every sentence has been carefully worked out before it is put down, although it is clear that he knows where he is going. He seems to allow himself the orator's freedom to develop individual points at will, but in accordance with the pattern of thought of the pamphlet as a whole. Something of this disciplined spontaneity has already been illustrated; a further example is provided by the end of a paragraph in which Burke has drawn attention to the feebleness of government under the court junta and to the way foreign governments can afford to ignore England's rightful demands.

> These demands (one of them at least) are hastening fast towards an acquittal by prescription. Oblivion begins to spread her cobwebs over all our spirited remonstrances. Some of the most

[1] *Works*, I, 329.

[2] In *Essays presented to D. Nichol Smith* (Oxford, 1945), p. 99.

valuable branches of our trade are also on the point of perishing from the same cause. I do not mean those branches which bear without the hand of the vine-dresser; I mean those which the policy of treaties had formerly secured to us; I mean to mark and distinguish the trade of Portugal, the loss of which, and the power of the cabal, have one and the same era.[1]

The image in this passage is certainly the vehicle of the argument and carries it along efficiently, but it gives one the impression that it occurred to Burke in the act of composition. He obviously intended to reach the point of isolating Portuguese trade as his main evidence, but the hesitant structure of the final sentence seems to indicate that the full extent of the image was unforeseen, as was its value in vivifying the argument, until Burke was actually putting pen to paper.

In the passage above it is a lack of purposeful human activity which is being observed and which the image pinpoints. The agent of the action is non-human, the vague abstract, 'oblivion', whose industry in covering the vines with cobwebs would be impossible if men were carrying out their proper function and attending to the health of the plants. What is presupposed here and elsewhere is the necessary collaboration between man and nature which is essential to the satisfactory functioning of both. Vines will grow, but if they are to be in the highest degree fruitful and beneficial man must co-operate; treaties are established on a basis of natural trust, but they require constant attention if their benefits are permanently to be secured. One is reminded of Thomas Hardy's character Giles in *The Woodlanders* who 'was a good man and *did good things*': goodness for Burke is an active quality and it is estimated by the extent to which man acts in accordance with natural laws.

The frequent appearance of natural imagery, in this work as in others, seems to confirm this view of its significance. Arguing that 'nothing can be more unnatural than the present convulsions of this country', Burke goes on to claim ironically that what seems to follow from the administration's argument is that the wealth of the nation is the cause of its discontent.

If our dominions abroad are the roots which feed all this rank luxuriance of sedition, [I imagine] it is not intended to cut them off in order to famish the fruit.[2]

[1] *Works*, I, 339.   [2] Ibid., I, 309.

Unnatural situations lead to remedies which are the reverse of what the natural process demands. Similarly, when he is speaking of the machinations of the Court to seize 'a degree of power which they could never hope to derive from natural influence' and which would never have the security such influence gives to power, Burke claims that they proceeded 'to destroy everything of strength which did not derive its principal nourishment from the immediate pleasure of the court'.[1] Having introduced this metaphor of the destruction of those natural growths which were not fed from one pre-selected and alien source, he shows how the Whig Party came under attack. Its power 'was rooted in the country'; it possessed a 'natural and fixed influence'; and in order to eradicate this permanent because natural power, the Court Party had 'to go to the root'.[2] Such an action inevitably resulted from the first unnatural step—that of trying to divorce the Court from the Administration, which together should have formed a natural alliance. On the other hand, a right assessment of and collaboration with natural forces leads to wisdom; decisions which may prove fatal to the security or peace of government, for example, will be avoided by these means.

> They who can read the political sky will see a hurricane in a cloud no bigger than a hand at the very edge of the horizon, and will run into the first harbour.[3]

Prudence, after all, is no small part of political wisdom. Above all, these same means teach men that natural virtues such as friendship, regard for others, or fidelity to 'dearest connections', lead inevitably to association with men of like interests on a basis of mutual trust.

> Commonwealths are made of families, free commonwealths of parties also; and we may as well affirm, that our natural regards and ties of blood tend inevitably to make men bad citizens, as that the bonds of our party weaken those by which we are held to our country.[4]

Emphasis on what promotes the natural well-being of a state and its people also produces, conversely, a concern with disease in the body politic. It is interesting, for instance, to find Burke comparing himself with the writer of a medical treatise.

---

[1] *Works*, I, 317-18. [2] Ibid., I, 318-19.
[3] Ibid., I, 336. [4] Ibid., I, 373-4.

My aim is to bring this matter into more public discussion. Let the sagacity of others work upon it. It is not uncommon for medical writers to describe histories of diseases very accurately, on whose cure they can say but very little.[1]

While it is untrue that Burke has no curative suggestions to offer, the comparison itself is significant. It is implied frequently in the use of such words as 'distemper', 'sickness', 'cure', and 'disorder', and on certain occasions these metaphors are more thoroughly exploited. For example:

> Particular punishments are the cure for accidental distempers in the state; they inflame rather than allay those heats which arise from the settled mismanagement of the government, or from a natural indisposition in the people.[2]

> the scheme of the junto under consideration, not only strikes a palsy into every nerve of our free constitution, but in the same degree benumbs and stupifies the whole executive power.[3]

> It would (among public misfortunes) be an evil more natural and tolerable, that the House of Commons should be infected with every epidemical phrensy of the people, as this would indicate some consanguinity, some sympathy of nature with their constituents, than that they should in all cases be wholly untouched by the opinions and feelings of the people out of doors.[4]

Such examples make it plain that when Burke is writing about the state he is not thinking of some nebulous abstract; in a traditional way the body politic imaginatively becomes a human body occasionally subject to disease, and it is the duty of the 'doctor of politics' (as he was later contemptuously to describe Richard Price) to propose remedial treatment. The advantage resulting from such an approach is obvious and need not be laboured: political disorders are translated into concrete terms of human living, and the desirability of natural activity and energetic life is constantly brought to the reader's notice.

And Burke's imaginative reasoning makes one conscious not only of an enduring world in which natural forces encourage and disease impedes human and political life; it also operates in a world which would, for his readers, be recognisably their own. Burke's metaphors introduce the constable who keeps the

[1] *Works*, I, 365. [2] Ibid., I, 310.
[3] Ibid., I, 338. [4] Ibid., I, 347.

peace;[1] the gaping multitudes such, perhaps, as those who might visit the fairs of the day and be taken in by 'a perspective view of the court, gorgeously painted, and finely illuminated from within';[2] the 'bitter waters' which flow through 'an hundred different conduits' and infect the drinker until he is 'ready to burst';[3] the plausible wisdom which is 'as current as copper coin, and about as valuable';[4] the eating of 'the roast beef of old England';[5] and the 'deepest and dirtiest pits' in which a man could be 'soused over head and ears'.[6] This is a world, too, which was accustomed to that vicious punishment of whipping at the cart's tail, and the allusion to this practice provides a fascinating illustration of the working of Burke's imaginative mind. Speaking with bitter irony of the time-server who conveniently discovers a fundamental disagreement with his party at the very moment when 'they lose power or he accepts a place', Burke comments:

> It is therefore very convenient to politicians, not to put the judgment of their conduct on overt-acts, cognizable in any ordinary court, but upon such matter as can be triable only in that secret tribunal, where they are sure of being heard with favour, or where at worst the sentence will only be private whipping.[7]

The imaginative evocation of the secret and indulgent courtroom of conscience where the place-man is judge, prisoner, jury, and hangman is brilliant. It would contrast sharply with the notoriously severe courts of the time where an offender was by no means sure of 'being heard with favour', and with the kind of scene witnessed by Parson Woodforde a few years later, in a Somerset town, when a man was whipped through the streets by a hangman, 'a most villainous looking Fellow indeed'.[8] The contrast between such a scene and the imaginative 'private whipping' would, for a contemporary, suggest the measure of Burke's bitterness.

Writing in his *Observations on 'the Present State of the Nation'* Burke accuses his opponent of attempting to raise 'by art magic

[1] *Works*, I, 309. [2] Ibid., I, 320.
[3] Ibid., I, 331. [4] Ibid., I, 376.
[5] Ibid., I, 341. [6] Ibid., I, 319.
[7] Ibid., I, 377.
[8] Ed. J. Beresford, *The Diary of a Country Parson* (1924), I, 209.

a thick mist before our eyes'.[1] This accusation cannot be made against Burke in the *Present Discontents*. Although he frequently raises issues of general, philosophical interest, he is vitally concerned with the actions of men in the real world, and, by the various means so far examined, he keeps his reader in contact with that world. Nevertheless, his object is philosophical enquiry and, by isolating examples of special uses of language, the character of his argumentative mode may have been obscured. To analyse the structure of a complete paragraph is the only satisfactory method. To avoid the charge of selecting only the best for analysis, and to choose a representative as well as a complete passage is difficult, the more so when each paragraph interlocks with a whole phase of the argument. As with Johnson and Gibbon, so with Burke the paragraph is his unit of composition; only this was sufficiently copious to encompass a single complex of thought.

The paragraph which follows forms part of Burke's handling of the issue of 'party' and 'faction'; supporters of the Administration had repeatedly tried to identify the two terms, arguing that all parties 'are in their nature factions, and ought to be dissipated and destroyed'. Burke's rejoinder begins:

It is indeed in no way wonderful, that such persons should make such declarations. That connexion and faction are equivalent terms, is an opinion which has been carefully inculcated at all times by unconstitutional statesmen. The reason is evident. Whilst men are linked together, they easily and speedily communicate the alarm of any evil design. They are enabled to fathom it with common counsel, and to oppose it with united strength. Whereas, when they lie dispersed, without concert, order, or discipline, communication is uncertain, counsel difficult, and resistance impracticable. Where men are not acquainted with each other's principles, nor experienced in each other's talents, nor at all practised in their mutual habitudes and dispositions by joint efforts in business; no personal confidence, no friendship, no common interest, subsisting among them; it is evidently impossible that they can act a public part with uniformity, perseverance, or efficacy. In a connexion, the most inconsiderable man, by adding to the weight of the whole, has his value, and his use; out of it, the greatest talents are wholly unserviceable to the public. No man, who is not inflamed by vain-glory into enthusiasm, can

[1] *Works*, I, 214.

flatter himself that his single, unsupported, desultory, un-systematic endeavours, are of power to defeat the subtle designs and united cabals of ambitious citizens. When bad men combine, the good must associate; else they will fall, one by one, an unpitied sacrifice in a contemptible struggle.[1]

The overall impression given by this passage—particularly out of its context—is of general wisdom: what Burke has to say is perhaps more relevant to the twentieth century than to the specific situation to which it refers. It lacks the particulars which Junius would have supplied and is more akin to the Johnsonian mode of writing; it excels this, however, by its range of political wisdom. Johnson was Burke's equal as a moral philosopher, but Burke's statements also carry the authority of a man of affairs. The grasp he shows of a party's response to an alarm—which he knew from first hand in his efforts to rally the Rockingham Whigs over the Wilkes case—is evidenced by the linguistic control early in the paragraph. There is operating, in effect, a 'submerged' military metaphor as Burke shows men linked together, communicating the alarm, and opposing evil 'with united strength', rather than lying dispersed without order and discipline, and resistance being impracticable.[2] This metaphor does not obtrude its presence but merges into the argument; it serves, however, to tighten the cohesion of Burke's description. For a time the prose then appropriately becomes looser as he remarks on the lack of unity if men are not intimately acquainted with one another in private or business life. And gradually a distinction is seen to emerge on which attention is focused for the remainder of the paragraph—the difference between men in private and in public life. In private life an individual can be self-sufficient, in public he is of value only when part of a larger effective whole. For it is to the question of effectiveness that Burke finally turns by means of the merest hint at the core of meaning in the parable of the talents—that talents are not to be hidden but put to their fullest use. In this context 'use' is equated

[1] *Works*, I, 372.
[2] It is interesting to note that Burke, writing to Rockingham, refers to the Marquess's supporters as 'the troops' and to the ensuing parliamentary session as 'the next Campain' (*Correspondence*, II, 411), so it may be that military metaphors came readily to his mind. They occur on major occasions elsewhere in the *Present Discontents*. See *Works*, I, 350, 373, 379.

with service to the public. There follows the emphatic declaration—beginning 'No man'—on the weakness of unconnected individuals against the power of a cabal; the statement carries the emphasis of the speaking voice, the rhythms (in this and the final sentence) are those of an orator. But this orator is also an imaginative writer: the military metaphor present at the beginning of the paragraph reappears in the final sentence as Burke contemplates isolated men falling 'one by one' in 'a contemptible struggle'. Again the metaphor is unobtrusive, but one becomes aware that as well as an argumentative development, there has been an imaginative logic running through the passage. The issue between good and evil men has been conceived, indeed, as a military conflict, with this level of imaginative thought never far below the level of conscious political theory.[1]

There is, as a result, an onward, inevitable movement about the style of this passage, common to the whole pamphlet. The thought, wholly related to the necessity for corporate action by all good men, is conveyed by a style which is itself urgent in tone and impact. Though it is a cultured style with its sentences of varied but balanced lengths, the use of assonance and alliteration, the accumulated phrases to produce an effect of weighty emphasis, the generally harmonious impression on the ear, and so on—it is also an aggressive style. With an average of one verbal construction to every line in the paragraph, one feels an active determination to reach a goal. This is precisely the effect which Burke's political argument requires to reinforce it. And though the conclusions of the phase of argument of which this paragraph is a part is reached only at a later point, one stage has been attained in the final emotive parallel between the action of evil and the essential counteraction of good men in political life.

As it stands, of course, there is no restriction placed on the relevance of Burke's final sentence: it could apply to what is required of good men under any circumstances in any century. This general validity of Burke's thought is a prominent feature of his achievement in the *Present Discontents*: while he keeps the

---

[1] This claim would seem to be supported by the close proximity of two of the more thoroughly developed military metaphors both also applied to the conflict between 'the king's men' and the Opposition. See *Works*, I, 371, 373.

immediate issue always before the reader's mind, he is constantly moving outwards from it, forcing his audience to recognise the fundamental questions which it raises. To give only one further example, in the middle of a long paragraph on the value of a place-bill the reader is confronted by a moral question of timeless relevance. Burke is considering whether men holding positions in the gift of the Government should be disqualified from holding a seat in Parliament; he observes that, if the Bill were passed, the powerful influence of Government would then operate, with increasing skill, underground instead of in the open. He continues:

> It is no inconsiderable part of wisdom, to know how much of an evil ought to be tolerated; lest, by attempting a degree of purity impracticable in degenerate times and manners, instead of cutting off the subsisting ill practices, new corruptions might be produced for the concealment and security of the old.[1]

Such a comment—which could be paralleled on numerous occasions—is obviously pertinent to the practical question under discussion, but it also forces the reader beyond it to a problem worthy of consideration in any age. A similar point could well be made about the effect of Burke's natural imagery and his reasoning in metaphor—both features vitalise the treatment of immediate issues while at the same time reminding one of the larger questions which are involved. It is on evidence of this kind that one can base a claim for the continuing greatness of the *Present Discontents*.

What, in comparison, can be said of the pamphlet which, on John Morley's reckoning, is its most formidable precessor: Swift's *Conduct of the Allies* (1711)? A claim for the same kind of greatness cannot be sustained. The two works present a sharp contrast. Swift says that he allowed other writers to publish their remarks on Marlborough's conduct of the War of the Spanish Succession before his own: 'they might argue very well . . . from general Topics and Reason, though they might be ignorant of several Facts, which I had the opportunity to know'.[2] It is with facts and arguments based on them that he is concerned; there is a minimum of the general wisdom to be found

---

[1] *Works*, I, 368.
[2] Ed. H. Davis, *Political Tracts 1711–1713* (Oxford, 1951), p. 53.

in Burke; indeed, Swift rarely allows the reader's mind to move out beyond immediate issues. His is writing which, like Junius's, impels to action—as it undoubtedly did—rather than to thought. As Junius kept his audience in the mêlée of current political activity, the doings of specific individuals and the outcome of particular policies, so Swift involves us with the actions of the Queen, Marlborough, the Spanish and French Kings, the Emperor, the soldiers, the monied interest—with everyone, in short, taking part in the main business of the war and negotiations for prolonging it or for making peace. There is, as a result, a perpetual motion, even a restlessness, about Swift's account; one's mind is not encouraged to branch out into any independent, abstract thinking, but is continually being jostled along by the pamphleteer. To take one example almost at random when Swift is describing what he calls 'the business of Toulon' and the Emperor Joseph's reluctance to see that city in the hands of the allies: we hear, in less than the space of two paragraphs, of the Emperor's contriving to send 'twelve or fifteen thousand men to seize *Naples*', of the Duke of Savoy, who is for attacking the enemy but only when the Mareschal de Thesse's troops arrive, of the Earl of Peterborough, who is despatched to Vienna, of the death of the Emperor, of Mr. Whitworth, who was also sent to Vienna[1]—and so the account rushes on. Throughout we are faced with 'plain Matters of Fact', to use Swift's own phrase; his constant use of numbers—of men, horses, regiments, ships, money—is one obvious sign of the factual bias; indeed, there are few statements without their reference to some piece of factual evidence. Where Johnson overwhelms the reader with the weight of philosophical disquisition, Swift overwhelms him by the accumulation of facts logically and astutely manipulated. Imagery is rigorously kept to a minimum. It is, generally speaking, limited to such metaphorical use of language as in the reference to the monied men 'whose perpetual Harvest is War',[2] to the constitution as 'a Healthy Body' dieted 'into a Consumption',[3] or to the Queen's ungrateful servants 'who as they wexed the Fatter, did but kick the more'.[4] This again is a sign of Swift's determination not to allow his audience's attention to be emotionally dissipated, but to keep it

[1] Ed. H. Davis, *Political Tracts 1711–1713*, pp. 35–6.
[2] Ibid., p. 41.   [3] Ibid., p. 58.   [4] Ibid., p. 43.

fixed on the evidence. He further controls the response to his pamphlet by frequent summaries of points already established, a careful division into sections and sub-sections (the latter being numbered to make clear the stages of his argument), and a general clarity of presentation. The presentation, then, perfectly mirrors the factual nature of the material Swift employs; it brings him closer to Paine than to Burke.

Swift was determined to promote, to the best of his ability, a specific and immediate object—the termination of the war. The contemporary renown of his pamphlet, of course, implies the correctness of our own feelings, that Swift's use of means to that particular end was brilliantly successful. One reads the *Conduct of the Allies* now for insights into his literary techniques, for his complete clarity, and his brisk, vital prose; for the handling of a single historical issue by an astute pamphleteer; but not for political or moral wisdom of permanent relevance. This last is where Burke triumphs; it gives his *Present Discontents* a lasting significance which Swift's pamphlet, by its very nature, cannot claim.

Nor can the claim be advanced, for similar reasons, for the Junius *Letters*. No one would read Junius for political wisdom; some might rightly urge a reading of Johnson for that purpose. On a comparative basis, however, Burke's range of political insights, and of the moral wisdom accompanying them, is far greater than Johnson's: one would expect as much from the professional politician. Moreover, there is a decided difference in tone between the work of the two men despite the apparent similarity of their prose styles. For example, the lofty sneer which occasionally occurs in Johnson is absent from Burke. 'Lampoon itself would disdain to speak ill of him of whom no man speaks well'—this has no parallel in Burke. His remark on Wilkes is:

> I will not believe, what no other man living believes, that Mr. Wilkes was punished for the indecency of his publications, or the impiety of his ransacked closet. . . . I must consider this as a shocking and shameless pretence.[1]

Burke's is personal, direct, and weighty; Johnson's by comparison is a sneering, verbal sleight of hand. If it be objected that it is in Burke's interests to uphold Wilkes and in Johnson's to

---

[1] *Works*, I, 353–4.

malign him, then Burke's treatment of Lord Bute—reputedly
the head of 'the king's friends'—can be adduced. He might indeed have wished to malign Bute, but:

> I have carefully avoided the introduction of personal reflections
> of any kind. Much the greater part of the topics which have been
> used to blacken this nobleman are either unjust or frivolous. At
> best, they have a tendency to give the resentment of this bitter
> calamity a wrong direction, and to turn a public grievance into
> a mean, personal, or a dangerous national quarrel.[1]

Such an attitude not only bespeaks political shrewdness, it also
carries the mark of humane feeling.

Furthermore, Burke does not distinguish between the cultured and the vulgar either in his general references to the people
or in the language he uses to refer to different social strata. This
is not to pretend that Burke was, like Paine, writing for a
'popular' audience—he strongly implies that he is not writing
'merely to please the popular palate'[2]—but to insist that, while
writing for predominantly upper-class readers, he does not score
cheap hits by jibing at the vulgar. That his audience was intended to be the cultured upper classes is not to be doubted.
The Latin quotations, the description of corruption being 'cast
down from court, as *Até* was from heaven',[3] the lines from
Addison,[4] the scholastic aphorism,[5] the eulogy on that 'wise
people', the Romans[6]—all such evidence points to a cultivated
reader. Burke probably had in mind those whom he describes
as 'the natural strength of the kingdom'—'the great peers, the
leading landed gentlemen, the opulent merchants and manufacturers, the substantial yeomanry'.[7] Within these circles he
was doubtless chiefly aware of the classes most directly interested
in the life and moral stature of Parliament—the peers and great
landed gentlemen, such as Rockingham, Portland, and Richmond, to whom he submitted the pamphlet before publication.
Describing the design of the court junta to weaken the position
of Parliament while strengthening its own, Burke says that
Parliament was to be taught 'by degrees a total indifference' to
the rank and abilities of ministers. He adds:

[1] *Works*, I, 330. [2] Ibid., I, 366.
[3] Ibid., I, 320. [4] Ibid., I, 375.
[5] Ibid., I, 378. [6] Ibid., I, 374.
[7] Ibid., I, 337.

It was to be avowed, as a constitutional maxim, that the king might appoint one of his footmen, or one of *your* footmen, for minister.[1]

This leaves no doubt of the identity of those whom he was primarily concerned to address. And yet Burke refers to 'the people' throughout without making any social distinctions:

> The people have no interest in disorder. When they do wrong, it is their error, and not their crime.[2]

> [The House of Commons] was not instituted to be a control *upon* the people. . . . It was designed as a control *for* the people.[3]

> The people will see the necessity for restoring public men to an attention to the public opinion. . . . [4]

The term is not being used in any democratic sense—'demos' was as much a bogey to Burke as it was to Johnson. By 'the people' Burke means chiefly those whose holding of property, in varying degrees, makes them responsible partners in the social body. Nevertheless, the fact that he does not find it necessary to make any distinctions either on the basis of class or of culture imparts to the tone of his writing the humanity and generosity of feeling which remain a hallmark of the *Present Discontents*.

[1] *Works*, I, 316 (my italics).   [2] Ibid., I, 310.
[3] Ibid., I, 348.   [4] Ibid., I, 380.

PART TWO

Political Controversy
1790–1793

VI

THE PUBLICATION OF BURKE'S *REFLECTIONS* AND THE SUBSEQUENT CONTROVERSY: A SURVEY

I

EARLY in November 1789 the first letter was written in the correspondence between Burke and the 'very young gentleman at Paris' which was to culminate a year later in the *Reflections*. Burke never publicly divulged the young man's name, but it is now known that his correspondent was Charles-Jean-François de Pont (at sixteen years of age in 1784 Advocate-General of the Parlement of Metz, and a *conseiller* of the Parlement of Paris in 1789).[1] In this first letter he asks Burke to assure him that the French are worthy to be free and that the Revolution will succeed. Burke's reply to this request—dated 'October 1789' though undoubtedly written in November[2]—contains a lengthy exposition of his opinions on the Revolution and principles of government. The germ of the *Reflections* is here: only the stimulus provided by later events was needed to precipitate the longer work. The concept of liberty as 'social freedom' synonymous with justice; the emphasis on security of property, respect for social status, and stable government; veneration of

---

[1] See H. V. F. Somerset, 'A Burke Discovery', *English* (1951), VIII, xlvi, 171–8.

[2] Ed. Fitzwilliam and Bourke, *Correspondence of Edmund Burke* (1844), III, 102–21.

the English system; his distaste for the 'rights of man' and insistence on the primary importance of 'man in the concrete'—concepts and arguments familiar to readers of the *Reflections*, all are here in little. Fearing that this letter might be opened *en route*, Burke preferred to detain it and to send in its place a short letter stating his reasons for the delay. In reply De Pont sent 'a new and pressing application'[1] in which he appeals to Burke:

> Ah daignex Monsieur daignex mon Maitre m'assurer que les differents evenements que nous avons essuyé étoient les suites necessaires d'un changement que les circonstances avoient rendu indispensable. Daignex enfin me donner l'espoir de voir ma Nation digne de jouir de la Liberté comme la nation Angloise. . . . Daignex Monsieur eclaircir mes doutes et ne laissez pas le prejugé de l'esprit de parti à un jeune homme qui a appris en Angleterre le danger de tous les prejugés.[2]

The reply to this appeal was the *Reflections*.

On the same day that De Pont began this correspondence, 4 November 1789, the Revolution Society held its annual meeting in London to commemorate the Revolution of 1688. In his *Discourse on the Love of our Country* Dr. Richard Price combined an examination of principles of government with a panegyric on the events in France. Here was the immediate stimulus Burke required: a Dissenting minister, in the person of the long-distrusted Richard Price, declaring from a pulpit that a nation has the right to choose its own governors, 'to cashier them for misconduct', and to frame a government for itself. Price, moreover, had dared to argue that the present state of England 'wanted the grand security of public liberty'; he signified the present time as favourable to the cause of liberty; and, referring to the action of the French, expressed his delight through the words of the 'Nunc Dimittis'. The final incentive—if one were still needed—was provided by the action of the Revolution Society in sending a congratulatory letter to the National Assembly. Burke could delay no longer.

Beyond doubt, the composition of the *Reflections* was proceeding in the early months of 1790, but Burke's first opportunity to declare his views came in the parliamentary debate on the Army

[1] *Reflections*, in *Works*, II, 277.
[2] Fitzwilliam MSS. (Northampton), A.ii.70. A translation of the letter is given in *English*, VIII, xlvi, 174–5.

Estimates, on 9 February.[1] In this speech he was concerned with the French example to England. The comparatively calm and rational approach to the subject in the letter to De Pont of November 1789 gives way to an impassioned denunciation of the chaos and barbarism in France, on lines which exactly foreshadow the *Reflections*. The present danger, he warns the Commons,

> is one of being led through an admiration of successful fraud and violence, to an imitation of the excesses of an irrational, unprincipled, proscribing, confiscating, plundering, ferocious, bloody, and tyrannical democracy.

His attack is directed at the example set by the Army, at the evil of adopting a new constitution 'when they were absolutely in the possession of a good one', at the States' exceeding the mandate from the people, and at the confiscation of Church property. Each of these objects is attacked on the same grounds in the *Reflections*. In this speech, too, he tacitly assumes that the only goal worthy of a national upheaval would be to obtain a constitution on the British model; the French are splenetically denounced because this was not their aim. To impress on his aristocratic audience their special danger if revolutionary principles spread in England Burke bids Members consider

> how they would like to have their mansions pulled down and pillaged, their persons abused, insulted, and destroyed; their title-deeds brought out and burned before their faces.

The pamphlet was certainly in existence at the time of this speech. Less than a week later Dodsley advertised as in the Press and 'speedily [to] be published', *Reflections on Certain Proceedings of the Revolution Society of the 4th November 1789, concerning the affairs of France*.[2] The prominence given to the Revolution Society in this title underlines Burke's immediate purpose: the seriousness of affairs in England. The French situation was chiefly important as a warning to England. It is also apparent that the pamphlet was at any rate partly in proof stage on 19 February when Sir Philip Francis thanks Burke in a letter for his trouble in 'sending for the printed paper'.[3] The radical, outspoken

---

[1] *Parliamentary History of England* (1816), XXVIII, 351 ff.
[2] *St. James's Chronicle*, 12 February 1790.
[3] Ed. Fitzwilliam and Bourke, *Correspondence of Edmund Burke*, III, 128.

Francis not only criticises the structure and style of the printed version as being much more exceptionable than the manuscript he had seen earlier, but advises Burke in the strongest terms not to publish it. He warns Burke of the unseemly 'war of pamphlets' which would follow publication, a prophecy which was amply realised. Burke was distressed by their disagreement, but in his reply, written immediately on receiving Francis's letter, he defends the composition against various criticisms, reaffirms his intention to publish, and states his aim in doing so:

> I intend no controversy with Dr. Price, or Lord Shelburne, or any other of their set. I mean to set in full view the danger from their wicked principles and their black hearts. I intend to state the true principles of our constitution in church and state, upon grounds opposite to theirs. . . . When I have done that, they may have the field to themselves.[1]

Still the pamphlet did not appear. At least one person— Thomas Paine—was awaiting the publication fully prepared to reply at once. He described to an unknown correspondent, on 16 April 1790, a visit to the bookseller Debrett, who informed him

> that Mr. Burke's pamphlet was in the press (he is not the publisher), that he believed Mr. Burke was much at a loss how to go on; that he had revised some of the sheets, six, seven, and one nine times![2]

A few days later Debrett told Paine that Burke had stopped the printing, leading Paine to the conclusion 'that after all this vaporing of Mr. B., he will not publish his pamphlet'.[3] Burke's intimate friends, however, were kept informed of its progress. Sir Gilbert Elliot, for example, told his wife that he had 'passed the forenoon' of 23 April in reading Burke's pamphlet which was 'just coming out on France, and the relation of that subject to England'.[4] But Burke's activities in the House—including speeches in support of the Test and Corporation Acts and his

---

[1] Ed. Fitzwilliam and Bourke. *Correspondence of Edmund Burke*, III, 140–1.
[2] Ed. P. S. Foner, *The Complete Writings of Thomas Paine* (New York, 1945), II, 1300.
[3] Ibid., II, 1301.
[4] Ed. Countess of Minto, *Life and Letters of Sir Gilbert Elliot, 1st Earl of Minto* (1874), I, 357.

part in the prosecution of Hastings—caused further delay. Yet writing continued throughout the summer. In July Richard Burke referred to the book on which his father had been employed '6 months in writing'.[1] Six weeks later he informed Fitzwilliam that 'The work which has been so long on the anvil is at last finish'd.'[2] On receiving this news Fitzwilliam wrote to Burke expressing his delight that 'the great work' was soon to appear and voicing the hope of his class and interests that it would correct the world's

> erroneous mode of viewing, & reasoning upon the art of government, & to teach it that true philosophy will place more dependence upon the experience of practice than upon the theories of speculation.[3]

Advance copies were sent to a select few (including Sir Philip Francis) during October, and on 23 October, in the *St. James's Chronicle*, Dodsley announced that

> On the 1st of November will be published, in Octavo, Price Five Shillings, Sewed, *Reflections on the Revolution in France, and on the Proceedings in Certain Societies in London relative to that Event*.

On 1 November the work appeared.

It was acclaimed immediately. Among the Fitzwilliam MSS. (Sheffield) are many letters typical, one may presume, of the congratulations and laudatory comments which Burke received; the writers include General Burgoyne, Horace Walpole, Sir Gilbert Elliot, Lord Loughborough, Richard Cumberland, and the Bishop of St. David's. Numerous diaries and letters of the time record the reactions of the upper classes, and so reflect the views of those to whom Burke particularly appealed. The success of his persuasion on such readers needs no emphasis. William Windham records in his diary on 7 November:

> On Thursday I conceive it was, that a material incident happened—the arrival of Mr. Burke's pamphlet. Never was there, I suppose, a work so valuable in its kind, or that displayed powers of so extraordinary a nature. It is a work that may seem capable

[1] Fitzwilliam MSS. (Northampton), A.iv.71. Letter to Fitzwilliam, 29 July 1790.
[2] Fitzwilliam MSS. (Northampton), A.iv.67. Letter, 8 September 1790.
[3] Fitzwilliam MSS. (Sheffield). Letter, 15 September 1790.

of overturning the National Assembly, and turning the stream of opinion throughout Europe.[1]

Horace Walpole, writing to Mary Berry the following day, is equally enthusiastic:

> the fatal blow has been at last given by Mr. *Burke*. His pamphlet . . . is far superior to what was expected even by his warmest admirers. I have read it twice, and though of 350 pages, I wish I could repeat every page by heart.[2]

Mrs. Montagu speaks of the 'admirable, excellent, incomparable pamphlet';[3] Fanny Burney considered it 'the noblest, deepest, most animated, and exalted work' she had ever read;[4] the King recommended it as a book every gentleman ought to read;[5] and members of Convocation of the University of Oxford petitioned the Vice-Chancellor for the award of the degree of LL.D. by diploma to Burke 'in Consideration of his very able Representation of the true Principles of our Constitution Ecclesiastical and Civil'.[6]

The sales of the *Reflections* were exceptional. Dodsley's printing-house had to work overtime in order to produce (according to a modern estimate[7]) the remarkable total of 5,500 copies in seventeen days. Throughout November the enormous demand was maintained, so that, on 29 November, Burke could justly claim:

> The public has been so favourable that the demand for this piece has been without example; and they are now in the sale of the twelfth thousand of their copies.[8]

---

[1] Ed. Mrs. H. Baring, *The Diary of the Rt. Hon. William Windham* (1866), pp. 212–13.

[2] Ed. W. S. Lewis, *Horace Walpole's Correspondence* (Yale, 1944), XI, 131–2.

[3] Ed. R. Blunt, *Mrs. Montagu: Her Letters and Friendships* (1923), II, 249.

[4] Ed. C. Barrett, *Diary and Letters of Madame D'Arblay* (1905), IV, 435.

[5] Cf. Sir P. Magnus, *Edmund Burke* (1939), p. 195.

[6] Undated petition (postmarked 'Oxford 90. DE. 9') in the Fitzwilliam Museum, Cambridge. Quoted by kind permission of the Syndics of the Museum.

[7] See William B. Todd, 'The Bibliographical History of Burke's *Reflections on the Revolution in France*', *The Library* (1951–52), 5th series, VI, 100–8.

[8] Ed. Countess of Minto, *Life and Letters of Sir Gilbert Elliot, 1st Earl of Minto*, I, 365–6.

This evidence makes acceptable Prior's claim that 'within the first year above 19,000 copies were sold in England', and 30,000 'within a few years'.[1] These vast sales meant considerable financial profit for Burke despite the newspaper report that he had 'given it to his bookseller before it appeared'.[2] A receipt exists, dated 26 May 1791, acknowledging the payment by Dodsley to Burke of £1,000 'in consideration of profits from the sale of *Reflections on the Revolution in France*'.[3] (To compare this sum with Burke's maximum salary of £300 per annum as editor of Dodsley's *Annual Register* is to get some idea of its magnitude.)

Foreign editions extend the view of the wide popularity of the *Reflections*. Not unexpectedly, the first country outside England where it appeared was France. The translator, now identified as Pierre-Gaëton Dupont[4] (a lawyer who visited England in 1788 or 1789 and made Burke's acquaintance), was at work on the proof-sheets before the publication of the first English edition. The translation was hastily completed, but was not issued in Paris until 29 November.[5] Even disregarding the compulsion under which he worked, it is not surprising that Dupont found his task exacting. Calonne—the former Minister and last great exponent of reform from above in France—gives good reasons for the defects in the translation, in a letter to Burke:

> I admit that Mr. Burke is not easy to translate . . . a style so full of metaphorical expressions, of words that have a profound meaning & many possible applications, of endless allusions drawn from the depths of the author's literary knowledge, & of turns of speech peculiar to his genius.[6]

Dupont was only too conscious of his errors. In several letters among the Fitzwilliam manuscripts he apologises to Burke,

---

[1] J. Prior, *Life of Burke* (5th edn., 1854), p. 311.

[2] *St. James's Chronicle*, 3 December 1790.

[3] *Historical MSS. Commission*, Appendix to 9th Report (1883), Part II, p. 484.

[4] T. W. Copeland, *Edmund Burke—Six Essays* (1949), pp. 205 ff. See also Hans A. Schmitt and John C. Weston, Jr., 'Ten Letters to Edmund Burke from the French Translator of the *Reflections on the Revolution in France*', *Journal of Modern History* (Chicago, 1952–53), XXIV, iv, 406–23; XXV, i, 49–61.

[5] T. Macknight, *Life and Times of Edmund Burke* (1860), III, 328.

[6] Fitzwilliam MSS. (Northampton), A.ix.60, 9 February 1791.

promising amendment in the next edition.[1] Nevertheless, he affirms that 2,500 copies were sold in the first two days, at the same time warning Burke that piratical attempts had been encountered.[2] In February 1791 he assures Burke:

> The demand with us is not at all abated, as you think it is. It still goes on, but not so fast as with the original, & perhaps it depends upon me, because many people are waiting for a new edition much more corrected, which has been promised to the public.[3]

In the same letter he estimates the total sale of the *Reflections*:

> I dare say—16 thousand in England—10 thousand from Paris—6 thousand from Lyon & Strasbourg, where I know the print-sellers have counterfeited editions for their account upon that of Paris.

Five months later, in July, a fifth Paris edition was printed[4] and in the same month Dupont remarks: 'en France plus de 16 mille exemplaires d'une méchante traduction ont été vendus'.[5] Germany had its edition by February 1791,[6] and at the end of July an Italian, Anthony Leonetti, informed Burke that he had prepared an Italian edition, offering to send a copy when it was printed.[7] There were in addition Irish and American reprints.[8] Nearly the whole of the Western world, therefore, was given the opportunity to read the *Reflections*. Burke's appeal, directed ultimately to Western civilisation at large, wherever established institutions were threatened, was evidently received with widespread eagerness.

[1] Fitzwilliam MSS. (Northampton), A.ix.4, 30 November 1790; A.ix.6, 13 December 1790; and A.ix.7, undated (*c.* 8 June 1791).

[2] Fitzwilliam MSS. (Northampton), A.ix.4. 30 November 1790.

[3] Fitzwilliam MSS. (Sheffield), 21 February 1791.

[4] Fitzwilliam MSS. (Northampton), A.ix.3. Letter, Dupont to Burke, 7 July 1791.

[5] Fitzwilliam MSS. (Northampton), A.ix.1. Letter, 14 July 1791.

[6] Fitzwilliam MSS. (Sheffield), 21 February 1791. A German edition of 1791 appears in the Sale Catalogue of the Library of Sir James Mackintosh. Editions of 1793 and 1794 appear in the Sale Catalogue of Burke's Library.

[7] Fitzwilliam MSS. (Sheffield), 30 July 1791.

[8] See E. J. Payne, *Burke, Select Works* (Oxford, 1898), II, 296.

II

Equally vigorous was the opposition to it. Many among the reform groups were horrified by what they read. That Burke, the former supporter of the American rebels, should denounce France where liberty was being re-born and should do so with such persuasive eloquence, incensed and appalled them.[1] Replies had to be made—they came in numbers, and at once. Within a fortnight of the appearance of the *Reflections* the first answer was on sale—*A Letter to the Right Hon. Edmund Burke, in Reply to his 'Reflections on the Revolution in France', &c. By a Member of the Revolution Society*.[2] Before the end of the year ten further replies were published, including the anonymous *Vindication of the Rights of Men*, which appeared in a second edition (bearing the name of the writer, Mary Wollstonecraft), in three weeks. In the two and a half years during which the controversy raged some seventy pamphlets were published.[3]

Though the controversy assumed no clearly defined shape and showed no signs of orderly development, it was the natural outcome of the complex political situation in 1790. The pamphleteers (the great majority of whom opposed Burke) were guided by their private political loyalties, their views on the whole question of reform, and their estimation of the value of the French example for the English reform movement. The anti-Burke writers had, then, a common adversary, but they wrote largely as individuals. The reason for this is not difficult to determine. The material of the *Reflections* is so far-ranging and Burke's attitude so provocative that there was no single and narrow point at issue. Writers were compelled to oppose Burke where they felt themselves attacked; the issue seemed to be between him and themselves as representative individuals, and consequently their tone is chiefly personal. Opposition came, then, from so many sides that there was no concerted effort, no

---

[1] Cf. W. Godwin, *Memoirs of the Author of the Vindication of the Rights of Woman* (2nd edn., 1798), p. 76.

[2] The author was Major John Scott, an intimate friend of Warren Hastings and at one time his agent.

[3] For a chronological list of the pamphlets in order of publication see Appendix.

possibility of mutual support. It thus becomes possible to classify the opposition only on the basis of the political groups to which writers were attached.

The danger in such a classification is that it results in over-simplification; it implies that there were no links between the groups. This would be a false view, as a few examples will demonstrate. There is Butler, 'the emblematical figure of an obscure citizen',[1] who though in the main politically close to the working-class reform movement and its concern with economic improvement rather than with political theory, did not share its contempt for tradition and outward ceremonial; he would have no sympathy for organisations like the Sheffield Constitutional Association, which studied and assented to Paine's principles. Samuel Parr, though himself an Anglican, links the Dissenters and Foxite Whigs by his friendship with, and respect for, Joseph Priestley. On the other hand, John Scott admits membership of the Revolution Society dominated by Dissenters, but dissociates himself from them on religious grounds;[2] Capel Lofft, a member of the same society, ranges himself against the Dissenters in his protest over the seizure of Church property in France.[3] Or there is the Unitarian Thomas Christie, who proclaims his affection for the institutions of government in England and whose general tone as well as his membership of 'The Friends of the People' places him with the radical Whigs, but, unlike the majority of this group, he clearly holds Paine in high regard.[4] Thus, though opposition to Burke is here divided into four main streams, it is essentially a division for the sake of clarity. With this proviso the opposition may be classified as follows: the 'popular' or lower-class party, allied to the extreme 'left-wing' but not wholly identified with it; the radical Whigs with their active but moderate demands for reform; the Dissenters, particularly the Unitarians, whose political and religious aims are indissoluble;

---

[1] John Butler, *Brief Reflections upon the Liberty of the British Subject* (Canterbury, n.d. [1791]), p. 143. His identity has not confidently been established. He was probably the Butler who published *An Address to the Inhabitants of the City of CANTERBURY, with several Remarks on the Proceedings of the late Election*, 1790. (Information from the City Librarian and Curator of Canterbury.)

[2] *Letter. . . . By a Member of the Revolution Society*, p. 2.

[3] *Remarks on the Letter of the Rt. Hon. Edmund Burke* (1790), pp. 63 f.

[4] *Letters on the Revolution of France*, Pt. I (1791), pp. 65–6.

and an indeterminate section seeking political and social changes on intellectual and humanitarian grounds.

Members of the many popular societies—and the Sheffield Constitutional Association may be taken as representative—regarded Burke as an eloquent advocate of the privileges of the ruling classes, the injustice of an oligarchy in control of the national system of taxes, and the contemptuous attitude towards the lower classes expressed in his scornful phrase, 'a swinish multitude'. A member of the Sheffield society, giving evidence at a State Trial in 1794, summarised their aims:

> To enlighten the people, to show the people the reason, the ground of all their complaints and sufferings; when a man works hard for thirteen or fourteen hours of the day, the week through, and is not able to maintain his family; that is what I understood of it; to show the people the ground of this; why they were not able.[1]

An energetic defiance of Burke and all he represented provided one method of achieving these aims. Members of the popular societies could resort to violence; they could publish propaganda in the shape of replies to the *Reflections*; or they could study other replies, disseminating the principles they contained. A discussion of these three courses of action leads to the heart of the popular reaction to Burke's pamphlet.

The first can be quickly dismissed, since it forms part of the broader question of the extent of the danger from popular violence in the 1790s. That there were some signs of outward opposition to Burke is, however, evident. The *Sheffield Register* recorded, on 30 November 1792, that during celebrations prompted by the success of the French armies an effigy of 'Burke riding on a swine' was exhibited. It was then two years after the famous reference to 'a swinish multitude', but it was still sufficiently vivid to provide the basis for a popular display. Another crosslight is thrown on the question of active opposition by a letter from John Nott, a button-burnisher of Birmingham, written to warn Burke that an order had been received from Sheffield and Birmingham for 3,000 buttons bearing the motto, 'Liberty and Equality'.[2] The emblems, Nott writes,

[1] Cited by P. A. Brown, *The French Revolution in English History* (1918), pp. 62–3.
[2] Fitzwilliam MSS. (Northampton), A.iv.30, 1792.

must be prepared before the 18th of January our Amiable Queen's Birthday as they [the consignees] are resolved to celebrate a Bloody day and not a Birthday.

Though this frantic warning may illustrate a type of hysteria aroused by the least sign of Jacobinism, it underlines the close affinity which was felt to exist between the aspirations of the French and those of the lower-class reform groups in England. That Burke had come to epitomise resistance to such aspirations is clear from Nott's action in writing to him.

The writings by and for the lower classes are of greater importance here. Though only one publication—*A Rhapsody to E—— B—— Esq.*, a composition in verse by J. Sharpe—can be directly connected with a popular society, several others were obviously intended for popular audiences.[1] Sharpe's pamphlet, published in Sheffield, consists of six quarto leaves of cheap paper; it appeared almost simultaneously with the exhibition of Burke's effigy in November 1792 and was presumably associated with this event.[2] Sharpe exposes the oppression which brought misery to the common people; he scoffs at the idea that merit is inherited with a title, a view attributed to Burke in the *Reflections*; he makes broad insinuations about Burke's pension and place-seeking, contrasting him with the honest Tom Paine; and he closes his poem with an ironical application of a liturgical petition, a practice later to become famous through William Hone's parodies of the Creed and Litany:

> . . . thou would'st preach 'tis right that they [Englishmen]
> Should unresisting sit and say
> *Lord have mercy upon us, and incline our hearts to keep this law.*

This pamphlet contains many of the features of literature addressed to the uneducated: protests against the economic system (especially the payment of tithes) which caused hardship; appeal to prejudice against the privileged classes; identification of Burke with these class interests; and the use of a crude irony to discredit Burke's persuasiveness. In most writings for the same

---

[1] E.g. Old Hubert [James Parkinson], *An Address to the Hon. Edmund Burke from the Swinish Multitude* (1793) and *Pearls cast before Swine, By Edmund Burke* (1793?); [Thomas Spence?], *Burke's Address to the Swinish Multitude* (1793?); [Daniel Eaton], *Hog's Wash, or A Salmagundy for Swine* (1793).

[2] For details of the illustrations to Sharpe's pamphlet see below, p. 259.

audience the connection between economic and political evils is particularly stressed. It is illustrated by the intention of the leaders of the Sheffield Association to publish, bound with a cheap edition of Paine's *Rights of Man*, 'an abstract of the iniquitous Corn Bill' of 1791.[1] Similarly, John Butler, the obscure citizen of Canterbury, relies mainly on the evidence of political and economic hardship he has experienced himself, a characteristic which led *The Monthly Review* to say of him: 'none can know better where the shoe pinches, than he that wears it'.[2] Butler thinks it sufficient bluntly and simply to oppose the 'true' picture to Burke's arguments in favour of the *status quo*. Daniel Eaton and Thomas Spence also exploit the connection between economic and social evils, though they seldom reveal Butler's patriotic sentiments. Their publications contain such articles as 'The Effects of the War on the Poor', 'Every Man is born with an imprescriptible Claim to a Portion of the Elements', and 'On a Life of Labour'; and their titles such as *Hog's Wash* and *Pigs' Meat* proclaim their direct opposition to the *Reflections*. Spence makes it clear that

> ... the thrones of true kings by the PEOPLE are made,
> And when kings become tyrants—submission is sin.[3]

And he boldly appeals to his readers:

> Hearken! O ye poor of the land! Do you fret and whine at oppression—'yes',—'Then, as ye do, so did your fathers before you'—and, if you *do no more*, your children may whine after you! Awake! Arise! arm yourselves—with truth, justice and reason— lay siege to corruption; and your unity and invincibility shall teach your oppressors terrible things.[4]

It is possible to overestimate the implications of such pronouncements, but this much is evident—the people were to obtain for themselves a more effective rôle in affairs of government. Though Spence explicitly says they were to arm themselves 'with truth, justice and reason', the example of the French might have suggested a more active interpretation of his words.

---

[1] See *Transactions of the Hunter Archaeological Society* (Sheffield, 1937), IV, 59.

[2] Op. cit. (May 1791), V, 109.

[3] *Pigs' Meat* (1793–95), I, 181.   [4] Ibid., II, 102.

The principal object of study of the popular reform groups was Thomas Paine's *Rights of Man*. Part I of this work, first published in February 1791 at half a crown[1]—half the cost of the *Reflections* (and very soon in much cheaper editions)—sold far more rapidly than Burke's pamphlet; nine editions were needed in less than twelve weeks. If we can accept Paine's own claim that the 'number of copies circulated in England, Scotland, and Ireland, besides translations into foreign languages, was between four and five hundred thousand',[2] the sale vastly exceeded that of the *Reflections*. Paine's modern editor asserts that the success of Part II (published a year later, in February 1792), was even greater, 'close to a million and a half copies being published in England during the author's lifetime'.[3] The reasons for the influence of the *Rights of Man* are explored in a later chapter, but if it is calculated on the basis of sales the size of the influence is indisputable.

Opposed at once to Paine and to the conservative Whiggism of Burke was a group of radical Whigs who, in April 1792, formed 'The Society of the Friends of the People'. They had withdrawn from 'The London Constitutional Society' when it was joined by Paine, Horne Tooke, Clio Rickman, and Thomas Holcroft, and the gulf between the two parties was at once apparent. Whereas the popular societies were mainly composed of working men and lower-middle-class tradespeople, the group of radical Whigs was largely made up of Members of Parliament, aristocratic and influential men who were inevitably linked with the Government and interested parties. They paid an annual subscription of one and a half guineas compared with the penny a week membership fee of many of the popular societies. The gulf was social and economic; it was also political. While the Constitutional and Reform Societies subscribed in varying degrees, though often in full, to the principles advocated by Paine, the radical Whigs broke off formal relations with the London Constitutional Society for that very reason—that it had sanctioned the full extent of Paine's theory. The Whigs were not prepared unconditionally to throw in their lot with the left

---

[1] Published by J. Johnson; it lacked Paine's preface which was included in the edition published by J. S. Jordan in March 1791 at a cost of 3s.

[2] Ed. P. S. Foner, *The Complete Writings of Thomas Paine*, II, 910.

[3] Ibid., I, 345.

wing; they wanted reform to come from inside Parliament rather than through pressure from without.

Their programme was clearly set out in the two parts of the declaration to which every member of the Society had to assent: 'To restore the Freedom of Election, and a more equal Representation of the People in Parliament', and 'To secure to the People a more frequent Exercise of their Right of electing their Representatives'.[1] It is obvious at once that in tone and content these aims differ considerably from the unequivocal demands of the Painites for absolute equality in representation. The radical Whigs were anxious to avoid sweeping political change because they were strongly connected with the existing system as a result of sentiment and hereditary wealth. One resolution of 1794 claims that they had never 'been betrayed into intemperate warmth';[2] it was this decorous moderation which distinguished them from both Burke and the left wing. The Friends of the People were indeed,

> strictly mediatory between the extremes of opinion, which marked that agitated time,—between the 'many honest men, who were driven into Toryism by their fears,' and the 'many sober men, who were driven into Republicanism by their enthusiasm.'[3]

Among the members listed in the initial *Regulations* are several who took part in the controversy over the *Reflections*: James Mackintosh, George Rous, Thomas Christie, Philip Francis, John Courtenay, John Scott, and Joseph Towers. Rous gives an admirable summary of their views:

> Should the exertions of the friends of parliamentary reform be found inadequate to surmount the interested defence of abuse, the next object ought to be to instil into the minds of the people a knowledge of the *true ends and nature* of all Government, and particularly to distinguish the *just principles* of our own constitution, that they may be taught to preserve its substance, and eradicate only its growing defects.[4]

[1] *Regulations of the Society of the Friends of the People* (1792).
[2] A. Cobban, *The Debate on the French Revolution* (1950), p. 136.
[3] Ed. R. J. Mackintosh, *Memoirs of the Life of Sir James Mackintosh* (1835), I, 80.
[4] *Thoughts on Government: occasioned by Mr. Burke's Reflections* (4th edn., 1791), p. 77.

Their objects—by no means revolutionary—were to be achieved through enlightenment, but, to strengthen their appeal, these writers guardedly pointed to the possibility of determined action if reform were not granted. Mackintosh remarks:

> It is because we sincerely love tranquil freedom, that we earnestly deprecate the moment when virtue and honour shall compel us to seek her with our swords.[1]

The French Revolution served a double purpose for these radical Whigs: it provided a blunt warning to a supposedly tyrannic government, and it was an example 'to invigorate the spirit of freedom'.[2] They enjoyed an optimistic confidence in the power of reason and were in general agreement on the necessity for secularising politics, at least to the extent that religious establishments could not endanger the progress of reason or the existence of the civil government itself; they demanded recognition of the administrative ability in the middle class, where, Mackintosh asserts, 'almost all the sense and virtue of society reside';[3] and they urged an extension of the franchise and the necessity for fiscal reform in the interests of the poor. For each of these arguments the French Revolution provided cogent illustrations.

The third principal section of opposition was determined to counter Burke's ideas on religion and its civil establishment. This group—which included many of the anonymous writers—was composed chiefly of Dissenters, the most important figures being Richard Price, Francis Stone—an Anglican parson who was later prosecuted for his Unitarian views and deprived of his living—and Joseph Priestley, who was described by one of Burke's supporters as 'by many degrees the ablest and most masterly of [Burke's] antagonists'.[4] These writers, like Price in his *Discourse*, claimed the right to liberty of conscience, the right to resist power when it is abused, and the right of a people to choose its own governors, to cashier them for misconduct, and to frame a government for itself. Such principles by themselves would not sharply distinguish this group from others already

[1] *Vindiciae Gallicae* (1791), p. 344.
[2] Ibid., pp. 346–7.
[3] Ibid., p. 129.
[4] E. Tatham, *Letters to the Rt. Hon. Edmund Burke on Politics* (Oxford, 1791), p. 61.

mentioned, but the writings of these men were given a particular bias by their conception of man's relationship with God. Price, Stone says,

> was convinced, that religion is a private concern between every man's conscience and his God, and in which no third party, either as one man, a set of men, or even the civil magistrate, has a right to interfere.[1]

This essential belief directed the Dissenters' attack on the *Reflections* and, owing to their anomalous political position, this private religious matter became indissolubly bound up with a public political issue. Their struggle was both for liberty of conscience and for the removal of civil disabilities. The vigour with which they pursued their objective led Burke to recognise the leading Dissenters as the most active enthusiasts for the French Revolution and the 'mortal and declared enemies' of his own party.[2]

Their enthusiasm was partly founded on the same optimistic confidence in the inevitable progress and reliability of reason which characterised Mackintosh and his associates. Also like the radical Whigs, the Dissenters laid stress on the value of popular enlightenment. The first of the three chief blessings, enumerated by Price, to be obtained for any country was knowledge. 'Enlighten [the people] and you will elevate them'; every piece of enlightenment 'helps to prepare the minds of men for the recovery of their rights, and hastens the overthrow of priestcraft and tyranny'.[3] Knowledge was the foundation of virtue and the key to liberty. But liberty for the Dissenters had the precise meaning already mentioned. It especially denoted the free exercise of reason and freedom in matters of conscience, together with the freedom to pursue any career according to talent. Consequently, they welcomed the French 'Declaration of Rights' and were particularly severe on Burke's defence of the Established Church. They expressed approval of the French confiscation of Church property and contempt for a man who could see without flinching 'a bishop of Durham, or a bishop of Winchester, in possession of ten thousand pounds a year';[4] they

---

[1] *An Examination of the Right Hon. Edmund Burke's Reflections* (1792), p. 30.
[2] Ed. Fitzwilliam and Bourke, *Correspondence of Edmund Burke*, III, 394.
[3] *A Discourse on the Love of our Country* (6th edn., 1790), p. 14.
[4] *Reflections*, in *Works*, II, 375.

considered religion 'a thing that requires no civil establishment whatever, and that its beneficial operation is injured by such establishment, and the more in proportion to its riches';[1] and they looked to America and France for the theory of 'a completely new government on the principles of *equal liberty* and the *rights of men*, without nobles, . . . without bishops, and without a king'.[2]

The final group, of indeterminate opposition, is inevitably less homogeneous than those already discussed. The writers necessarily vary in their approach, but, while expressing individual views, they were doubtless representative of a great body of opinion. There were many who favoured reform but who were not attracted by the extreme left-wing policy of Paine, the moderate radicalism of Mackintosh, or the religio-political arguments of the Dissenters; yet they were not unmoved by the French Revolution and considered the *Reflections* erroneous and unfeeling. In many ways typical of such people was Sir Brooke Boothby, a member of the Lichfield circle of Darwin, Day, and the Edgeworths, and described by *The Monthly Review* as 'an elegant, a well-bred, and a well-informed English gentleman'.[3] He owns himself an admirer of Burke, but feels compelled to warn those who were about to feed on the 'well-flavoured and high-seasoned dish that "there is death in the pot" '.[4] More vigorous still is his warning to readers of Paine in a later pamphlet. He asserts that the *Rights of Man*

> proposes no less than to destroy every moral, and religious, and political establishment in the world. . . . It is a sketch of a complete code of destruction.[5]

Boothby and his kind eschewed both extremes, but felt the greater kinship for Burke. Yet they saw a real significance in the French Revolution. When the French people are judged by the unerring standard of 'our own revered Revolution' (when James was 'cashiered' and William 'elected') Boothby finds them justified in their action against despotism. Again unlike Burke, he is

[1] Priestley, *Letters to the Right Honourable Edmund Burke* (1791), p. 53.
[2] Ibid., p. 40.
[3] Op. cit. (May 1791), V, 71.
[4] *A Letter to the Right Honourable Edmund Burke* (1791), p. 4.
[5] *Observations on the Appeal from the New to the Old Whigs, and on Mr. Paine's Rights of Man* (1792), pp. 107–8.

prepared to suspend judgment on the wisdom and virtue of the French revolutionary leaders, believing they had an unparalleled opportunity to achieve fame if they completed 'what they have so gloriously began'.[1] He also claims that he is not so blinded by the magnificence of the French Court that he ignores the interests of the common people. Moreover, he is mystified by Burke's apparent defence of the Roman Catholic Church, which, in his view, is the prime obstacle to liberty; he thinks the French set a worthy example by curbing the papal power. Yet despite Boothby's zeal for a degree of reform in harmony with writers previously noticed, in other respects he supports the *status quo*. He clearly sympathises with Burke's veneration of monarchy, and gives his approval to the existing system of representation. He maintains that 'the extreme inequality of representation which sounds so ill in theory almost disappears in practice',[2] since the English system is a happy blend of democracy, monarchy, and aristocracy, all holding 'a joint undivided property'. Boothby, then, held a mixture of opinions peculiar to Burke and to his opponents, an amalgam doubtless common in England in the 1790s. The mixture was, however, insecure. The trend of affairs in France, robbing him of confidence in the virtue and rightness of the revolutionists, would almost inevitably dictate a swing towards full acceptance of Burke's position.

More proof against such a tendency would be Mary Wollstonecraft and others like her whose opposition to Burke was basically humanitarian. Like William Wilberforce and John Howard, she was moved by the miseries of the oppressed members of society. Though her attention inevitably turned to the political system which was responsible for the oppression and which Burke defended, her indignation was principally aroused by the attitude crystallised in his assertion:

> To be enabled to acquire, the people, without being servile, must be tractable and obedient. . . . They must respect that property of which they cannot partake. They must labour to obtain what by labour can be obtained; and when they find, as they commonly do, the success disproportioned to the endeavour, they must be taught their consolation in the final proportions of eternal justice.[3]

---

[1] *A Letter to the Right Honourable Edmund Burke*, p. 38.
[2] Ibid., pp. 30–1.   [3] *Reflections*, in *Works*, II, 514.

There was small wonder that Mary Wollstonecraft considered hereditary property and honours the chief obstacles to civilisation, or that she passionately accused Burke of allowing his respect for rank to swallow up 'the common feelings of humanity'.[1] She identified herself with the poor suffering from heavy taxes, from press-gangs, game-laws, and a corrupt government; she demanded economic reform and, to achieve this, reform of the constitution 'if such an heterogeneous mass deserve that name'. Her principal charge against the constitution was that it originated in ages unsanctified by 'the *regal* stamp of reason',[2] and against Burke that his imagination had usurped the place of reason, the only legitimate judge.

Another writer who can fairly be included among the indeterminate opposition to Burke is Arthur Young, whose *Travels in France* (1792–94), though essentially apart from the controversy over the *Reflections*, reinforced the arguments of all sympathisers with the Revolution. The book (which is more fully examined later) not only corrected Burke on several points of fact; it weakened his contention that France in 1789 had the elements of a good constitution and that the Revolution was unnecessary. On the contrary, Young insists that

> when the extent and universality of the oppression under which the people groaned [is understood]—oppression which bore upon them from every quarter, it will scarcely be attempted to be urged, that a revolution was not absolutely necessary to the welfare of the kingdom.[3]

Yet it is noteworthy that later, under the same influences as those which it is suggested would operate on Boothby, he fully adopted the anti-French position in a pamphlet, *The Example of France, a Warning to Britain* (1793). Burke's relief at gaining such an ally is obvious from a congratulatory letter to Young in which the pamphlet is described as 'incomparably well done'.[4]

Finally, though it is detached from the main body of English opposition, is a reply which must be noticed—that of the recipient of the *Reflections*. The result of De Pont's appeal for advice was far from his expectations. Dupont, the translator, informed

[1] *A Vindication of the Rights of Men* (2nd edn., 1790), p. 32.
[2] Ibid., p. 68.
[3] Ed. M. Betham-Edwards, *Travels in France* (2nd edn., 1889), p. 323.
[4] Fitzwilliam MSS. (Northampton), A.iv.27. 5 March 1793.

Burke that De Pont is accused 'd'être au plus profond de la démocratie',[1] a view which is borne out by the latter's indignant letter to Burke, 6 December 1790,[2] which later appeared, edited and translated, as an *Answer to the Reflections of the Right Hon. Edmund Burke* (1791). De Pont addresses Burke very firmly:

> When I took the liberty, last year, of asking your opinion on the political events in France, I had certainly no idea that my letter would lead to the publication of the work you have so kindly sent me. I will even confess that I should never have made the request, had I been able to foresee its effect; and that if I had at that time known your opinions, far from begging you to express them, I should have besought you not to make them public.

De Pont anticipated that the man who had supported the American Revolution would defend a revolution in France; Paine had been of the same opinion. In Burke's eyes, however, the Americans had been struggling to assert their right to share in the traditional liberty of the British subject as expressed in the British constitution; the French, having a constitution which could be reformed, had violently and wantonly overthrown it. Therefore, though the American action was admirable, the French was despicable. In his letter De Pont writes as a loyal Frenchman. He fears that Burke's eminence might incite the French nobility to seditious activities, thus exposing them to fresh dangers and the country to civil war. On several points of fact and principle De Pont corrects Burke with a vigour and conviction born of intimate knowledge of his own country and an ardent wish to see her restored to peace.

In contrast with the capacity for argument and the literary ability shown by Burke's opponents, his supporters in the controversy are remarkably inept. Friedrich von Gentz (in a survey of the controversy appended to his translation of the *Reflections*), asserts that not one among them is worthy of consideration.[3] Undoubtedly Burke's position would be weakened rather than strengthened by their efforts. The verse compositions addressed to Burke, such as William Bowles's *Poetical Address to the Rt. Hon. Edmund Burke* (1791) or George L. Schoen's *Innovation* (1793), are

---

[1] Fitzwilliam MSS. (Northampton), A.ix.6. 13 December 1790.
[2] Printed in *English*, VIII, xlvi, 175–8.
[3] *Betrachtungen über die französische Revolution* (Berlin, 1793), pp. 313–14.

flat and uninspired; they lack the vigour and wit of Courtenay's *Poetical and Philosophical Essay* (1793) or the anonymous *Heroic Epistle to the Rt. Hon. Edmund Burke* (1791) and *Reflections on Reflections* (1791?), written in opposition. Among others in support of Burke is the Hon. Frederick Hervey's prose pamphlet, *A New Friend on an Old Subject* (1791); it is a competent piece of writing, but, like the poem *Innovation*, it relies too greatly on sensationalist stories of French barbarism, and would succeed only with those readers predisposed to agree. There are two longer works, *A Vindication of the Rt. Hon. Edmund Burke's Reflections* (1791)[1] and Edward Tatham's *Letters to the Rt. Hon. Edmund Burke on Politics* (1791): the tone of the former is virulent and bitterly sarcastic and of the latter arrogant in the extreme; both are marked by contempt for Dissenters and a too obvious intention to vindicate the Church Establishment. Burke's supporters, indeed, do not merit, either for the style or content of their pamphlets, the attention given to his opponents. They wrote under the shadow of Burke's own success in the *Reflections*; their style must have been, to their detriment, subject to comparison with his; and there was little which they could hope to achieve which had not already been accomplished by him. Except as tokens of agreement with his principles and attempts to parry some of the attacks on particular details of the *Reflections*, their efforts would be largely unavailing save among Burke's convinced—and undiscriminating—sympathisers.

The controversy over the *Reflections* virtually came to an end in 1793. The appearance of new publications by Burke drew off some critics of the earlier work; the growing likelihood of war with France, increasingly oppressive measures by the Government at home, and the impossibility of sustaining interest in a particular aspect of a larger issue over a period of years, all contributed to hasten its end. War came with France in February 1793. Henceforth, evidence of sympathy for France in any shape was proof of sedition, even of treason.

---

[1] See J. Kennedy *et al.*, *Dictionary of Anonymous and Pseudonymous English Literature* (Halkett and Laing), New edn. (1932), VI, 174, where this work is attributed (without evidence) to Burke himself. On stylistic grounds the attribution seems unlikely to be correct.

VII

EDMUND BURKE:
REFLECTIONS ON THE
REVOLUTION IN FRANCE

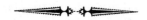

I

Not only were numerous opponents quick to proclaim the errors in Burke's facts and question his conclusions, as soon as the *Reflections* was published, but the process has continued ever since. As Raymond Williams observes, 'the confutation of Burke on the French Revolution is now a one-finger exercise in politics and history'.[1] Yet, in this century at any rate, little has been done thoroughly to account for the continuing impact of the book from 1790 to our own day, except on the level of abstract theory. It is abundantly evident, however, that the response of Burke's contemporaries was not only to a body of ideas but rather to a complete literary achievement, a mode of writing effectively designed to convey a particular manner of thinking; when they attacked or praised the book it was that complete achievement they had in mind. Paine or Mackintosh, for example, were alive to the intimate relationship that exists between Burke's philosophical reflection and his literary techniques, and it is surprising to find critics who examine his political thought without recognising that literary criticism is essential to their purpose. To use John Holloway's remark on the Victorian 'sage', what Burke 'has to say is not a matter just of "content" or narrow paraphrasable meaning, but is transfused by the whole texture of his writing as it constitutes an experience

---

[1] *Culture and Society, 1780–1950* (Pelican edn., 1961), p. 24.

for the reader'.[1] Burke was not only a great thinker, he was also an imaginative writer who requires a response from the reader as a whole man and not simply as a creature of intellect. Consequently his exposition—the play of imaginative insights as well as the statement of logical argument—itself becomes 'proof' in this special sense that it communicates, and affirms while communicating, the rich complexity of a philosophy of life; it does not merely demonstrate the truth of a set of propositions.

This chapter attempts to identify the qualities of a prose which, by its very rhythmic subtleties, its suggestive power, its imagery, or its emotive strength, reinforces by its own texture the ideas it expresses on the surface. Further, the claim will be advanced that the 'apostrophe' to the French Queen has a special function in acting as the centrepiece of the *Reflections*: it is central because it is the most memorable passage—a fact of vital importance in a piece of persuasive writing—and because it is central to the argument, the passage which gathers up the principal ideas Burke has previously expressed, invests them with a new quality, and then acts as a kind of supercharger for the argument that follows. At this rhetorical and philosophical centrepoint Burke's vision of moral disorder contrasted with the symbol of the moral order he venerates reaches climactic proportions, and the principles underlying his vision receive their most startling evocation.

First, then, the nature of the ideas concentred in the apostrophe. It should be recognised at the outset that Burke's attention is not restricted to a local, French situation; he sees the Revolution in terms of its significance for and effect on the whole of Christian culture and civilisation. (This has an important bearing on his literary methods and should not be lost sight of.) The French, he declares in the first of the *Letters on a Regicide Peace*, have 'made a schism with the whole universe', a 'violent breach of the community of Europe', and he elaborates a picture of a common culture with 'a similitude throughout Europe of religion, laws, and manners'. This was the culture 'which softened, blended, and harmonized the colours of the whole' Christian world, and which the French have rejected.[2] It is as if, with Macbeth, they had said, 'let the frame of things disjoint'

---

[1] *The Victorian Sage* (1953), pp. 10–11.
[2] *Letters on a Regicide Peace* (1796), in *Works*, V, 214–15.

—and Burke intended the same universal implications as are found in Shakespeare's vision of the symbolic overthrow of order in the universe by the arrogance, atheism, and self-centred morality of an individual. (It is, perhaps, not accidental that Burke makes imaginative reference to *Macbeth* in the course of the *Reflections*.[1]) 'Every thing seems out of nature',[2] Burke declares, and he means not merely in France but, potentially at least, in the cosmos.

The existence of such a cosmic view is substantiated by Burke's frequent reference to the divinely ordained moral order with which a properly designed mode of government is harmoniously integrated. 'Our political system,' he tells his young correspondent, De Pont, in the *Reflections*,

> is placed in a just correspondence and symmetry with the order of the world, and with the mode of existence decreed to a permanent body composed of transitory parts; wherein, by the disposition of a stupendous wisdom, moulding together the great mysterious incorporation of the human race, the whole . . . moves on through the varied tenor of perpetual decay, fall, renovation, and progression.[3]

What may be regarded as a first premise for this claim is his assertion

> that the awful Author of our being is the Author of our place in the order of existence; and that having disposed and marshalled us by a divine tactic, not according to our will, but according to his, he has, in and by that disposition, virtually subjected us to act the part which belongs to the place assigned us.[4]

Political systems, then, and the relation of the individual to them are part of a divine order; the moral ties and obligations recognised as existing between individuals exist with the same reality between man and the system of which he is a part. 'We have given to our frame of polity the image of a relation in blood . . . keeping inseparable . . . our state, our hearths, our sepulchres, and our altars.[5] Political institutions, the bond of human relations, a noble tradition, and 'the spirit of religion' are indissolubly bound in a mysterious and immutable order. Rebellion in one quarter means the disintegration of the whole.

[1] *Works*, II, 343.   [2] Ibid., II, 284.   [3] Ibid., II, 307.
[4] *An Appeal from the New to the Old Whigs* (1791), in *Works*, III, 79.
[5] *Reflections*, in *Works*, II, 307.

Such a cosmic pattern ensures 'a noble freedom'; it also involves 'the discipline of perfect freedom', obligations as well as privileges. 'We have obligations to mankind at large, which are not in consequence of any special voluntary pact. They arise from the relation of man to man, and the relation of man to God, which relations are not matters of choice.'[1] And, as a corollary, 'the presumed consent of every rational creature is in unison with the predisposed order of things'. It is this kind of thinking that lies behind Burke's claim that Englishmen have chosen their 'nature' rather than their 'speculations' to 'preserve a rational and manly freedom'.[2] 'Nature' here presupposes harmony between the individual, humbly acknowledging his personal insufficiency, and the 'predisposed order of things'; it implies the danger of proud and wilful passions but the signal importance of natural feelings.

An important consequence of these attitudes is that Burke considers the immediate event against 'a standard of virtue and wisdom, beyond the vulgar practice of the hour'.[3] Frequent reiteration of words like 'harmony' and 'balance' involves not mere questions of expediency or maintenance of the *status quo*; it involves a noble vision of an order of things which, while it certainly requires 'natural authority and legitimate subordination', transcends individual selfishness; it recognises immediate needs and circumstances but regards humanity from

> that elevation of reason, which places centuries under our eye, and brings things to the true point of comparison, . . . and to which nothing can ascend but the spirit and moral quality of human actions.[4]

It is from this elevated position that Burke regards the French Revolution. A key passage for the understanding of his attitude to it—and of the centrality of the apostrophe in the *Reflections*—is found in the *Letters on a Regicide Peace*. He has examined the 'establishments of regicide, of jacobinism, and of atheism' which he claims to see in France; he then turns to '*the correspondent system of manners*'.

> Manners are of more importance than laws. Upon them, in a great measure, the laws depend. The law touches us but here and

[1] *An Appeal*, in *Works*, III, 79.
[2] *Reflections*, in *Works*, II, 308.　　[3] Ibid., II, 309.　　[4] Ibid., II, 414.

there, and now and then. Manners are what vex or soothe, corrupt or purify, exalt or debase, barbarise or refine us, by a constant, steady, uniform, insensible operation, like that of the air we breathe in. They give their whole form and colour to our lives. According to their quality, they aid morals, they supply them, or they totally destroy them. Of this the new French legislators were aware; therefore, with the same method, and under the same authority, they settled a system of manners, the most licentious, prostitute, and abandoned, that ever has been known, and at the same time the most coarse, rude, savage, and ferocious.[1]

It is a passage of profound importance; it is certainly fundamental to a grasp of the significance of the apostrophe. This last (as we shall see subsequently) has its roots in the description of the events of 6 October 1789, and within a page or two after it Burke faintly apologises for devoting so much attention to this day, but claims that it was the 'occasion of the most important of all revolutions . . . a revolution in sentiments, manners, and moral opinions'.[2] Here indeed is the crucial test: evidence of moral degeneracy, of a corrupting of the values and behaviour of the people affected by the political change, is proof that the change itself is politically evil. 'What in the result is likely to produce evil, is politically false: that which is productive of good, politically true.'[3] Burke himself never forgets that politics do not concern abstractions but the welfare of sentient human beings, whereas in France the revolutionists 'are so taken up with their theories about the rights of man, that they have totally forgotten his nature. Without opening one new avenue to the understanding, they have succeeded in stopping up those that lead to the heart.'[4] The moral consequences are disastrous: the individual becomes the source of a private morality and no corporate values remain; 'humanity and compassion are ridiculed as the fruits of superstition and ignorance', and 'tenderness to individuals is considered as treason to the public'.[5] In fact, 'benevolence to the whole species' drives out feeling for the single human being.[6] This, in Burke's view, leads to the disintegration of a society. He is convinced that a love of country

[1] *Works*, V, 208.   [2] *Reflections*, in *Works*, II, 352.
[3] *An Appeal*, in *Works*, III, 81.   [4] *Reflections*, in *Works*, II, 337.
[5] Ibid., II, 341.
[6] *A Letter to a Member of the National Assembly*, in *Works*, II, 537.

proceeds from a love of individuals, of 'the little platoon we belong to in society',[1] whereas the revolutionists are destroying the very source of such love, the family itself.[2] The French have acted in this instance according to the principles of Rousseau and have corrupted morality; they have also corrupted public taste. 'Taste and elegance, though they are reckoned only among the smaller and secondary morals, yet are of no mean importance in the regulation of life'—but they are rejected because to the French, 'all refinement has an aristocratic character'.[3]

This thoroughgoing condemnation of the revolution in France (not of all revolution) is above all pragmatic. Burke starts from the individual human being with his feelings, prejudices, and shortcomings; he knows that man is fallible and weak, and therefore needs direction—'Government is a contrivance of human wisdom to provide for human *wants*';[4] and he observes what happens to this fallible creature when the critical, analytical, unfeeling reason is elevated by abstract theories to the position of moral dictator. This abstract reason banishes the affections; it is the prime mover 'of this barbarous philosophy, which is the offspring of cold hearts and muddy understandings';[5] and instead of an auxiliary it assumes a dominant rôle. Men who are guided by it develop a 'complexional disposition . . . to pull every thing in pieces', but what is worse, because they are continually employed in finding faults, they come to hate 'vices too much . . . [and] to love men too little'.[6] 'The true lawgiver', on the other hand, 'ought to have a heart full of sensibility. He ought to love and respect his kind, and to fear himself.'[7]

From this brief glance at Burke's philosophical principles[8] certain important features emerge: these are the features which are conveyed in the very texture of Burke's prose and are concentred in the apostrophe. Burke insists on the universal significance of the total event; there is a 'pattern of nature' with which

---

[1] *Reflections*, in *Works*, II, 320.
[2] Cf. *A Letter*, in *Works*, II, 538–40; *Regicide Peace*, in *Works*, V, 208–12.
[3] *A Letter*, in *Works*, II, 539.
[4] *Reflections*, in *Works*, II, 333.   [5] Ibid., II, 350.
[6] Ibid., II, 441.   [7] Ibid., II, 439.
[8] For a full and incisive examination of them see Charles Parkin, *The Moral Basis of Burke's Political Thought* (Cambridge, 1956).

a constitution and civil society should be in accord,[1] but in France 'everything seems out of nature'; change is necessary, but it should be governed by reverence for antiquity and awareness of 'analogical precedent, authority, and example';[2] individuals, like political societies, should be in harmony with 'the order of the world', otherwise selfishness and self-sufficiency take the place of humility and veneration of 'the disposition of a stupendous wisdom'; a consciousness of a noble tradition of privileges and obligations leads to reverence for that tradition and also for individuals on account of their age and descent. Finally, and perhaps most important, it is essential to recognise man's 'nature', to acknowledge him as a rational but fallible creature of emotions and prejudices, and to act accordingly. There are corollaries which have already been touched on—the value of traditional wisdom precisely because of man's fallibility, and the importance of taste and elegance in helping attain a mode of life appropriate to a divinely ordered universe—but these and others will emerge as and when necessary.

II

What we must now attend to is the living quality of Burke's insight, the ways in which the principles outlined above are conveyed and reinforced through imagery, the accumulated significances of key-terms, the power of suggestion, the variations of mood and prose-rhythm, and so forth—in fact that part of his argument which cannot be paraphrased or summarised but yields its characteristics only to literary analysis. The problem is—to use John Holloway's terminology—to show how exposition becomes proof. Burke certainly does make use of logical argument, but there is much more to his *Reflections* than this; it is the 'much more' that one remembers, what Hazlitt described as Burke's 'impatience to transfer his conceptions entire, living, in all their rapidity, strength, and glancing variety, to the minds of others'.[3] If we are to account for the rich complexity of this impact made by the book in 1790 or later we must examine the subtle control that Burke exercises over the reader's response. And to this end close analysis of his prose-texture is essential.

[1] *Reflections*, in *Works*, II, 307.   [2] Ibid., II, 305.
[3] Ed. P. P. Howe, *Works* (1930–34), VII, 229.

Perhaps the dominant impression given by the *Reflections* is of a relentless pace in the writing: the imperative tone, the cumulative effect of image and illustration, the apparently inexhaustible fertility of Burke's mind, all combine to forbid effective reply except from the most incisive minds. Burke remarks at the beginning of his book that he indulges in 'the freedom of epistolary intercourse', and it is notable that, apart from the explanatory preface, he never stands aside to look at France with his English audience; from the first word, 'You', to the end he does not distinguish between his correspondent, De Pont, and the general reader. He addresses both with the same degree of intimacy—'I do not often quote Bolingbroke' or 'Mr. Hume told me';[1] he confides in them, telling them, for example, that he quoted Aristotle from memory when drafting the *Reflections* and that 'a learned friend' has since found the exact quotation for him;[2] or he puts both in the shoes of the imaginary interlocutor who objects to his ridicule of the Crown in the new French constitution:

> Oh! but I don't do justice to the talents of the legislators: I don't allow, as I ought to do, for necessity. Their scheme of executive force was not their choice. This pageant must be kept. The people would not consent to part with it. Right; I understand you.[3]

And the objection is ruthlessly swept aside. Burke is placing every reader in the position of De Pont, addressing each one with urgent directness, and demanding concurrence rather than eliciting agreement. The literary impression given, then, is one of relentless inevitability; this is also the dialectical object Burke aims at, since inevitability is a prominent feature of the formal argument. Certain forces, he would have us believe, have been let loose which will necessarily lead to chaos and violent anarchy; other forces there are which would with equal certainty ward off such results and sustain universal contentment and harmony. In both cases Burke intends to give precisely this feeling of inevitability: it is the characteristic of his writing and of his thinking.

'It was inevitable; it was necessary; it was planted in the nature of things.'[4] Here in a nutshell is the reader's response and

---

[1] *Reflections*, in *Works*, II, 397, 441.   [2] Ibid., II, 396 n.
[3] Ibid., II, 473–4.   [4] Ibid., II, 316.

Burke's fundamental premise. As a premise it is appropriate to either the 'natural order'—that which depends on authority, precedent, and antiquity, and is creative and beautifying—or the 'unnatural' disorder—that which depends on metaphysical theory, which denies the value of the wisdom of the race, which grows by what it feeds on, destruction, violence, dismemberment. 'A good tree cannot bring forth evil fruit; neither can a corrupt tree bring forth good fruit.' The biblical words illustrate Burke's point: whether there is order or disorder there will be fruition; the product may be evil, but there will be organic growth. This attitude—expressed in various ways, as will be shown—engenders an onward, inevitable movement which both dominates the total literary experience and is a primary element in Burke's argument.

It cannot be doubted that Burke conceives of a disorder which, once set in motion, generates its own motive power: the sentence quoted at the beginning of the preceding paragraph is applied directly to it. A few pages earlier, after condemning the treachery of the French leaders to a mild king, he states: 'This was unnatural. The rest is in order.'[1] There follows a paragraph describing France in terms which signify the overthrow of traditional order. 'Overturned', 'without vigour', 'expiring', 'pillaged', 'anarchy', 'tottering power', 'impoverished fraud and beggared rapine'—the list does not exhaust the references to the features of the unnatural situation. Such terms have a paraphrasable significance, but, by their number, their associations with a traditional mode of thinking, their reiterated stress on poverty, evil growth, chaos, and utter ruin, they have an immeasurable and cumulative emotive force which is beyond paraphrase. The association of chaos with the perversion of a religious sanction is also made plain: the French people 'have not the engagement of nature' to choose deputies 'upon whom they lay their ordaining hands'.[2] In fact, the corruption involves the whole nation, not simply a handful of leaders. 'At present, you seem in everything to have strayed out of the high road of nature';[3] 'the levellers only change and pervert the natural order of things';[4] to force 'tailors and carpenters' into the rôle of governors is 'an usurpation on the prerogatives of nature';[5]

[1] *Reflections*, in *Works*, II, 312.   [2] Ibid., II, 314.
[3] Ibid., II, 325.   [4] Ibid., II, 322.   [5] Ibid., II, 322.

indeed, 'everything seems out of nature in this strange chaos of levity and ferocity, and of all sorts of crimes jumbled together with all sorts of follies'.[1]

Such is the state of society when nature is overthrown—and, in words like 'overturned', 'pillaged', 'pervert', and 'usurpation', Burke is asserting that the subversion was deliberate, and that the results were (philosophically) 'necessary'. It is a topic to which we shall return, but it is interesting now to consider the contrasting state. There is little doubt that Burke intended the reader to be assaulted by opposing sets of values from the outset until the climactic illustration, the barbarous treatment of the royal family, preceding the apostrophe. Immediately following the last quotation (which comes very early in the book) we find:

> In viewing this monstrous tragi-comic scene, the most opposite passions necessarily succeed, and sometimes mix with each other in the mind; alternate contempt and indignation; alternate laughter and tears; alternate scorn and horror.

It is this condition of emotional flux—which 'necessarily' or inevitably arises—that is sustained, to be most fully exploited immediately before the apostrophe and 'cashed' in it.

So far we have been concerned with the primitive, uncivilised situation, the Hobbesian nature, 'nasty' and 'brutish'. For his part, Burke has 'in [his] contemplation the civil social man, and no other',[2] and (in what is for him a rather unusual image) he invokes the authority of Newton to show the difference:

> metaphysic rights entering into common life, like rays of light which pierce into a dense medium, are, by the laws of nature, refracted from their straight line.[3]

A kind of inevitability, as certain as the immutable laws of Newtonian physics, requires that primitive 'rights' be abated or modified in the interests of a civil community. 'Government is not made in virtue of natural rights' but to satisfy human needs.[4]

Burke's conception of civilised 'nature' is both stern and generous. That it imposes its own discipline and involves an inexorable principle of growth has already been noted; it also requires men to perform 'the functions which belong to them',[5]

---

[1] *Reflections*, in *Works*, II, 284.   [2] Ibid., II, 332.
[3] Ibid., II, 334.   [4] Ibid., II, 332.   [5] Ibid., II, 317.

and to remain within 'their natural spheres of action'.[1] 'Perpetual decay' and 'fall' are features of 'the method of nature', but so also are 'renovation and progression'.[2] And for this reason renovation cannot be undertaken lightly: care must be taken 'not to inoculate any scion alien to the nature of the original plant'.[3] Here again the metaphor (anticipating Coleridge) emphasises the principle of inevitable growth, a process which must not be tampered with except by 'those whom nature has qualified'.[4] 'The harmony of the world' depends on this same process seen in its cosmic significance; it clearly involves the reciprocal counteracting of opposing powers 'in the natural and in the political world', and such counteraction frequently requires compromise 'which naturally begets moderation'.[5] It becomes clear that while the same word is being used Burke expands or contracts its meaning at will but carries over the implications from one usage to the others. 'Nature' may refer to the universal order; it may—as in 'nature teaches us to revere individual men; on account of their age, and on account of those from whom they are descended'[6]—refer to the moral force which requires the acceptance of a divinely fashioned, hierarchical, and fundamentally unchanging society; or it may simply refer to the character of the living object. But whatever the specific usage, the connotations of the word in other contexts— all suggestive of harmony and continuity, life and organic development—are invoked and enrich the immediate significance.

The impression of inevitability is heightened by the frequent use of other key-terms such as 'order' and 'antiquity'. 'Order' is itself often linked with 'natural' (as in some of the examples above) and invariably suggests the idea of an unchanging permanence.

> The institutions of policy, the goods of fortune, the gifts of providence, are handed down to us, and from us, in the same course and order. Our political system is placed in a just correspondence and symmetry with the order of the world.[7]

Here the implications of the word merge with those of 'nature' previously discussed. Again, Burke speaks of 'any fixed order of

[1] *Reflections*, in *Works*, II, 319.   [2] Ibid., II, 307.
[3] Ibid., II, 305.   [4] Ibid., II, 304.   [5] Ibid., II, 308-9.
[6] Ibid., II, 308.   [7] Ibid., II, 307.

things';[1] he associates order with peace in an ideal state;[2] and he asserts that 'the order of civil life' provides a defence for the humble as well as eminence for the superior members of society.[3] This concept, then, like 'nature', is at once stern and generous; it imposes its own discipline but gives its own rewards. Both are involved with the third concept, 'antiquity'. The order Burke has in mind is fixed from time immemorial; antiquity and the wisdom it represents (and therefore the ordered thinking it enforces) are a country's 'capital' which it flings away at its peril;[4] a 'pre-possession towards antiquity', such as exists in England, ensures that a constitution and its laws are regarded as an 'inheritance' not willingly dispensed with; and men who are aware of this heritage act under the impetus of noble example and not according to 'the vulgar practice of the hour'. The long paragraph in which Burke surveys the possibilities of action open to France in 1789 is permeated with references to 'antiquity' and 'ancestors'; these in turn are surrounded by noble, high-sounding terms such as 'wise', 'pious', 'privileges', 'loyalty and honour'.[5] By such means an emotive picture suggesting great potentialities is given, only to be followed with the sharpest of contrasts:

> Compute your gains: see what is got by those extravagant and presumptuous speculations which have taught your leaders to despise all their predecessors, and all their contemporaries. . . .

Respect for the wisdom of the race, Burke claims, is the test of man's moral worth: it requires that he acknowledge his own fallibility.

These frequently used concepts ('nature' more than forty times in the first quarter of the book) cohere to provide a powerful impression of a natural order of great antiquity and therefore of great authority, and of universal reference. It is reinforced by words—'world', 'universe', 'earth', 'mankind'—which expressly convey the same view. Thus, a constitution developed by men who acknowledge Burke's natural order is 'in just correspondence and symmetry with the order of the world'; the emergence of natural leaders is 'to illuminate and beautify the world';[6]

---

[1] *Reflections*, in *Works*, II, 320. [2] Ibid., II, 283.
[3] Ibid., II, 310. [4] Ibid., II, 309.
[5] Ibid., II, 309–11. [6] Ibid., II, 321.

and an order that recognises the importance of natural affections unites mankind by a universal love.[1] On the other hand, when such values are rejected 'universal anarchy' ensues;[2] when men wilfully disregard traditional usages and are governed by pride (the Satanic sin) 'nothing in heaven or upon earth can serve as a control on them'.[3] For these reasons the events of 1789 represent a crisis 'not of the affairs of France alone, but of all Europe, perhaps of more than Europe . . . the French Revolution is the most astonishing that has hitherto happened in the world'.[4] Burke's numerous quotations from classical authors keep the reader constantly aware of a European and ancient tradition of culture which depended on the values he advances and which the Revolution threatens; the quotations from English laws, while they serve to reinforce the authority of antiquity and precedent, also represent a part of 'the old common law of Europe' which is endangered. In other words, the texture of the prose itself, giving evidence of the weight and beauty of ancient (literary and legal) traditions, proves the point Burke is arguing more formally.

There are other key-words—'authority', 'religion', 'morality', 'law', 'principles', among others—but enough has been done to prove that Burke understood the value of a vague, cumulative use of terms which convey more than their surface meaning and whose suggestiveness enlarges with each successive usage. As he had remarked over thirty years earlier in the *Enquiry into . . . the Sublime and Beautiful*, 'it is one thing to make an idea clear, and another to make it *affecting* to the imagination'.[5] Affecting to the imagination he meant the *Reflections* to be and the literary technique just discussed contributes to this end; it also adds to the prose a richness, a generosity of feeling, and a 'noble dignity', qualities with which, on the level of argument, he wishes to invest a society organised after the principles he advocates. (He may also have been guided by his views on another source of the sublime, 'magnificence', defined in the *Enquiry* as 'a great profusion of things, which are splendid or valuable in themselves' and which suggest grandeur.[6])

An 'apparent disorder,' Burke claims, 'augments the

---

[1] *Reflections*, in *Works*, II, 320. [2] Ibid., II, 327.
[3] Ibid., II, 318. [4] Ibid., II, 284.
[5] *Works*, I, 90. [6] Ibid., I, 105.

grandeur.' The feeling of a grand disorder is a common response to the *Reflections*, but it is not the result of careless extravagance on Burke's part. An examination of his imagery will demonstrate that the sources for his images are limited, and seem purposefully selected, since the emotions they arouse harmonise with the effect of the key-terms analysed above, and the total result is inextricably involved with the ideas he wishes to establish. In connection with the approved kind of order Burke uses four principal sources of imagery: nature, the Bible, the noble house or castle, and, most important of all, the human family. Natural imagery has already been touched on: to point out that Burke frequently uses metaphorically such nouns as 'plant', 'body', 'root', and 'stock', and verbs like 'inoculate' and 'grafts', is enough to show that the ideas previously discussed are embedded in the texture of the prose. The Bible is used allusively rather than by direct reference. It is true that on one occasion, when he wishes to substantiate his claim that egalitarianism is 'at war with nature', Burke gives exact quotations from *Ecclesiasticus*,[1] but in the main he works through overtones in metaphorical language so as to invoke biblical authority for what is being stated. For example, by introducing the phrase, 'the cup of their abominations' he associates the French and their English admirers with the lascivious woman in *Revelation*;[2] behind the statement, 'to guard the treasure of our liberty, not only from invasion, but from decay and corruption',[3] lies the biblical command, 'lay up for yourselves treasure in heaven where neither moth nor rust doth corrupt, and where thieves do not break through nor steal'; and when Burke compares the actual state of affairs in France to 'the situation to which you were called',[4] he is invoking the Prayer Book injunction that the individual be content with 'that state of life unto which it shall please God to call him'. 'When words commonly sacred to great occasions are used, we are affected by them even without the occasions'[5]—so said Burke in the *Enquiry*, and his reasoning there is applicable to his practice in the *Reflections*. The emotive power of his biblical (and classical) allusions provides links with a sanctified tradition which is unassailable and not to be questioned; by so doing they contribute to the impression which Burke seeks to convey on the

---

[1] *Reflections*, in *Works*, II, 322–3 n.   [2] Ibid., II, 377.
[3] Ibid., II, 327.   [4] Ibid., II, 326.   [5] *Works*, I, 172.

surface of his argument, that to subvert an established tradition is both ignoble and sacrilegious.

Imagery from architecture is used in a similar fashion. Whereas the French in their lust for change demolish what is established and 'like their ornamental gardeners, [form] everything into an exact level',[1] Burke's veneration for stability, dignity, and a cultural tradition is transmitted through the image of the noble country-house or castle. (In this respect he is in the tradition of Ben Jonson, Marvell, Pope, and, later, Yeats, whose use of the same concept serves an analogous purpose.) For instance, he states that in 1660 and 1688 the English nation

> had lost the bond of union in their ancient edifice; they did not, however, dissolve the whole fabric. On the contrary, in both cases they regenerated the deficient part of the old constitution through the parts which were not impaired. They kept these old parts exactly as they were, that the part recovered might be suited to them.[2]

Here antiquity and the suggestion of a noble tradition, organic conservation and development are given almost concrete reality; the idea behind 'the part recovered' being 'suited to' the existing building is exactly parallel to that which informs the claim that 'we have taken care not to inoculate any scion alien to the nature of the existing plant'; and there is, through the whole image, that sense of security, solidity, and confidence which Burke argues is true of the English constitution. Fully developed images of the same kind, as well as allusive statements, are frequently found. De Pont is told that France in 1789

> possessed in some parts the walls, and, in all, the foundations, of a noble and venerable castle. You might have repaired those walls; you might have built on those old foundations.[3]

He is warned that

> it is with infinite caution that any man ought to venture upon pulling down an edifice, which has answered in any tolerable degree for ages the common purposes of society, or on building it up again, without having models and patterns of approved utility before his eyes.[4]

[1] *Reflections*, in *Works*, II, 443.   [2] Ibid., II, 295.
[3] Ibid., II, 308.   [4] Ibid., II, 334.

He is reminded that the 'temple of honour ought to be seated on an eminence',[1] advice which might—however far-fetched the notion may seem—come from a landscape-gardener designing the grounds of a noble house; and when Burke says that the revolutionists, 'without opening one new avenue to the understanding, . . . have succeeded in stopping up those that lead to the heart',[2] again he appears to be thinking of such grounds and (in Johnson's definition) 'the walk of trees before a house'. And the image reappears in the savage comment that 'in the groves of [the revolutionists'] academy' (not here a country-house but a place of theory), 'at the end of every vista, you see nothing but the gallows'.[3] This type of imagery diffuses its influence through the *Reflections*; it is undoubtedly responsible for a great deal of the veneration, permanence, traditional grace, and solid beauty with which Burke invests the natural order of things. Literary technique has in fact become part of the substantiation of the outlook he is seeking to establish.

Closely related to this last type of imagery is Burke's central symbol, the family. Burke regards the family as a natural and, at the same time, a sacred and indissoluble unity (a sharp contrast to the disintegration and atheism consequent upon the revolutionary philosophy); it is a principal source of 'the peace, happiness, settlement, and civilisation of the world.'[4] As a symbol the family fuses some of Burke's most passionately held ideas: that a love of country and of mankind proceeds from a love of 'the little platoon we belong to in society'; that the wisdom of the race is transmitted generation by generation to the present; that a tradition binds together past and present, and involves thought for the future; that moral obligations are essential to the well-being of society; and that human relationships and affections, emotions and prejudices are primary considerations. It is by this symbol (which has about it some of the 'obscurity' that fascinated him in the *Enquiry*), that Burke gives to his argument a large part of its emotional fervour and its power to allay intellectual analysis. Around it cluster the numerous references to 'inheritance', 'fore-fathers', 'posterity', 'records', 'titles', and the like, and while it would be tedious to detail his every use of such words, an examination of two paragraphs in which the

---

[1] *Reflections*, in *Works*, II, 323–4.   [2] Ibid., II, 337.
[3] Ibid., II, 350.   [4] *Regicide Peace*, in *Works*, V, 209.

symbol is most fully developed before the apostrophe, is instructive.[1] These paragraphs, it is important to note, represent the climax to the long discussion of Price's 'bill of rights' and precede a closer attention to the causes of events in France; this in its turn leads up to the events of 6 October 1789 and then to the apostrophe. We are dealing, therefore, with the emotional 'peak' before that which concerns the most significant family, the French royal family, and particularly the Queen herself.

By means of quotations from Acts of Parliament and liberal use of emotive terms Burke brings to the centre the idea that English liberties are 'an *entailed inheritance* derived to us from our fore-fathers, and to be transmitted to our posterity'. Increasingly, then, the nation is being regarded as a family, with all the privileges and obligations that involves. The idea gradually becomes a concrete image: 'Whatever advantages are obtained by a state proceeding on these maxims, are locked fast as in a sort of family settlement; grasped as in a kind of mortmain for ever.' Such a situation means that the nation functions 'after the pattern of nature': 'we receive, we hold, we transmit our government and our privileges, in the same manner in which we enjoy and transmit our property and our lives'. (It will be noticed that the dominant ideas linked with 'nature' and 'order', as discussed earlier, become involved with the family symbol, and as this is further developed more and more ideas are made interdependent.) The process described means also that 'the gifts of providence are handed down to us, and from us, in the same course and order'. It is, then, a universe whose pattern is divinely ordained; to be 'natural' in the sense of a nation's acting as a family is to carry out the divine plan. Neither the universal order, the constitution, nor the family are ever 'old, or middle-aged, or young', but 'in a condition of unchangeable constancy'. Burke then fully presents his 'philosophic analogy':

> In this choice of inheritance we have given to our frame of polity the image of a relation in blood; binding up the constitution of our country with our dearest domestic ties; adopting our fundamental laws into the bosom of our family affections; keeping inseparable, and cherishing with the warmth of all their combined and mutually reflected charities, our state, our hearths, our sepulchres, and our altars.

[1] *Reflections*, in *Works*, II, 307–8.

Here the truths carried on the surface of formal argument are expressed with imaginative insight; the family-symbol with its gradually accumulated features—unity, inheritance, the closest human affinities and obligations, powerful emotions, and loyalties both ancestral and religious—itself takes over the burden of the argument.

Burke has by now established the principle of 'conformity to nature', and he goes on to speak of the benefits that ensue. In this he relies entirely on the ideas and emotions fused in the family-symbol. The whole weight of this symbol—which is impressive but not over-precise—is transferred to the freedom that is achieved by a nation in harmony with the natural order. The family and its privileges becomes, as it were, imaginatively identified. Liberties are 'an inheritance'; awareness of 'canonized forefathers' tempers freedom 'with an awful gravity'; and the idea of 'a liberal descent' militates against the excesses of upstarts not accustomed to these privileges and encourages 'an habitual native dignity'.

> By this means our liberty becomes a noble freedom. It carries an imposing and majestic aspect. It has a pedigree and illustrating ancestors. It has its bearings and its ensigns armorial. It has its gallery of portraits; its monumental inscriptions; its records, evidences, and titles.

This passage is an excellent achievement by Burke's imaginative reason; a philosophic concept is given concrete reality; the implications of the preceding argument are drawn together into an impressive unity; and the family-symbol (with some features of the image of the noble house) is exploited to carry the full weight of Burke's political philosophy and to give it an imaginative grandeur. More than that, the apostrophe, which is placed in a distinctly 'family' setting, is prepared for by language which has the flavour of an 'age of chivalry' and of a civilisation which was founded on 'the spirit of a gentleman, and the spirit of religion'.[1]

When we turn to Burke's handling of the 'unnatural' as opposed to the 'natural order' we find the same disciplined imagination at work. The imagery, again drawn from a few selected sources, reinforces the impression, produced by formal

[1] *Reflections*, in *Works*, II, 351.

argument, of the destructive violence and selfish arrogance of revolutionists. The sources which account for nine-tenths of this imagery are prophecy, intoxicants, medicine, and trade. The first two, which can conveniently be taken together, are closely related.

The connection between them is made clearer by reference to Swift's 'Digression concerning Madness' in *A Tale of a Tub*. Unless both Swift and Burke were drawing on an earlier source there may be some grounds for conjecturing that Burke was indebted to his fellow-countryman, with whose general political and philosophical outlook he would have considerable sympathy. (He certainly had Swift in mind later in the *Reflections*, where he makes direct reference to *Gulliver's Travels*.[1]) In the Digression Swift accounts for

> the greatest Actions that have been performed in the World, under the Influence of Single Men; which are, *The Establishment of New Empires by Conquest: The Advance and Progress of New Schemes in Philosophy: and the contriving, as well as the propagating of New Religions.*

He argues that in all cases the 'natural Reason' of such men 'hath admitted great Revolutions'; the 'Human Understanding' has been 'troubled and overspread by Vapours, ascending from the lower Faculties'. His first illustrative example is 'Harry the Great of France', who was operated on by 'a certain *State-Surgeon*' (Ravaillac, his assassin). The arrogant presumption of 'Introducers of new Schemes in Philosophy' is also attributed to vapours that 'overshadow the Brain' and lead to '*Madness* or *Phrenzy*'. In this way Swift disposes of all who indulged in 'Metaphysical Cobweb Problems'. And then follows his principal contention:

> For, the Brain, in its natural Position and State of Serenity, disposeth its Owner to pass his Life in the common Forms, without any Thought of subduing Multitudes to his own *Power*, his *Reasons* or his *Visions*; and the more he shapes his Understanding by the Pattern of Human Learning, the less he is inclined to form Parties after his particular Notions; because that instructs him in his private Infirmities, as well as in the stubborn Ignorance

[1] Ibid., II, 404 n. (Two copies of *Gulliver's Travels* and two sets of Swift's *Works* are listed in the *Catalogue of the Sale of Burke's Library*, items nos. 487, 488, 554, 730.)

of the People. But when a Man's Fancy gets *astride* on his Reason, when Imagination is at Cuffs with the Senses, and common Understanding, as well as common Sense, is Kickt out of Doors; the first Proselyte he makes, is Himself, and when that is once compass'd, the Difficulty is not so great in bringing over others.

Both the details and the terminology, and the philosophy underlying Swift's irony bear a striking resemblance to Burke's imagery and indeed to his thinking. Both writers imply that when men arrogantly imagine that their private ideas are superior to traditionally accepted notions an unnatural state of irresponsibility and a dangerous lack of rational control inevitably follow.

Burke refers to the 'tavern' in which the Revolution Society held their meeting;[1] he speaks of the 'address' sent by the Society to the National Assembly as being 'passed by those who came reeking from the effect of the sermon';[2] the petty lawyers in the Assembly are 'intoxicated with their unprepared greatness';[3] and almost all the 'high-bred republicans' of Burke's day had slighted their opponents 'in the pride and intoxication of their theories'.[4] All such references suggest an irresponsibility which is coupled with an aggressive arrogance and self-sufficiency and results in the natural equilibrium being destroyed and reason being out of control. The link with imagery drawn from prophecy is obvious. ('Prophecy' for Burke is chiefly pejorative and signifies 'a vain confidence of divine favour' or 'heat of imagination', Johnson's definitions of 'enthusiasm'.) Whenever Price appears Burke makes it clear that, in Swift's phrase, 'common Sense is Kickt out of Doors'. Price '*philippizes*, and chants his prophetic song';[5] he deals in 'delusive, gipsy predictions';[6] he uses 'the confused jargon of Babylonian pulpits';[7] and he moved the address to the National Assembly when 'the fumes of his oracular tripod were not entirely evaporated'.[8] In each of these references (and there are others similar) there is a strong feeling of irresponsibility, a confused brain, and pride; 'gipsy' is defined by Johnson as 'a vagabond who pretends to foretel futurity, commonly by palmestry or physiognomy', and in his use of the word Burke obviously intends to

---

[1] *Reflections*, in *Works*, II, 280. [2] Ibid., II, 285.
[3] Ibid., II, 316. [4] Ibid., II, 336. [5] Ibid., II, 285.
[6] Ibid., II, 291. [7] Ibid., II, 303. [8] Ibid., II, 339.

suggest both instability and charlatanism; and the element of capriciousness recalls Swift's picture of 'a Man's Fancy . . . *astride* on his Reason'.

The condemnation of pride—which accompanies 'enthusiasm' for both Swift and Burke—is reinforced by two comparisons between Price and the Pope[1] (a sardonic type of humour in view of Price's vigorous anti-papalism and an example of the same linking of opposites that Swift uses when he identifies Peter with Jack in *A Tale of a Tub*). But more frequently there is a strong suggestion of heathenism; Burke grants Price's religiosity but implies that it is pre-Christian, even barbarous.[2] The very term 'prophecy' is so controlled as to suggest pre- or non-Christian cults; 'Babylonian' and 'oracular tripod' strengthen this impression with overtones of heathen worship. Burke's control over the reader's response is also notable when he claims that Price uses the *Nunc Dimittis*, a 'beautiful and prophetic ejaculation' (the controlling epithet is the first), 'with an inhuman and unnatural rapture' and 'unhallowed transports'.[3] Here 'prophecy'—linked with the infant Christ—is approved, but the terms applied to Price indicate that the use to which it is put is barbarous; this impression is immediately confirmed by a comparison between the French treatment of Louis and a band of Indians returning from a scalping raid. By such means Burke associates Price and the revolutionists with savage heathenism, which points to either ignorance or rejection of Christian ethics. The metaphor applied to France—'everything human and divine sacrified to the idol of public credit'[4]—unobtrusively strengthens this association.

Frequent imaginative references to medicine substantiate the charge of pride which Burke directs against all subverters of natural order: Price and his kind are presumptuous in their claim to be 'qualified' by 'nature' to administer a 'bitter potion to a distempered state'.[5] There is also a link—especially in a phrase like 'epidemical fanaticism'[6]—with the imagery previously

---

[1] *Reflections*, in *Works*, II, 287, 289.

[2] Cf. Samuel Butler, 'A Modern Statesman', *Characters* (1759): 'The *Heathen* Priests of old never delivered Oracles but when they were drunk, and mad or distracted, and who knows why our modern Oracles may not as well use the same Method in all their Proceedings.'

[3] *Works*, II, 339-, 340.   [4] Ibid., II, 312.

[5] Ibid., II, 304.   [6] Ibid., II, 424.

examined in that, to use Swift's words, a man cannot be 'in the natural State, or Course of Thinking . . . to reduce the Notions of all Mankind, exactly to the same Length, and Breadth, and Heighth of his own'. Moreover, if Burke had Swift in mind, the term, 'State-Surgeon', which so aptly epitomises his view of Price, may have been a further controlling factor.[1] Burke's type of humour would certainly associate Doctor Price, Doctor Hugh Peters, and perhaps Doctor Joseph Priestley, with state-surgery. Price is a 'spiritual doctor of politics';[2] he and his kind, while setting up as 'doctors of the rights of men',[3] are not practical, experienced 'physicians' but 'professors of meta-physics';[4] they irritate a calm love of liberty by 'making the extreme medicine of the constitution its daily bread' and rendering 'the habit of society dangerously valetudinary'.[5] The French, for their part, 'have seen the medicine of the state corrupted into its poison';[6] indeed, their 'present confusion, like a palsy, has attacked the fountain of life itself'.[7] Such a plethora of images—and there are others—builds up a powerful association between revolutionism and disease; revolutionists are always on the watch for serious ailments in the body-politic, with the result that they come to love corruption too much and contented human nature too little. Indeed, they have no conception of tender solicitude, but develop a pathological inclination for brutality. They do not hesitate 'to cut up the infant for the sake of an experiment' nor, like the daughters of Peleas, 'to hack that aged parent [their country] in pieces, and put him into the kettle of magicians'.[8] (Hobbes' specific use of the same Greek legend[9] serves incidentally to point up the difference between his habit of direct reference and Burke's allusive method, which increases the suggestive richness of his prose.) The contrast Burke makes us aware of is with 'the healing voice of Christian charity'.[10]

The last of the main sources of anti-revolution imagery is

---

[1] See also Samuel Butler, 'The Seditious Man', *Characters*: 'He is a State-Mountebank, whose Business is to persuade the People that they are not well in Health, that he may get their Money to make them worse.'

[2] *Reflections*, in *Works*, II, 288.   [3] Ibid., II, 297.

[4] Ibid., II, 333.   [5] Ibid., II, 335.   [6] Ibid., II, 312.

[7] Ibid., II, 322.   [8] Ibid., II, 436–7, 368.

[9] Ed. M. Oakeshott, *Leviathan* (Oxford, 1946), p. 222.

[10] *Reflections*, in *Works*, II, 286.

trade. The contemporary interest in this type of reference need not be insisted on; there may be the further hint (such as is commonly found in Swift) of the link between trade and dissent; but, most significant, the practical and concrete features of trade contrast vividly with the alleged flimsiness and impracticability of abstract theories. Actually to speak of these theories in terms of trade is to get the advantage of irony. Books circulated by the Constitutional Society may, 'like goods not in request here', have found 'a market' in France;[1] Burke warns De Pont that both England and France must avoid allowing themselves 'to be imposed upon by the counterfeit wares' which are exported to France 'as raw commodities of British growth, though wholly alien to our soil' ('unnatural' in the wide sense discussed earlier), and smuggled back as if 'after the newest Paris fashion';[2] and he declares that France has set up 'trade without a capital' (having rejected the accumulated wisdom of centuries).[3] The same type of image provides the irony in Burke's comment on those who find

> nothing to satisfy their pious fancies in the old staple of the national church, or in all the rich variety to be found in the well-assorted warehouses of the dissenting congregations.[4]

Even from this brief quotation it is worth noting that, by precise choice of single words, Burke retains his grip on his central thesis. 'Staple' is defined by Johnson as 'a settled mart, an established emporium'; Burke's use of 'warehouses' coupled with derisive alliteration suggests transitoriness and lesser quality. On the other hand, Burke can derive an approving response from this type of imagery which he normally uses for the purpose of irony or censure. In a passage on 'the real rights of men' Burke gives this illustrative metaphor (added to the text in the third edition):

> In this partner-ship [of civil society] all men have equal rights; but not to equal things. He that has but five shillings in the partnership, has as good a right to it, as he that has five hundred pounds has to his larger proportion. But he has not a right to an equal dividend in the product of the joint stock. . . .[5]

[1] *Reflections*, in *Works*, II, 279.   [2] Ibid., II, 299.
[3] Ibid., II, 309.   [4] Ibid., II, 286.
[5] Ibid., II, 332. In the 3rd edn. the last word of the quotation was 'estate'; it was replaced by 'stock' in the 5th.

Basically the image derives from the same source as 'goods', 'wares', and 'trade', but by a subtle movement from vulgar commercial traffic to the principles of a capitalist economy he achieves the opposite response. We move away from 'trade' to the 'capital' on which it depends; from, as it were, the counter to the board-room. And finally, in a famous passage, by similar means Burke imaginatively establishes his claims for traditional wisdom.

> We are afraid to put men to live and trade each on his own private stock of reason; because we suspect that this stock in each man is small, and that the individuals would do better to avail themselves of the general bank and capital of nations and of ages.[1]

Not only is the limited and insecure 'stock' of the private trader directly contrasted with 'general bank' and 'capital', the inexhaustible wealth of corporate human resources, but the movement of the prose and character of the diction subtly enforce the contrast. As far as the word 'small', the diction is predominantly monosyllabic and its motion relatively staccato, whereas the final long clause is appropriately richer in polysyllables and rhythmic fluency.

One point at least emerges clearly from this discussion of imagery and key-terms: though contemporary critics denounced Burke for the seeming extravagance and grand disorder of the *Reflections*, he was writing within an imaginative discipline. It makes for a wholeness and coherence which provide permanent delight; it also gave Burke an immediate polemical advantage. Though there is an abundance of imagery, by selecting it largely from a limited number of sources Burke ensured that his readers would associate certain attitudes, values, and emotions with tradition and order, on the one hand, and with revolution and disorder, on the other. For he was not working for what, in the *Enquiry*, he called 'a clear expression' but for 'a strong expression':

> The former regards the understanding; the latter belongs to the passions. The one describes a thing as it is; the other describes it as it is felt.[2]

---

[1] *Reflections*, in *Works*, II, 359.   [2] *Works*, I, 180.

In other words, he writes not simply as a political philosopher but as an imaginative artist; the ideas of the philosopher are conveyed in the texture of the prose with a potency and wholeness possible only to a man employing imaginative language. Burke did not only cogitate about the issues confronting him but also felt passionately about them. Indeed, the very strength of his feelings is a salient feature of the case he is arguing: the traditional order takes full account of natural feelings; the revolutionists deny them. Seen from this angle, his emotive prose is the embodiment of the fundamental nature of his thought.

> Why do I feel so differently from the Reverend Dr. Price, and those of his lay flock who will choose to adopt the sentiments of his discourse?—For this plain reason—because it is *natural* I should; because we are so made, as to be affected at such spectacles with melancholy sentiments . . . because in those natural feelings we learn great lessons; because in events like these our passions instruct our reason.[1]

The *Reflections* exists as proof of this philosophy, giving evidence of natural emotions and the lessons they teach. Emotive techniques are then more than persuasive methods: they convey the essence of Burke's philosophic position.

It may be objected, however, that this judgment cannot be indiscriminately applied to the whole of the *Reflections*, that Burke was not above exploiting emotionalism merely to secure immediate assent from a particular audience. It is, of course, true that the whole work is geared to making a profound appeal to the conservative mind: the character of the prose style, the emphasis on traditionalism, the stress on the importance of property, of the religious basis of society, or of the country gentlemen as opposed to the urban masses are all obvious enough. Burke is also capable of an inflated, windy eloquence in which his critical mind is inactive; part of the passage on the divine origin of civil society provides one example:

> [The English people] conceive that He who gave our nature to be perfected by our virtue, willed also the necessary means of its perfection.—He willed therefore the state—He willed its connexion with the source and original archetype of all perfection. They who are convinced of this his will, which is the law of laws,

---

[1] *Reflections*, in *Works*, II, 352–3.

and the sovereign of sovereigns, cannot think it reprehensible
that this our corporate fealty and homage, that this our recognition of a signiory paramount, I had almost said this oblation of
the state itself, as a worthy offering on the high altar of universal
praise, should be performed . . . with mild majesty and sober
pomp.[1]

Here words are heaped on words, a specious kind of Prayer
Book idiom and rhythm ('this our sacrifice of praise and thanksgiving', 'this our bounden duty and service') takes control, and
as the rhythms move gradually farther from those of common
speech the language is falsely overheightened. The same easy
command of emotive verbiage is also at Burke's disposal to bol-
ster up a weak argument. In his defence of the monks whose
property had been confiscated he elaborates in paragraph after
paragraph a case which rests on the flimsy premise that the
monks are desirable landowners because they are no worse than
other men.[2] It is the verbal weight which is used to cow
readers into submission. Burke is guilty too of hysterical outbursts—

> Massacre, torture, hanging! These are your rights of men!
> These are the fruit of metaphysic declarations wantonly made,
> and shamefully retracted.[3]

of sophistry—

> Habitual dissoluteness of manners [among the French nobility]
> continued beyond the pardonable period of life.[4]

and of gross overwriting—

> the painted booths and sordid sties of vice and luxury . . . the
> momentary receptacles of transient voluptuousness.[5]

The fact is therefore inescapable that the central importance
of 'natural feelings' in Burke's philosophy, which properly makes
his emotive prose itself a weighty proof of the case he argues on
a formal level, also allows him to exploit emotionalism of a
specious kind. Nevertheless, Bentham overstates the case against
him: 'the power [Burke] trusted to was *oratory—rhetoric*—the art
of misrepresentation—the art of misdirecting the judgment by

---

[1] *Reflections*, in *Works*, II, 370.
[2] Ibid., II, 428–34.   [3] Ibid., II, 491.
[4] Ibid., II, 409.   [5] Ibid., II, 432.

agitating and inflaming the passions'.[1] This ignores the organic relationship between Burke's style and his thought; it also ignores the imaginative discipline of which evidence has been given and the literary sensitivity which enabled him to achieve immediate effectiveness combined with lasting and complex pleasure.

Even at moments when Bentham would say Burke is most characteristically himself, as in his denunciation of the rejection of prescriptive rights in France, when he adopts the tone of a prophet.

> I see, in a country very near us ... I see the National Assembly ... I see a practice perfectly correspondent ... I see the confiscators ... I see the princes of the blood. ...

and when he goes to the very edge between decorum and excess—

> Flushed with the insolence of their first inglorious victories, and pressed by the distresses caused by their lust of unhallowed lucre. ...

where he risks in prose a Miltonic grandiloquence, he is aware of the value of verbal contrast to jolt his reader into alertness:

> What vestiges of liberty or property have they left? The tenant-right of a cabbage-garden, a year's interest in a hovel, the good-will of an ale-house or a baker's shop ... are more ceremoniously treated in our parliament.[2]

Here and frequently elsewhere Burke disregards a contemporary theorist of rhetoric like George Campbell who insists on the desirability of 'reputable' language and the danger of 'vulgarisms',[3] and switches from heightened to common speech to increase the impact of both. The immensity of the vision in the well-known passage beginning, 'Society is indeed a contract', with its view of 'a partnership not only between those who are living, but between those who are living, those who are dead, and those who are to be born', has its own dignity and grandeur; but it is set off by the clash between this kind of prose

[1] *Works* (Edinburgh, 1843), X, 510.
[2] *Reflections*, in *Works*, II, 422–3.
[3] *The Philosophy of Rhetoric* (1776), I, 345 ff.

fluency (contrasting sharply with Paine's defiant abruptness when he contests the argument) and the sentence:

> the state ought not to be considered as nothing better than a partnership agreement in a trade of pepper and coffee, calico or tobacco, or some other such low concern.[1]

Both the idiom and the petulant rhythm throw into relief the grand conception to follow. And, of course, this command of vulgar speech is serviceable for denigrating the narrow vision of the revolutionists:

> It is nothing but plain impudence.[2]

> Such a machine . . . is not worth the grease of its wheels.[3]

> [Members of a Dundee club] would not give a dog's-ear of their most rumpled and ragged Scotch paper for twenty of your fairest *assignats*.[4]

The range of Burke's verbal and imaginative ability is obvious. He is not confined, as for the most part are, say, Paine, Mackintosh, or Godwin, within a single style, but rather his literary scope corresponds to the comprehensiveness of his political wisdom. The wisdom without the literary skill would be hamstrung. His ability to distil into a terse maxim some idea of political morality is not only the mark of an incisive intelligence; it is also the proof of Burke's understanding of a polemical situation. Such pungent sentences as—

> Kings will be tyrants from policy, when subjects are rebels from principle.[5]

> Equal neglect is not impartial kindness.[6]

> It is not from impotence we are to expect the tasks of power[7]

are at once intellectually stimulating and memorable; they sum up features of the argument in a way that would stick in the reader's mind, provide him with easily quotable phrases, and thus extend Burke's authority. The only writer in the controversy with a comparable skill is Paine, but his aphorisms are less satisfying and less packed with general insight. He was incapable of the combination of idea, verbal economy, and rhythmic sense

---

[1] *Reflections*, in *Works*, II, 368. [2] Ibid., II, 395.
[3] Ibid., II, 473. [4] Ibid., II, 509. [5] Ibid., II, 350.
[6] Ibid., II, 421. [7] Ibid., II, 470.

that Burke achieves in: 'Wisdom cannot create materials; they are the gifts of nature or of chance; her pride is in the use.'[1]

The tone of this sentence is imperiously assured, but, as other quotations have demonstrated, Burke's range in this respect, too, is vast. He was well aware of the importance of variety. Though he expected his audience to endure argument sustained at greater length than Paine imposed on his readers, Burke recognised that 'fatigue must give bounds to the discussion of subjects, which in themselves have hardly any limits'.[2] Wit, literary allusions, variation in idiom, tone of voice, and prose rhythm were all manipulated to keep the reader alert. The living audience of 'not the least learned and reflecting part'[3] of the community were to receive Burke's message through a literary experience they would not easily forget.

The resourcefulness of which he is capable is partly illustrated by a portion from his onslaught on the speculation in land encouraged by the new French constitution.[4] One paragraph finishes thus:

> They have reversed the Latonian kindness to the landed property of Delos. They have sent theirs to be blown about, like the light fragments of a wreck, *oras et littora circum*.

Here the charge that the Assembly has destroyed the stability of landed property is made obliquely through a witty reference to Greek legend reinforced by the Virgilian quotation. A paragraph of sustained attack follows. It begins with an ironic glance at the 'holy bishop' (Talleyrand) and his approval of 'enlightened' usury as a spur to agriculture, which Burke directly challenges with his denial that 'a man's not believing in God can teach him to cultivate the earth with the least of any additional skill or encouragement'; it then moves through a reminder of Cicero by way of the quotation, '*Diis immortalibus sero*', and an ironic comment on the usurers—'These gentlemen are too wise in their generation'—which carries biblical implications, to the observation on 'their great precursor and prototype', Alphius. He, in Horace's second Epode, begins by celebrating the charms of a pastoral life—'*Beatus ille*'—and ends by succumbing to his lust for money. The reader, who has been

---

[1] *Reflections*, in *Works*, II, 428.   [2] Ibid., II, 475.
[3] Ibid., II, 369.   [4] Ibid., II, 461–3.

flattered by the assumption that he will respond to the quotations and allusions and delighted by the writer's fertility, comes to the end of the paragraph with its play on words, irony, and scathing use of biblical overtones:

> They will cultivate the *Caisse d'Église*, under the sacred auspices of this prelate, with much more profit than its vineyards and its corn-fields. They will employ their talents according to their habits and their interests. They will not follow the plough whilst they can direct treasuries, and govern provinces.

Once Burke's feelings, whether of scorn, anger, or admiration, fire his imagination, such sustained verbal brilliance invariably results. His literary experience is always at hand to add an extra level of pleasure, enforcing the impact of what is said and deepening the hold it takes on the reader's mind. The famous question, 'Who now reads Bolingbroke?' is vivid in its contemptuous sharpness, but it gains an added piquancy if it recalls Pope's, 'Who now reads Cowley?'[1] Again, Pope's line, 'But soft —by regular approach—not yet', from the description of the obstacles confronting a visitor to Timon's villa, becomes 'But soft—by regular degrees, not yet' and carries the Popeian irony and comedy into Burke's attack on the involved French electoral system.[2] 'Some great offences in France must cry to heaven' inevitably reminds one of Claudius's confession in *Hamlet*[3] and 'such unfeathered two-legged things' equally recalls Dryden in *Absalom and Achitophel*, as well as Plato's description of man which lies behind that.[4] On other occasions another kind of recall operates.

> They took an old huge full-bottomed periwig out of the wardrobe of the antiquated frippery of Louis the Fourteenth, to cover the premature baldness of the National Assembly.[5]

Here it is a similarity of conception and comic vision rather than verbal echoes which calls up Swift's picture of Dryden (in *The Battle of the Books*) swaggering under his large helmet 'like a

---

[1] *Reflections*, in *Works*, II, 361, cf. Pope, *The First Epistle of the Second Book of Horace*, l. 75.
[2] Ibid., II, 445, cf. Pope, *Epistle to Burlington*, l. 129.
[3] Ibid., II, 465–6, cf. Shakespeare, *Hamlet*, III, iii, 36.
[4] Ibid., II, 494, cf. Dryden, *Absalom and Achitophel*, l. 170.
[5] Ibid., II, 500.

shrivled Beau from within the Pent-house of a modern Pere-
wig'.[1] In these and other instances Burke shows a thorough
understanding (greater than, say, Hobbes or Godwin) of the
power of allusive reference to strengthen the punch of his
writing and enrich the audience's response.

At every turn there is evidence of Burke's artistic awareness.
An examination of his textual revisions (through to the eleventh
edition) would merely serve to reinforce the same point. Indeed, to read the *Reflections* as Burke intended—not only with
the political consciousness but also with imagination and
literary intelligence—is a complex experience. The whole texture of the writing constitutes the experience. This has been
demonstrated in the detail; what remains is to show that, in the
part of the *Reflections* which has caught the attention of his critics
almost without exception, Burke's imaginative discipline and
the full range of his techniques are effectively deployed on the
larger scale. That part is the apostrophe to the French Queen
and the paragraphs which provide the setting for it.

III

The apostrophe is not a sudden eruption; it is prepared for
with immense care. As Burke approaches it he stresses increasingly the brutality and moral depravity which are eventually to
be contrasted with the beauty, civilised grace, taste, and
courtesy epitomised by the Queen. She is a product of a way of
life which gives a central place to human affections and the
family, and thus reflects a universal harmony. This is vitally important. Admiration and emotional attachment ('Who is it that
admires, and from the heart is attached to . . .'[2]) are Burke's
standards of value here, admiration (as Johnson defines it)
carrying the sense of regarding with love as well as with wonder.
He proposes to show in the act of writing and in the presentation
of events that ordered institutions are 'embodied . . . in persons;
so as to create in us love, veneration, admiration, or attachment'.[3] This attitude both controls, and is exemplified in his
handling of, the revolutionary treatment of the French royal
family.

[1] Ed. H. Davis, *Prose Works of Swift* (Oxford, 1939), I, 157.
[2] *Reflections*, in *Works*, II, 341.   [3] Ibid., II, 350.

The events of 6 October (the attack on Versailles) which prepare for the apostrophe are preceded by a description of political
and moral 'distortion'.[1] The National Assembly has neither
responsibility nor authority, and spectators take precedence over
the elected deputies; Louis and his ministers are powerless;
criminals are exalted and the virtuous forced into crime; women
are defeminised; destruction (not natural creation) triumphs;
manners and good breeding are replaced by murder and
assassination. 'They have inverted order in all things'; 'the
moral taste of every well-born mind' is outraged. And in this
context Burke fastens on what he considers an insulting Address
from the Assembly to Louis and on Price's 'triumph' over the
fallen monarch.[2] Consequently, before he comes to the detail of
6 October Burke has established his values by these emotive
means. It is notable too that the picture becomes more and more
particularised; we move from a generalised description of chaos
and its attendant evils to a specific illustration. Gradually, then,
the reader is being put into the position Burke considered essential: 'I must see with mine own eyes, I must, in a manner, touch
with my own hands, not only the fixed but the momentary circumstances.'[3] Attention to the 'momentary circumstances' of
any event had a philosophical significance for Burke as well as
making for greater rhetorical effectiveness. (It is no accident
that the apostrophe opens with a reference to actual personal
experience.)

Immediately following a renewed stress on Louis' bitter
humiliation (achieved through medical imagery), heightened
by an allusion to Macbeth's mental agony, we come to the concrete event: 'on the morning of the 6th of October, 1789'.[4]

[1] *Reflections*, in *Works*, II, 340–1.
[2] It is of interest to remember Price's rejection of Burke's charge, since
it may prove Burke guilty of calculated misrepresentation. Price claimed
that his use of the *Nunc Dimittis* referred to the events of 14 July and not
6 October 1789: 'I am indeed surprised that Mr. Burke could want candour
so much as to suppose that I had other events in view.' The protest becomes
more damning when Price continues: 'The letters quoted by [Burke] on
p. 99 and 128 [Bohn, II, 338 n., 358–9 n.], were dated in *July* 1789, and
might have shewn him that he was injuring both me and the writer of those
letters.' (*A Discourse on the Love of our Country*, p. vi.)
[3] *A Letter to a Member of the National Assembly*, in *Works*, II, 549.
[4] *Reflections*, in *Works*, II, 343.

(From here to the apostrophe with its mood of exalted reflection, action is the key-note, a fact which contributes to the splendid isolation of the Queen in that passage.) In his account of the attack on Versailles Burke selects for emphasis human emotions, loyalty, the family relationship, and the love it entails: the guard's fidelity to the point of death,[1] the Queen's love of and trust in Louis, who is both 'king and husband', and the family—'this king . . . and this queen, and their infant children'. The violent slaughter and bestiality which surround them seem intended by contrast to stress the family as a life-giving source. A further profound contrast follows—suggesting the values which are involved in this event—between Christianity and heathenism. 'Consecrated', 'altars', 'thanksgiving', 'divine humanity', and 'fervent prayer' are opposed to 'Theban and Thracian orgies' and the kind of 'prophetic enthusiasm' examined previously. The point of the contrast is to underline the marked difference between the 'humanity' of Christ and the depraving philosophy of revolution in their several effects on men's actions. Burke is in fact compelling our attention not to abstractions but to human beings in the actual business of living, invariably a prominent feature in all his thinking. Religious fanaticism—which is the impression given of Price and the French by the account of the alleged plan for the murder of the bishops—breeds the sort of proud self-sufficiency and irresponsibility Swift noted in his Digression; Christian culture (the foundation for 'the age of chivalry'), on the other hand, encourages humanity, sensibility, humility and moral purity. 'Inborn feelings of [human] nature' are at once the test and the proof of this culture: it is they which direct Burke's reactions to the events described.

Burke's natural feelings become dominant and they are displayed in response to the plight of a family of rank, beauty, ancient lineage, and 'tender age'.[2] Here the symbol of the family is actualised: an institution is embodied in persons worthy of 'admiration' (in the Johnsonian sense). Furthermore,

---

[1] It is noteworthy that Burke never deleted the reference to the death of the guard, though, even if not at the time of writing, certainly before many editions were out, he must have known it was false. Several of his opponents in the subsequent controversy informed him of it.

[2] *Reflections*, in *Works*, II, 347.

in the act of writing itself Burke is giving evidence of 'generous loyalty to rank and sex' and 'sensibility of principle', qualities which, in the apostrophe, he attributes to the age of chivalry—and this at the same time as he presents a contrast with the heartlessness of the 'new-sprung modern light'. The feelings of Louis, as prince but also as husband, are reported as facts, and his 'humanity' is honoured.

The Queen, therefore, comes to the centre of the stage amid references to the family and to natural emotions. The intensity of the writing is heightened by emphasis on her beauty and her suffering, and the weight of a whole paragraph is thrown forward to the contemplation of her death. Moreover, Burke does not underestimate the value of sex-appeal, particularly when it is associated with a woman of rank, courage, beauty, and sensibility. She is important, then, as a particular woman; she is equally significant (whatever the truth about her personal life), as a symbol of nobility and grace, the source of life and growth and continuity. The Queen in fact embodies some of the fundamentals of Burke's political thought. These are the same features which predominate in the apostrophe, where philosophical implications are concentred in a memorable literary achievement.

There can be little doubt that the apostrophe represents an imaginative re-creation of Burke's feelings when he saw Marie Antoinette in 1773, under the stress of his acute reaction to her situation in 1789. And there is equally little doubt that his literary theory, outlined in the *Enquiry*, directed to some extent at least his writing in this passage. The apostrophe demonstrates his preference for a 'strong' over a 'clear expression'; it illustrates his contention that imaginative literature should convey the effect of the object described on the feelings of the writer. This last was exactly his aim. For the revolutionary philosophers 'a queen is but a woman; a woman is but an animal; and an animal not of the highest order';[1] for Burke she is a symbolic creature seen through the medium of what he called 'a moral imagination'. 'A clear expression' would be appropriate to the 'new conquering empire of light and reason', showing the object as it is and appealing to the intellect; a 'strong expression', showing the Queen as transfigured by Burke's emotions, is a

---

[1] *Reflections*, in *Works*, II, 349.

persuasive factor in support of his own outlook. His technique is also foreshadowed in the *Enquiry*, where he says of Priam's account of Helen that it does not contain 'one word . . . of the particulars of her beauty; nothing which can in the least help us to any precise idea of her person', yet it is more affecting than a long and detailed account.[1] The same comment is applicable to Burke's description of the Queen. Indeed, it is rather an evocation than a description—an evocation of a woman symbolising 'conscious dignity, noble pride, and a generous sense of glory',[2] qualities which he has previously attributed to the French nation. Burke avoids physical attributes and emphasises the Queen's ethereal beauty. As was noticed earlier in speaking of the universal imagery Burke employs, it is a world which is involved here: 'never alighted on this orb', 'just above the horizon', 'glittering like the morning-star'. This last phrase exploits biblical associations from a passage in *Ecclesiasticus* (quoted in the *Enquiry*[3]), which is shot through with brilliant images of splendour, holiness, and dignity. The reference is, then, in harmony with an elevated language which powerfully suggests visionary radiance and unearthly qualities. The dominant impression is conveyed by a word-pattern which includes 'orb', 'delightful', 'decorating', 'cheering', 'glittering', 'splendour', 'joy', and 'love'; they are terms that involve the reader in the imaginative experience Burke presents; and they invoke ideas of grace, dignity, elegance, and taste, ideas which he has related to the approved order of things since the beginning of the book. And yet the change in values initiated by the Revolution is, as it were, carried along in an undercurrent—'that elevation and that fall', 'Little did I dream', 'disgrace', 'disasters'—which comes gradually nearer the surface with 'sophisters, economists, and calculators', 'extinguished for ever', 'never, never more', 'it is gone'. The Queen symbolises all that is finest in a whole civilisation, and with her perish the benefits which society derived from that civilisation: dignified obedience, exalted freedom, the unifying and ennobling power of human emotions. The vague, emotive phrases—so difficult briefly to paraphrase—

---

[1] *Works*, I, 177.
[2] *Reflections*, in *Works*, II, 322.
[3] *Works*, I, 106. (The phrase also occurs in the Office of the Blessed Virgin Mary.)

in which Burke indulges are not mere extravagances of the moment; in them is concentrated much of the significance of the preceding argument. The hyperbole—'I thought ten thousand swords must have leaped from their scabbards to avenge even a look that threatened her with insult'—similarly focuses a great deal of earlier suggestion. The exaggeration one feels is conscious; it gives heightened expression—which can be ridiculed but not forgotten—to that notion of the instinctive defence of womanhood which is the traditional proof of humane feelings. In France these feelings are atrophied; the unnatural coldness of revolutionary philosophy inhibits the normal response; and the noble because natural, ancient system of manners is subverted. The degradation of this woman, then, involves the symbolic destruction of ancient governmental institutions which were embodied 'in persons so as to create in us love, veneration, admiration, or attachment'. And the whole process is presented to the reader by means of intense emotion, the human quality most despised by the revolutionists.

What follows the apostrophe depends upon it. Henceforward Burke is concerned to show the results of a philosophy that leaves nothing 'which engages the affections on the part of the commonwealth';[1] that rejects the civilisation and system of manners founded on the two principles, 'the spirit of a gentleman, and the spirit of religion';[2] that despises the natural feelings which would have scorned to humiliate a beautiful, nobly descended queen; and that, elevating the individual at the expense of the community, provokes both moral and political disintegration. The values given particular embodiment in the apostrophe are those by which the English and French constitutions are measured in the remainder of the *Reflections*.

The apostrophe is central to the work as a whole. At the risk of being censured by some for excessive emotionalism, Burke provides a memorable centrepiece which, in symbolic terms, focuses the philosophical significance of all that goes before it and acts as a seminal passage for what follows. Even if it is considered a sample of the 'marvellous' according to his own definition—that which will 'strike and interest the public'[3]—it is

[1] *Reflections*, in *Works*, II, 350.
[2] Ibid., II, 351.
[3] Ibid., II, 441.

highly functional: after the apostrophe Burke is more and more concerned with the detail of governmental organisation which may well become confused in the reader's memory; this passage remains in the mind by its imaginative force and persuasive suggestiveness.

VIII

THOMAS PAINE'S *RIGHTS OF MAN*: THE VULGAR STYLE

J UST over three months after the appearance of Burke's
Reflections Paine published his *Rights of Man* (Part I), one
of the most widely read pamphlets of all time. It is an example
of political prose written for a relatively uneducated audience,
a literary kind which presents the critic with difficult problems
of analysis and evaluation. Writers—such as those examined by
John Holloway in *The Victorian Sage*—who cater for an audience
alert to subtleties of allusion, tone, rhythm, imagery, and so
forth, and who in consequence are able to manipulate a large
range of literary techniques, confident of their readers' response
—such writers lend themselves readily to conventional literary
analysis. But because our critical tools are not normally sharpened on his kind of writing, an author like Tom Paine tends to
be ignored. He receives a nod from compilers of 'social settings'
and 'literary scenes', as if what he had to say and the manner of
saying it can safely be disregarded, but no serious critical attention.

It is noticeable that no attempt has been made by literary
critics to account for the remarkable impact of the *Rights of
Man*. There is no need to insist on the reality of Paine's influence in his own day, it is too well known (though the reminder
may be timely in view of the complete absence of his name from
the *Pelican Guide to English Literature* covering the Revolutionary
period). And it is not adequate to leave it to the political
historian to explain this influence, or merely to claim, with some

eighteenth-century critics, that Paine's was an appeal to the political have-nots against the ruling class. When it is remembered that upwards of seventy books and pamphlets were written in reply to Burke's *Reflections*, many of them addressed to the same audience as Paine's, this explanation obviously does not account for the distinctive success of the *Rights of Man* or for the sale (according to Paine) of 'between four and five hundred thousand' copies within ten years of publication.[1]

One principal reason for Paine's success was the apparent simplicity of his revolutionary doctrine and the lucid directness with which he expressed it. For example, he enters the great eighteenth-century debate on social contract; he rejects the notion that government is a compact between 'those who govern and those who are governed' as 'putting the effect before the cause', and asserts that initially

> the *individuals themselves*, each in his own personal and sovereign right, *entered into a compact with each other* to produce a government: and this is the only mode in which governments have a right to arise, and the only principle on which they have a right to exist.[2]

Any government that, like the British, was the result of conquest and was founded on the power of a ruling caste and not on the free choice of the people was, *ipso facto*, no true government. Paine will have no truck with Burkean arguments which start from the idea that man is the product of countless ages of human and political development; as in the above quotation he insists on beginning *ab initio*, 'when man came from the hand of his Maker. What was he then? Man. Man was his high and only title, and a higher cannot be given him.'[3] The argument is naïve, but its persuasive force lies in its simplicity; only by its consequences does the reader recognise how deceptive and how rigorous is the apparent simplicity—man's essential equality is established, privileges claimed as a result of so-called noble descent or hereditary succession vanish, and it is an easy step to the assertion that sovereignty resides in the collective will of a nation (expressed by its freely elected representatives) and not in a single man who has come by chance to the position of king.

---

[1] Ed. P. S. Foner, *Complete Writings*, II, 910.
[2] Ibid., I, 278.   [3] Ibid., I, 273.

From the same source springs the belief that 'Man is not the enemy of man, but through the medium of a false system of government',[1] or, as he expresses it in Part II of the *Rights of Man* (published 1792), 'man, were he not corrupted by governments, is naturally the friend of man, and human nature is not of itself vicious'.[2] From this premise, expressed with such disarming directness, there follows a conclusion of vast importance for an age of dynastic conflicts: wars are the means by which non-representative governments maintain their power and wealth. (There is little wonder that Horace Walpole was perturbed when 'vast numbers of Paine's pamphlet were distributed both to regiments and ships' on the second anniversary of the fall of the Bastille.[3])

Time and again Paine makes statements which appear commonplace in a context of political theory; they prove to be revolutionary in their implications.

> The duty of man . . . is plain and simple, and consists but of two points. His duty to God, which every man must feel; and with respect to his neighbour, to do as he would be done by.[4]

The assertion seems innocuous enough, but, as in Swift's writings, only when the reader has swallowed the bait does he realise how firmly he is hooked. The duty to one's neighbour should be recognised by all men, by rulers as well as the ruled; Paine's reader then discovers that the moral injunction has become a means by which rulers are to be assessed and that those who act well according to this principle will be respected, those who do not will be despised; and finally, the last jerk on the hook, 'with regard to those to whom no power is delegated, but who assume it, the rational world can know nothing of them'. The logic by which this last position is reached is not unimpeachable, but there is sufficient appearance of logic to obtain general acceptance of the conclusion from a quite impeccable premise.

There is no need to labour the point or to outline Paine's political philosophy in full detail; based on the French 'Declaration of the Rights of Man and of Citizens' (which Paine includes in translation), his own doctrine has the same clarity that marks the deceptive simplicity of that document. Furthermore, it is

---

[1] *Complete Writings*, I, 343.   [2] *Ibid.*, I, 397.
[3] Ed. W. S. Lewis, *Horace Walpole's Correspondence*, XI, 318.
[4] *Complete Writings*, I, 275.

reinforced by Paine's buoyant confidence: the 'system of principles as universal as truth and the existence of man' which had
been operative in the revolutions of America and France would
inevitably operate throughout Europe. It would, therefore, 'be
an act of wisdom to anticipate their approach, and produce
revolutions by reason and accommodation, rather than commit
them to the issue of convulsions'. This conclusion to Part I is
matched by the equally confident finish to Part II with its
allegory of the budding of trees in February:

> . . . though the vegetable sleep will continue longer on some
> trees and plants than on others, and though some of them may
> not *blossom* for two or three years, all will be in leaf in the summer,
> except those which are *rotten*. What pace the political summer
> may keep with the natural, no human foresight can determine. It
> is, however, not difficult to perceive that the spring is begun.

The allegory is as simple as biblical parable, its message is clear
and the experience it draws on is universal; moreover, the writer
has succeeded in detaching himself from his own powerful feelings and has embodied them in a vivid and concrete image
which precisely conveys the desired sense of inevitability. Paine
is indeed a conscious artist.

This conclusion so far lacks convincing evidence to support
it, but it is necessary to introduce it at an early stage. Paine was
aware that he was doing something new in the art of political
pamphleteering; the first part of the *Rights of Man* was intended
to test 'the manner in which a work, written in a style of thinking and expression different to what had been customary in
England, would be received'.[1] Immediate reactions to the
literary quality of the pamphlet were, of course, coloured by
political prejudice, but they remain important for our purpose.
For Horace Walpole Paine's style 'is so coarse, that you would
think he means to degrade the language as much as the
government';[2] Sir Brooke Boothby thought Paine had 'the
natural eloquence of a night-cellar' and found his book 'written
in a kind of specious jargon, well enough calculated to impose
upon the vulgar';[3] and *The Monthly Review*, to some extent

[1] *Complete Writings*, I, 348–9.
[2] Ed. W. S. Lewis, *Correspondence*, XI, 239.
[3] *Observations on the Appeal from the New to the Old Whigs, and on Mr. Paine's
Rights of Man*, pp. 106 n., 273–4.

sympathetic to Paine's politics (it found his principles 'just and right on the whole'), felt obliged to remark that his style

> is desultory, uncouth, and inelegant. His wit is coarse, and sometimes disgraced by wretched puns; and his language, though energetic, is awkward, ungrammatical, and often debased by vulgar phraseology.[1]

On the other hand, Fox is reported as saying of the *Rights of Man* that 'it seems as clear and simple as the first rule in arithmetic'.[2]

Both extremes are to some extent right. The books is 'clear', but it is also inelegant and occasionally ungrammatical; Paine can certainly be said to use 'vulgar phraseology'. Yet it was an effective piece of pamphleteering, it 'worked': T. J. Mathias, writing in 1797, observed that 'our peasantry now read the *Rights of Man* on mountains, and moors, and by the wayside';[3] it handled serious and fundamental issues; and it provided a healthy counterblast to Burke. Moreover, it remains readable. The modern critic, then, finds himself in the position of having to accept that, given the urgency of the situation and the needs of the audience, Paine's effectiveness depended in part at least on his 'vulgarity'. Now 'vulgarity' in normal critical terminology is pejorative; it is the term used by a Boothby or an eighteenth-century reviewer accustomed to aristocratic standards of accepted literary excellence; it is the term associated with the word 'mob' as Ian Watt has shown it to have been used in Augustan prose;[4] and it is, of course, still current. But when the term is applied to Paine and his style the pejorative is completely out of place; 'vulgar' is necessary as a critical word, but it should be descriptive, meaning, not boorish or debased, but plain, of the people, *vulgus*. Reluctance to accept this view leads to an unnecessarily restrictive limitation on the scope of literary criticism; criticism, then, is in danger of forgetting the principle of the suitability of means to ends and of becoming confined for its standards to those works only which are considered fit for aesthetic 'contemplation'.

[1] Op. cit. (May 1791), V, 93.
[2] *Atlantic Monthly* (Boston, 1859), IV, 694.
[3] *The Pursuits of Literature*, IV, ii.
[4] 'The Ironic Tradition in Augustan Prose from Swift to Johnson', A Paper at the Third Clark Library Seminar (University of California, 1956).

Admitting, therefore, that Paine's achievement in the *Rights of Man* has little to offer to the 'contemplative', what can the critic say about the vulgar style? Take, for example, a passage ironically described by Walpole as one of Paine's 'delicate paragraphs':

> It is easy to conceive, that a band of interested men, such as placemen, pensioners, lords of the bed-chamber, lords of the kitchen, lords of the necessary-house, and the Lord knows what besides, can find as many reasons for monarchy as their salaries, paid at the expense of the country, amount to.[1]

The humour is crude, decorum is absent, the alliteration is of the kind that occurs in agitated conversation, and the logic is questionable (for others besides sycophants can justify monarchy)—but what are the advantages of such a style? In the first place there is—here and throughout the book—a philosophical claim inherent in the language used: Paine is suggesting, by his choice of idiom, tone, and rhythm, that the issues he is treating can and ought to be discussed in the language of common speech; that these issues have a direct bearing on man's ordinary existence—monarchy involves the citizen in heavy taxation for its support; and that they ought not to be reserved (as Burke's language implies they should) for language whose aura of biblical sanctity suggests that such issues are above the head of the common man. Paine's language, his 'vulgarity', is indeed part of his critical method; to use a colloquial idiom about issues which Burke treats with great solemnity and linguistic complexity at once goes some way towards establishing the points just mentioned. Secondly, of course, Paine's style gains in intelligibility and immediacy, and, as one result, his readers were provided with quotable phrases which would become part of their verbal armoury for use against the *status quo*. And, thirdly, there is a rumbustious energy (such as Burke lacked) about this writing; it marks out the writer as a man of vigorous and healthy common sense. Paine, in fact, is creating an image of himself as one of the vulgar, using the language of the masses with just sufficient subtlety to induce their acceptance of his views. (His understanding of the importance of a *persona* is further illustrated and confirmed in the second part of the

---

[1] *Complete Writings*, I, 326–7.

pamphlet, where, for example, his sympathy with the economic circumstances of his poorer readers prompts him to remind them: 'my parents were not able to give me a shilling, beyond what they gave me in education; and to do this they distressed themselves'.[1]) If one may accept Paine's own phraseology as describing his intended audience—'the farmer, the manufacturer, the merchant, the tradesman, and down through all the occupations of life to the common labourer'[2]—then his is the kind of idiom to make a direct impact.

It is, moreover, all of a piece with Paine's criticism of Burke's language. More attention will be given to this matter later, but it might be observed here how frequently Paine selects a passage from the *Reflections* in order to point out the obscurity of Burke's meaning.

> As the wondering audience, whom Mr. Burke supposes himself talking to, may not understand all this learned jargon, I will undertake to be its interpreter.[3]

Not only does this kind of remark cement the link between Paine and his unlearned reader, and give him an opportunity to score a witty point through the interpretation that follows, it also implies that the supporters of the *status quo* wrap up their sophistries in elevated obscurity. By translating Burke's language into the idiom of every day Paine diminishes his opponent's stature and suggests that his seeming authority resides in the bombastic quality of his diction rather than in the validity of his argument. Paine, on the other hand, is seen to make his points in words that are readily understood; he does not have recourse (so he would have us believe) to any jargon, learned or unlearned, but uses vulgar speech, the language of common sense and common experience.

As his diction is of every day, so Paine's imagery and allusions are drawn from the common stock. He claims, for instance, that by requiring wisdom as an attribute of kingship Burke has, 'to use a sailor's phrase . . . *swabbed the deck*';[4] Court popularity, he says, 'sprung up like a mushroom in a night';[5] a State-Church

---

[1] *Complete Writings*, I, 414.
[2] Ibid., I, 327.
[3] Ibid., I, 319.
[4] Ibid., I, 318.
[5] Ibid., I, 328.

is 'a sort of mule-animal, capable only of destroying, and not of breeding up';[1] or his famous comment that Burke 'pities the plumage, but forgets the dying bird'.[2] Immediately intelligible as they are, such phrases also suggest (as do similar ones in Bunyan) the writer's nearness to and feeling for the life lived by his readers; he is using their phrases, and thus infers his oneness with their political position. He is, furthermore, adding to the status of vulgar speech (as Wordsworth did in the first *Lyrical Ballads*) by showing its capacity for dealing with important issues at a fundamental level; Burke's language, on the other hand, suggests that these issues are the exclusive concern of men using a refined and aristocratic medium.

Similar remarks are prompted by Paine's limited use of literary allusion. Burke's adulation of chivalry is ridiculed by a reference to Quixote and the windmills;[3] the interrelation (for the French) between the fall of the Bastille and the fall of despotism is described as 'a compounded image . . . as figuratively united as Bunyan's Doubting Castle and Giant Despair';[4] Burke's researches into antiquity are not rigorously pursued, Paine asserts, in case 'some robber, or some Robin Hood, should rise' and claim to be the origin of monarchy;[5] or again he enquires whether the 'metaphor' of the Crown operates 'like Fortunatus' wishing-cap, or Harlequin's wooden sword'.[6] Where Paine refers beyond what might be called folk literature (and *Don Quixote* had assumed this character in England), he requires little in the way of literary training: a reference to the *Comedy of Errors*, for example, is valuable only for what is invoked by the title itself; it does not depend for its effectiveness, as do some of Burke's Shakespearean allusions, on a knowledge of the play. The only literary knowledge on which Paine counts to any extent is a knowledge of the Bible and the Book of Common Prayer. He is confident that an allusion to the Israelites' struggle for freedom, through the mention of 'bondmen and bondwomen',[7] will suggest an analogy with contemporary affairs; he clearly expects the language and rhythm of, 'our inquiries find a resting place, and our reason finds a home',[8] to be evocative, and the Litany to be recalled by, 'From such principles, and such

---

[1] *Complete Writings*, I, 292. [2] Ibid., I, 260. [3] Ibid., I, 259.
[4] Ibid., I, 261. [5] Ibid., I, 319. [6] Ibid., I, 325.
[7] Ibid., I, 296. [8] Ibid., I, 273.

ignorance, Good Lord deliver the world.'[1] It is noticeable, too, that on the only occasion when irony depends on a literary allusion, a biblical reference is used. Having asserted that a love of aristocratic titles is childish, Paine goes on: 'A certain writer, of some antiquity, says: "*When I was a child, I thought as a child* . . .".'[2] The irony is, of course, directed at Burke's love of antiquity and precedents, but the interesting point is that Paine is attributing to the ordinary man the literary alertness to appreciate the irony. But, for the most part, Paine relies on the force of his facts and the arguments based on them, and thereafter only on his audience's response to the metaphorical use of language which demanded a minimum of literary awareness. The metaphors involved in the description of the Bastille as 'the high altar and castle of despotism'[3] rely for their effect on political and religious prejudice; the claim that France had 'outgrown the baby-clothes of *count* and *duke*, and breeched itself in manhood'[4] requires none but normal experience to achieve its persuasive effect.

As in this last Paine frequently relies on metaphors which are rooted in popular experience. The experiments in aeronautics in the nine years preceding the publication of the *Rights of Man* —culminating in the Channel flight of Blanchard and Jeffries in 1785—probably account for the charge that Burke has 'mounted in the air like a balloon, to draw the eyes of the multitude from the ground they stand upon'.[5] This charge is reiterated elsewhere, but here Paine gives it imaginative embodiment in a way that would have popular appeal. Again, Paine draws heavily on what Mr. Christopher Hill has called the 'Norman Yoke' tradition in English political literature, the theory that before 1066 the Anglo-Saxons were blessed with liberty and representative government, whereas the coming of the Normans meant the end of both and the establishment of oppressive monarchy and oligarchy.[6] The theory had been current since at least the sixteenth century, it gained new vitality in the writings of the Civil War period, it reappeared in Defoe, and then, most vociferously, in Paine. When, therefore, Paine

---

[1] *Complete Writings*, I, 325.   [2] Ibid., I, 286.   [3] Ibid., I, 264.
[4] Ibid., I, 286.   [5] Ibid., I, 282.
[6] See Christopher Hill, *Puritanism and Revolution* (1958), Chap. 3, especially pp. 99–109.

refers to 'the vassalage class of manners'[1] that leads subjects to humble themselves in the presence of kings, or describes William the Conqueror as 'the son of a prostitute and the plunderer of the English nation',[2] he is writing within a popular tradition which would excite even the most unsophisticated among his readers. Their tendency to look back to a golden age before the advent of tyrannic government would be powerfully stimulated by allusions to this unhistorical but very emotive and widely held theory. But the kind of popular experience most often exploited by Paine is the dramatic and theatrical. The century abounded with farces, ballad-operas, 'entertainments', pantomime, and such-like theatrical performances; he clearly felt able to rely on experience of them. As Gay had satirised the Walpole 'gang' on the stage, so Paine uses stage-terms in his prose effectively to convey his contempt for the Court and aristocracy. The unnatural degradation of the masses results, he says, in bringing forward 'with greater glare, the puppet-show of state and aristocracy';[3] courtiers may despise the monarchy, but 'they are in the condition of men who get their living by a show, and to whom the folly of that show is so familiar that they ridicule it';[4] and the enigma of the identity of a monarch in 'a mixed government', when king, cabinet, and dominant parliamentary group are barely distinguishable, is described as 'this pantomimical contrivance' in which 'the parts help each other out in matters which neither of them singly would assume to act'.[5] Furthermore, we hear of 'the Pantomime of Hush', of Fortunatus and Harlequin (favourite characters of pantomime), and of the magic lanthorn. The achievement of this frame of reference is important. It obviously shows Paine drawing on experiences shared with his readers, and this is a significant factor in persuasion. It also allows him to ridicule the constitution Burke defends and generally to identify it as a mode of comic entertainment (since Paine's theatrical allusions are invariably used for the purpose of attack). Consequently, the common reader is induced to regard the constitution in the same light and with the same insouciance as he viewed his kind of dramatic entertainment. Some humorous as well as some serious purpose is involved. And it is noteworthy that while Burke

---

[1] *Complete Writings*, I, 296.   [2] Ibid., I, 320.   [3] Ibid., I, 267.
[4] Ibid., I, 296.   [5] Ibid., I, 340.

himself frequently refers to the drama in the *Reflections*, his is a different purpose: it is more obviously to arouse the emotional fervour normally associated with serious drama and to suggest that the proper state of mind for observers of the French Revolution is that appropriate to watching a tragedy.

To recognise that Paine also conducts a great deal of his literary criticism of the *Reflections* in terms of dramatic criticism is to see that the concept of drama is more than simply a persuasive technique: it embodies something central in Paine's own thesis. In his 'Conclusion' he lays it down as an axiom that 'Reason and Ignorance, the opposites of each other, influence the great bulk of mankind' and that the Government in any country is determined by whichever of these principles is dominant. Reason leads to government by election and representation, ignorance to government by hereditary succession. Leaving aside the logic of this assertion, it becomes plain that the axiom is organic with Paine's choice of literary methods and the nature of his attack on Burke. It may have been no more than fortuitous that what he felt to be a popular interest—theatrical entertainment—provided him with a key metaphor to focus his analysis of Burke's arguments and literary techniques; what is certain is that the essential business of drama—the imaginative interpretation of reality in terms of figures created to embody the dramatist's attitudes and values—perfectly focuses Paine's charges against Burke. (In this sense, for example, Burke 'created' the Marie Antoinette who appears in the *Reflections*; he did not present the woman from the world of fact.) Used as a metaphor, the drama draws attention to the dichotomy between reason and ignorance, or reality and appearance, life and art, fact and fiction—between, indeed, the position claimed by Paine and the one he attributed to Burke. This is the conflict with which, in some shape or another, Paine constantly faces his readers; his choice of metaphor by which to conduct the argument suggests insight of no ordinary kind.

Once this is grasped, the references to drama fall into place. Burke, says Paine, is 'not affected by the reality of distress touching his heart, but by the showy resemblance of it striking his imagination'; he 'degenerates into a composition of art'; and he chooses to present a hero or a heroine, 'a tragedy-victim expiring in show', rather than 'the real prisoner of misery' dying in jail.[1] Again, Burke makes 'a tragic scene' out of the executions following the fall of the Bastille; unlike Paine, he does not relate the factual circumstances which gave rise to the event.

> As to the tragic paintings by which Mr. Burke has outraged his own imagination, and seeks to work upon that of his readers, they are very well calculated for theatrical representation, where facts are manufactured for the sake of show, and accommodated to produce, through the weakness of sympathy, a weeping effect. But Mr. Burke should recollect that he is writing history, and not *plays*, and that his readers will expect truth, and not the spouting rant of high-toned exclamation.[2]

> I cannot consider Mr. Burke's book in scarcely any other light than a dramatic performance; and he must, I think, have considered it in the same light himself, by the poetical liberties he has taken of omitting some facts, distorting others, and making the whole machinery bend to produce a stage effect. Of this kind is his account of the expedition to Versailles.[3]

These are statements at length of Paine's literary-political criticism of Burke; in them the clash between truth and fiction, reality and art, reason and imagination, concentred by the metaphor of the drama, is evident enough. Proof of what is essentially the same approach occurs frequently elsewhere. Seen in this light, Paine's frequent use of factual information takes on an extra significance. He charges Burke with focusing attention solely on the deleterious effects of the Revolution and of ignoring the facts which made it necessary and inevitable.

> It suits his purpose to exhibit consequences without their causes. It is one of the arts of the drama to do so. If the crimes of men were exhibited with their sufferings, the stage effect would sometimes be lost, and the audience would be inclined to approve where it was intended they should commiserate.[4]

Consequently, when Paine provides factual details he is not only giving information to justify and propagate his own political attitudes; his intention is to confront 'art' with 'life' and to shatter what he considers is an imaginative façade; he is also attempting to dispel the ignorance which Burke fosters by his 'dramatic method' (as defined above) and which encourages the

---

[1] *Complete Writings*, I, 260. [2] Ibid., I, 258.
[3] Ibid., I, 267–8. [4] Ibid., I, 268.

continued existence of despotic government. It is not necessary to labour any claim for Paine's accuracy as literary critic, although, speaking generally, his line of approach is sound. Burke merits comparison with a dramatist; he concentrates attention on single human figures who embody attitudes and values he regards as important (or despicable); his narrative of events is essentially conducted by 'scenes'; he stresses human actions to convey the character of a political movement; he does, in a sense, make a tragic heroine out of Marie Antoinette, and so forth. Paine, on his side, is justified in trying to break down the splendid, tragic isolation with which Burke invests the Queen; he is equally shrewd in trying to shift the emphasis that Burke places on Louis as the personal object of revolutionary assault, on to an issue of principle. There is, then, substance in Paine's literary-critical approach; he shows, perhaps, more insight in this respect than many later critics of Burke; but what is chiefly important here is the way in which his literary criticism coheres with his larger political theory.

The corollary to his critical onslaught on Burke is that Paine should show himself guided by reason, that his style—by its simplicity and lucidity—should mirror his emphasis on fact and common sense. He should, in other words, write the plain vulgar style in contrast to (what he would describe as) the refined and lofty obscurity of his opponent. If Burke 'confounds everything'[1] by failing to make distinctions and refusing to define his terms, Paine should work by definition and clarity; if Burke's book is 'a pathless wilderness of rhapsodies',[2] then Paine's should be well ordered and comprehensible. If Paine's writing is found to possess these desired characteristics one's conclusion will not necessarily be that he is superior to Burke as a writer, but rather that his style and literary methods embody his political and moral values as effectively as Burke's quite different style and methods are an embodiment of his.

In part, the shape of the *Rights of Man* is dictated by Paine's task: to refute the *Reflections*. He was compelled to take up separate claims advanced by his antagonist; where he felt it necessary he had to provide evidence omitted by Burke, as in his account of the Versailles incident or his review of the influences leading to the outbreak of the Revolution; and he had to argue

[1] *Complete Writings*, I, 278.   [2] Ibid., I, 272.

his own political theory. The nature of his task led, then, to some disjointedness; he was determined to reason 'from minutiae to magnitude'.[1] Again, the presence of a 'Miscellaneous Chapter' may be urged as proof of disorderliness. There is, in fact, some truth in *The Monthly Review*'s charge of desultoriness in presentation. Yet there is a sense in which this had to be. Some roughness of style, the absence of refinement and decorum, an energy that mirrored a scarcely controllable anger on behalf of the poor and unenfranchised—these things were signs of political good faith and honesty of purpose. From the nature of the theory argued in Paine's book, he had to eschew the literary methods associated with an aristocratic culture linked, in its turn, with the politics of the establishment.[2] There is, then, a significant truth in Sir Brooke Boothby's sneering comment that Paine 'writes in defiance of grammar, as if syntax were an aristocratical invention'.[3]

Whatever one's final judgment on the mode of presentation, there is no doubt that Paine's writing is simple and lucid.

> There never did, there never will, and there never can exist a parliament, or any description of men, or any generation of men, in any country, possessed of the right or the power of binding and controlling posterity to the '*end of time*' . . .[4]

> When we survey the wretched condition of man under the monarchical and hereditary systems of government, dragged from his home by one power, or driven by another, and impoverished by taxes more than by enemies, it becomes evident that those systems are bad, and that a general revolution in the principle and construction of governments is necessary.[5]

Writing such as this—and the examples are innumerable—has the merits of clarity, directness, energy, and the powerful conviction carried by the speaking voice. There is a balance about

---

[1] *Complete Writings*, I, 282.

[2] Cf. Professor Leslie A. Fiedler's remark on the typical young British writer of our own day that 'when he is boorish rather than well-behaved, rudely angry than ironically amused . . . even when he merely writes badly, he can feel he is performing a service for literature, liberating it from the tyranny of a taste based on a world of wealth and leisure which has become quite unreal' (*Encounter* (1958), X, i, 9).

[3] *Observations . . . on Mr. Paine's Rights of Man*, p. 106 n.

[4] *Complete Writings*, I, 251.

[5] Ibid., I, 341.

the phrasing which is not 'literary' but vulgar in the non-pejorative sense; it results from a determination to ensure the reader's agreement by insistent affirmation, the accumulation of facts, and the colloquial phrasing of an accomplished popular orator. Where Paine attempts the kind of 'literary' style that is Burke's province he fails utterly:

> In the declaratory exordium which prefaces the Declaration of Rights, we see the solemn and majestic spectacle of a nation opening its commission, under the auspices of its Creator, to establish a Government; a scene so new, and so transcendently unequalled by anything in the European world, that the name of a Revolution is diminutive of its character, and it rises into a regeneration of man.[1]

This is rhetoric of the worst kind; it is vague and rhapsodic, pretentious and inflated—it is, indeed, guilty of the faults with which Paine charges Burke. But it is not normal: the two examples previously quoted are more representative of Paine's general style. He is invariably concerned to place his views 'in a clearer light';[2] to enable us 'to possess ourselves of a clear idea of what government is, or ought to be';[3] and to avoid any word 'which describes nothing' and consequently 'means nothing'.[4]

Paine obviously felt that an argument visibly divided into sections was necessary for his audience; his readers presumably required the kind of signposting denoted by phrases such as, 'I will here cease the comparison . . . and conclude this part of the subject', or, 'it is time to proceed to a new subject'. Occasionally he contrives to turn what is avowedly a transition into an opening for humour:

> Hitherto we have considered aristocracy chiefly in one point of view. We have now to consider it in another. But whether we view it before or behind, or sideways, or any way else, domestically or publicly, it is still a monster.[5]

The use of clearly defined stages is a pointer to Paine's understanding of the capacity of his readers. They required guidance and reassurance; they were not to lose themselves in 'a pathless wilderness'. Nor could Paine count on a willingness

---

[1] *Complete Writings*, I, 317.   [2] Ibid., I, 277.
[3] Ibid., I, 278.   [4] Ibid., I, 287.
[5] Ibid., I, 288.

in his audience to follow a lengthy discussion of abstract theory
—hence his use of anecdote, of plain narrative carefully punctuated with information about the passing of time ('He arrived
at Versailles between ten and eleven at night', 'It was now about
one in the morning'[1]), of snatches of conversation with an
ordinary soldier or a plain-speaking American, of humorous
interjections, and the like. Paine was, indeed, well aware of the
necessity 'of relieving the fatigue of argument'.[2] And the constant
use of facts, the frequent recourse to definition, the impress of
personal authority and experience ('I wrote to [Burke] last
winter from Paris, and gave him an account how prosperously
matters were going on'[3]), the enumeration of points established
—in fact, the general concreteness of reference recalling Defoe
or the Swift of the *Drapier's Letters* is based on a thorough understanding of the needs of his audience.

'When men are sore with the sense of oppressions, and men-
aced with the prospect of new ones, is the calmness of philosophy, or the palsy of insensibility to be looked for?'[4] Paine's
rhetorical question brings sharply into focus the difficulty posed
by his kind of writing for the literary critic. However astute
Paine's motives in 1791, the *Rights of Man* does not give the
reader the same degree of permanent pleasure that he experiences from reading the *Reflections*; Paine cannot command that
complex subtlety of style and sensitivity to the resources of
language displayed by Burke. Yet, as the Paisley weaver poet,
Alexander Wilson, put it:

> . . . Tammy Paine the buik has penned,
> And lent the courts a lounder.[5]

The audience for which Paine designed his work were convinced that he had dealt a 'wallop' to the political establishment, and because he had successfully created that audience
for himself by the first part of his pamphlet—hence the
greater attention to it here—the influence of Part II was
even more immense. Paine's distinction, then, is that he per-
fected an idiom appropriate to his deceptively simple philosophy

---

[1] *Complete Writings*, I, 270–1.   [2] Ibid., I, 285.
[3] Ibid., I, 297.   [4] Ibid., I, 265.
[5] Cited by D. Craig, *Scottish Literature and the Scottish People: 1680–1830*
(1961), p. 77.

as well as to his culturally unsophisticated readers; his manner of defiant abruptness suited the urgency of the times and the seriousness of the issues from the standpoint of the oppressed members of society; and he proved himself the master of a single, highly flexible style. Its pugnacity, its lucidity, and those features of it we can properly call vulgar confirm Paine's mastery of rhetorical techniques which the particular situation demanded.

IX

VINDICIAE GALLICAE

THERE can be no doubt that Paine's was the most popular reply to Burke and among the most significant contributions to the language of political controversy in the late eighteenth century. Other participants in the controversy, however, were influential in their day, and their pamphlets offer an opportunity to analyse a fascinating variety of polemical methods. From James Mackintosh and Mary Wollstonecraft to the Scottish intellectual Thomas Christie and the obscure citizen, 'honest John Butler' (as *The Monthly Review* called him[1]), all Burke's opponents were convinced that theirs was the true morality, that Burke had deliberately obscured and misrepresented the issues raised by the Revolution for England and mankind, and that the clear light of reason would reveal the truth about them while exposing Burke's multiple errors of fact and interpretation. (As Wollstonecraft remarked: 'True morality shuns not the day.'[2]) Yet, however justified these beliefs may have been, problems remained. The liberal writers had to reach an audience, dislodge the vast influence already achieved by the *Reflections*, and secure acceptance of their own views. To do this required them to write in a manner which would initially capture the attention and then engage the imagination of their readers, and continue to be memorable. But how was this to be done if they were to display their confidence in the primacy of reason and avoid relying on those emotive techniques used in the *Reflections*? In other words,

---

[1] Op. cit. (May 1791), V, 108.
[2] *Vindication of the Rights of Men*, p. 131.

could they achieve what any controversialist aims at—the conviction of his readers to the extent that right action will inevitably follow—without using the same literary methods for which they denounced Burke?

To answer these questions three writers have been selected for detailed examination, and others for more general treatment. Foremost in the first group is James Mackintosh, who wrote for the intelligent middle and upper classes—Burke's own audience—to whom Paine's matter and manner were repellent. Though he later renounced his youthful enthusiasm for the Revolution, the effect of the *Vindiciae Gallicae*, described here by Thomas Campbell, Mackintosh could not undo.

> In the better educated classes of society, there was a general proneness to go with Burke; and it is my sincere opinion, that that proneness would have become universal, if such a mind as Mackintosh's had not presented itself, like a breakwater, to the general spring-tide of Burkism.[1]

Also addressed to a middle-class audience there is, secondly, Mary Wollstonecraft's *Vindication of the Rights of Men*, one of the earliest replies to the *Reflections*; published within a month of Burke's book, it went into a second edition in three weeks and, according to Godwin, 'obtained extraordinary notice'.[2] And the last of this trio is the work described by John Morley as 'the substantial and decisive reply to Burke', Arthur Young's *Travels in France*, a book 'worth a hundred times more than Burke, Mackintosh, and Paine all put together'.[3]

JAMES MACKINTOSH: *Vindiciae Gallicae* (1791)

> It was time that men should learn to tolerate nothing ancient that reason does not respect, and to shrink from no novelty to which reason may conduct. . . . It was time, as it has been wisely and eloquently said, that Legislators, instead of that narrow and dastardly *coasting* which never ventures to lose sight of usage and precedent, should, guided by the *polarity* of reason, hazard a bolder navigation, and discover, in unexplored regions, the treasure of public felicity.[4]

[1] Ed. R. J. Mackintosh, *Memoirs of the Life of Sir James Mackintosh*, I, 59.
[2] *Memoirs of the Author of a Vindication of the Rights of Woman*, p. 75.
[3] *Burke* (1879), p. 162.
[4] *Vindiciae Gallicae*, pp. 116–17.

This credo—urgent in spite of its formal and complicated structure—focuses attention both on Mackintosh's ideas and on his mode of writing. It not only represents a complete rejection of Burke's contempt for unaided reason and signifies the writer's view of events in France, it is also central to his analysis of Burke's persuasive methods and indicates the principal character of his own. 'Analysis and method,' Mackintosh claims, level all the writers participating in the controversy:[1] what is merely 'ornamental' in the *Reflections* will disappear under analysis; methodical presentation will allow opposing arguments to make their own forceful impact on the reader's mind. Mackintosh's confidence in such a procedure is clear from the tone of the passage quoted; it is equally evident in what follows when he considers Burke's attitude towards 'theory':

> If by theory be understood vague conjecture, the objection is not worth discussion; but if by theory be meant inference from the moral nature and political state of man, then I assert, that whatever such theory pronounces to be true, must be practicable, and that whatever on the subject is impracticable, must be false.[2]

Here the prose is nervous and reminds one of the fervour of Keats' famous claim about the truth of imaginative perception. Indeed, Mackintosh's belief in the power of reason was intensely and emotionally felt; his problem was to maintain a rational poise while communicating the intensity of his own belief.

That this was a real problem is suggested by the analogy with which Mackintosh illustrates the last statement:

> Geometry . . . bears nearly the same relation to mechanics that abstract reasoning does to politics. The *moral forces* which are employed in politics are the passions and interests of men, of which it is the province of metaphysics to teach the nature and calculate the strength, as mathematics do those of the mechanical powers.

He goes on to quote the example of a technological discovery which is immediately adopted because it makes an incontrovertible appeal to reason. Why, he infers, should not discoveries made in political science be adopted with equal readiness? The argumentative weakness is obvious: men and human institutions

---

[1] *Vindiciae Gallicae*, p. vii. [2] Ibid., p. 118.

are not, like mechanics, amenable to strict laws of causation. As D. H. Lawrence pointed out, while we must be alert and intelligent about social change, the change 'must *happen*. You can't drive it like a steam-engine.'[1] But in addition to the philosophical weakness, the analogy itself lacks fire; it is the product of (in Coleridge's terms) the fancy rather than the imagination; it is a 'dry, cold, formal deduction of the understanding',[2] and the intensity of belief is missing.

His faith in the efficacy of reason, coupled with the conviction that 'society is inevitably progressive',[3] leads him to take up a characteristic position: 'It is absurd to *expect*, but it is not absurd to *pursue* perfection.'[4] Mackintosh refuses to share the view he attributes to Burke: 'an arrogant confidence in our attainments' mixed with 'an abject distrust of our powers'. On the contrary, he is sceptical about the political progress so far achieved and puts his trust in 'the human understanding' to produce governments which are 'the work of art' and not the result of 'chance'.[5] Hence, of course, his approval of the French Revolution. The French had made intelligent use of human experience to imitate the good and reject the evil in existing forms of government; in other words, they had trusted in man's power of choice and discrimination. That this had involved the overthrow of the *ancien régime* was merely evidence of the revolutionists' consistency; they could not build on old foundations (as Burke had advised), since the foundations themselves were imperfect.

These views were all of a piece with Mackintosh's attitude to the contemporary English political situation. He believed that man's intelligence should be given an opportunity to reform the corrupt and unjust constitution. The key to reform lay in changes in the franchise and parliamentary representation: 'From this radical improvement all subaltern reform would naturally and peaceably arise.'[6] The example of France had demonstrated what achievements were possible by the exercise of reason:

[1] In 'The State of Funk', *Sex, Literature and Censorship* (ed. H. T. Moore, 1955), p. 135.
[2] Hazlitt, *Works*, XI, 100.
[3] *Vindiciae Gallicae*, p. 197.   [4] Ibid., p. 114.
[5] Ibid., p. 115.   [6] Ibid., p. 343.

The shock that destroyed the despotism of France has widely dispersed the clouds that intercepted reason from the political and moral world; and we cannot suppose, that England is the only spot that has not been reached by this flood of light that has burst in on the human race.[1]

Mackintosh is confident that the same power of reason will counteract his opponent's emotive appeal and secure assent from his own audience, and from the outset his mode of argument accurately embodies this confidence. The first sentence challenges Burke's failure to define his terms; he has not, Mackintosh asserts, even defined the term 'French Revolution'. It is capable of at least three meanings: the occasion when the States-General was admitted to an active share in government, the union of the three orders in one Assembly, or the formation of a new constitution by that Assembly. Each of these was a revolutionary act, but Burke had used the descriptive term without signifying to which he referred. Thus, one of Mackintosh's objects was to 'extricate [Burke's language] from this ambiguity'[2] and to allow the light of reason to expose his persuasive obscurities. Time and again he returns to this task. He carefully examines the meaning of 'experience', which, according to the *Reflections*, the French have ignored,[3] or reproves Burke for deliberately attaching an imprecise meaning to the final word in Price's claim that the nation has a right 'to cashier our governors for misconduct'. 'A plain man'—one who interprets according to the context of a word and by the aid of his common sense—'could have foreseen scarcely any diversity of opinion'.[4] Mackintosh despises what he elsewhere describes as 'a mode of proceeding more remarkable for controversial dexterity than for candor';[5] he insists that Burke is attributing 'loose and indefinite' meanings to a word whose context permits only one sense: 'that precise species of misconduct for which James II was dethroned—A CONSPIRACY AGAINST THE LIBERTY OF HIS COUNTRY'.[6]

Such an analytic method achieves, of course, more than one result. It suggests that Burke's manner of presenting his case was deceitful; it implies that he was incapable of thinking clearly (or

---

[1] *Vindiciae Gallicae*, p. 345.
[2] Ibid., p. 17.
[3] Ibid., pp. 111–12.
[4] Ibid., p. 301.
[5] Ibid., p. 181 n.
[6] Ibid., pp. 302–3.

that he intentionally dissembled when the plain truth was un-congenial); and it warns the reader against an unquestioning acceptance of any of Burke's statements. In addition, it provides documentary evidence of Mackintosh's own clarity of mind, honesty, and scrupulous attention to fact. It is a method, too, that inspires trust between writer and reader: if Mackintosh applies this scrutiny to Burke's language the inference is that he is prepared for it to be applied to his own.

These same qualities of clarity, honesty, analytic thinking, and constant reference to factual evidence are established by the conduct of the *Vindiciae Gallicae* as a whole. Mackintosh draws attention to the lack of order in the *Reflections*, observing that for Burke to begin with an attack on the English admirers of the Revolution was to determine 'the propriety of approbation . . . before discussing the merit or demerit of what was approved'.[1] For his part Mackintosh sees 'a natural order' which his work must follow. (The word 'natural' has not the conno-tative aura that it has for Burke; it clearly denotes 'logical' or 'rational', a meaning which, in the light of the earlier analysis of the *Reflections*, at once suggests an important difference between the two men.) Logically the first topic is whether a revolution was necessary and expedient, and, since Burke ignored it, a consideration of the Revolution as an historical sequence of events. Following this, logic again demands that the Assembly, the body which legislated for the Revolution, be considered; then the 'popular excesses' to which Burke had given prominence; then the new Constitution; and finally, the conduct of the English admirers.[2] There is an undeniable naturalness in this ordering of topics, and again the reader is led to believe that he is in the hands of a competent, trust-worthy writer who will rely on no sleight of hand to obtain his agreement. Mackintosh desires 'a fair audience at the bar of reason';[3] the initial frankness with which he states his intention goes a long way to secure it.

[1] *Vindiciae Gallicae*, p. viii.

[2] It is noteworthy that the compiler of *A Comparative Display of the Different Opinions of the most distinguished British Writers on the subject of the French Revolution* (1793) adopted Mackintosh's divisions for his own chapter headings.

[3] Op. cit., p. 85.

Of course, *Vindiciae Gallicae* is not a mere documentary account; it is not an objective view of French affairs, and Mackintosh does not try to delude his readers into believing that it is. He makes it plain when describing the meeting of the States-General at Versailles, 5 May 1789, that his object is 'not to narrate events, but to seize their spirit';[1] it is abundantly clear too from his tone and enthusiasm that he is one of those who 'can never cease to rejoice' that 'the year 1789 has furnished one spot on which the eye of humanity may with complacence dwell'.[2] Yet, as subsequent analysis will show, his literary manner is for the most part proof that Mackintosh is a writer whose enthusiasm is under the control of his reason. We do not meet with intemperate outbursts of invective levelled at Burke, and although de Calonne—whose book, *De l'État de la France présent et à venir* (1790), Mackintosh answers along with the *Reflections*—is described as 'an exiled robber' he is rather despised than abused. Indeed, abuse seems too crude a method for Mackintosh to handle. His patience is frequently tried, but his audience was not Paine's, and the intelligent reader for whom he wrote would admire his restraint. For instance, when he examines Burke's passionate denunciation of the seizure of church property in France, Mackintosh writes:

> What immediately follows this contemptuous passage is so outrageously offensive to candor and urbanity, that an honourable adversary will disdain to avail himself of it.[3]

Despite the seeming self-righteousness when the sentence is out of context, it is as an 'honourable adversary' that Mackintosh appears. He is not one of the 'frivolous and puerile adversaries' who rely on refuting Burke by convicting him of 'some minute errors'.[4] He certainly points to such factual mistakes, but does not rest his case on them. And he is always ready to concede points to his opponent or to record his agreement with Burke when this is appropriate. Even though Burke was wrong to announce the death of the sentinel when Versailles was attacked, or to claim with certainty that the Queen's chamber was invaded, 'these slight corrections palliate little the atrocity';[5]

---

[1] *Vindiciae Gallicae*, p. 39.   [2] Ibid., p. 125.
[3] Ibid., pp. 83–4.   [4] Ibid., p. 185.
[5] Ibid., pp. 185–6.

with Burke Mackintosh reprobates the franchise-qualification decided upon by the National Assembly, and disagrees with another liberal pamphleteer, Mrs. Macaulay Graham, on this score;[1] or again, he disapproves of excluding ministers from seats in the Assembly.[2] 'Blind and servile applause'[3] is no more Mackintosh's natural mode than virulent abuse, and he indulges in neither.

Sober, honest, plain-speaking but temperate as Mackintosh undoubtedly appears, he does not lack shrewdness or decisiveness as an opponent. He recognises, for example, the emotive and argumentative uses Burke makes of individuals to arouse strong feelings on behalf of those who suffered and to create the impression that the Revolution in France and the reverberations in England were the work of self-interested men. Mackintosh makes strenuous efforts to destroy this view and to undermine the emotive appeal. 'A Revolution which the *people* have made':[4] this is the keynote which is sounded again and again in *Vindiciae Gallicae*. It gives to Mackintosh's account a nobility and generalised emotiveness which would move those readers who were interested in historical or philosophical issues, but which would fail to stir readers who looked for sensational events involving the names of famous individuals. 'To become the advocate of *individuals*, were to forget the dignity of a discussion that regards the rights and interests of an emancipated nation.'[5] This is the level at which Mackintosh prefers to conduct his argument; he employs detail, of course, to support his views, and is often forced to discuss the individuals to whom Burke gave prominence, but only this approach will, for him, establish the true nature of the Revolution in France. It was, in his eyes, a spontaneous movement by a whole people influenced by general causes (philosophical as well as political, moral as well as social), and owing 'almost nothing to the schemes and the ascendant of individuals'.[6] For this among other reasons it was *sui generis*:

> Among many circumstances which distinguished that event, as unexampled in history, it was none of the least extraordinary, that it might truly be said to have been a REVOLUTION *without*

[1] *Vindiciae Gallicae*, pp. 224-6. [2] Ibid., p. 270.
[3] Ibid., p. 227. [4] Ibid., p. 182.
[5] Ibid., p. 190. [6] Ibid., p. 59.

Leaders. It was the effect of general causes operating on the people. It was the revolt of a nation enlightened from a common source.[1]

The central figure in *Vindiciae Gallicae* is the French nation imbued with an infectious vitality (which made its impact on English liberals) and a love of liberty too great for the private interests of individuals to be matters of moment.

Mackintosh is also alive to another of Burke's principal themes in the *Reflections*: the disintegration of France into a confederacy of separate units. Indeed, he reverses Burke's emphasis; he claims that France was dismembered before the Revolution and united as a result of it. In his opening chapter Mackintosh represents French society before 1789 as one made up of 'ranks' and privileged orders 'which divided France into distinct nations',[2] whereas the Revolution inspired 'democratic sentiments' and a sense of nationhood. In his discussion of the French Constitution he returns to Burke's charge, arguing from detail that

> the Legislators of France have solicitously provided more elaborate precautions against this dismemberment than have been adopted by any recorded Government.[3]

Under the *ancien régime* the country was 'an aggregate of independent States', each with its distinct character, laws, and privileges; the removal of 'the compressing force of despotism' which held them together would have led them to resume their independent status; and consequently, the new division of the kingdom by the Assembly had the merit of recognising local distinctions while emphasising 'the common center of the national system'.[4]

Such refutation of his opponent's claims is carried out with explicit reference to Burke's statements; the reader is presented with both points of view and encouraged to prefer Mackintosh's. This method, however, is not invariable. On several occasions Mackintosh establishes principles without drawing attention to Burke's contrary views. For example, Burke had expressed contempt for the 'turbulent and discontented' noblemen who joined the Tiers Etat in the new Assembly, and sneered at the

[1] *Vindiciae Gallicae*, pp. 127–8. [2] Ibid., p. 73.
[3] Ibid., p. 233. [4] Ibid., p. 237.

'large proportion of mere country curates' in that body. Mackintosh quite unostentatiously corrects this picture. The leaders of the third estate

> were seconded in the Chamber of the Noblesse by a minority eminently distinguished for rank, character, and talent. The obscure and useful portion of the Clergy . . . naturally coalesced with the Commons.[1]

The account is presented as factual and not as a matter of dispute; Mackintosh claims distinction for the nobles, but honestly confines them to a 'minority'; and although he concedes the obscurity of the clergy, the word 'useful' corrects the Burkean unbalance. Again, Burke had invested Louis XVI with a blameless if vacillating disposition; without drawing attention to this portrait Mackintosh strips off its persuasive veneer and shows Louis as a feeble, yielding instrument of ambitious men, lacking any deep concern for the welfare of his people.[2] This method of persuasion (frequently employed) has several advantages. It diminishes the need for direct reference to the *Reflections*, and thus lessens the number of occasions when the audience is reminded of Burke; it lends a positive air to the writing and reduces the element of bickering controversy; and, most important, sceptical readers or the Burke-partisan are not constantly kept on the *qui vive*. They are not warned to prepare defensive positions and may discover too late that they have assented to views which make Burkean opinions untenable.

A variant on this rhetorical method reminds us of the audience Mackintosh is addressing. Burke's sneers at the 'usurers' who had bought confiscated Church property in France but who would soon exchange land for money, had culminated in a quotation from Horace's second Epode about the money-lender, Alphius. When Mackintosh takes up this issue he remarks:

> The heir of the stock jobbing *Alpheus* may acquire as perfectly the habits of an active improver of his patrimonial estate, as the children of *Cincinnatus*, or *Cato* the *Censor*.[3]

Unobtrusively he has paid Burke in his own coinage, demonstrated his own easy acquaintance with classical literature, and

---

[1] *Vindiciae Gallicae*, p. 40.   [2] Ibid., pp. 45–6.
[3] Ibid., p. 160. (Cf. p. 125 above.)

strengthened the link with a cultured audience. That this was Mackintosh's audience is clear; his dignified restraint, urbanity, literary references, choice of idiom, and the build of his paragraphs reinforce the general impression that he wrote for people accustomed to reading Johnson or Burke rather than Paine. The presence through quotation, in the final paragraph of *Vindiciae Gallicae*, of both Johnson and Lucan is significant enough. Nevertheless, though Mackintosh was convinced that it was among the 'middle rank [that] . . . almost all the sense and virtue of society reside',[1] he is not guilty of class conceit; he will have no truck with 'the arrogance of rank and letters' which has 'ignominiously confounded under the denomination of the vulgar' the 'great body of mankind'.[2] His aim was to write a work 'addressed to popular conviction',[3] and though we obviously cannot attach to the word 'popular' the meaning it carries when applied to Paine's *Rights of Man*, the intention was undoubtedly genuine.

Any reader with some literary training, a mind alert to the vigorous presentation of an argument, and ready to respond to the sympathetic personality behind the writing would, for the most part, find *Vindiciae Gallicae* a stimulating experience. He would, of course, find some faults. Occasionally he would meet with bigotry, as in Mackintosh's assault on monasticism: 'The dens of fanaticism, where they did not become the recesses of sensuality, were converted into the styes of indolence and apathy.'[4] Mackintosh's normal composure has here given way and bombast is the result. It is a fault never far off in his prose; without the conscious discipline and the careful choice of word and image that he usually employs, the lofty commonplace or cliché appears.

> [The revolutionists of 1688] wrested the sceptre from superstition, and dragged prejudice in triumph. They destroyed the arsenal whence despotism had borrowed her thunders and her chains.[5]

> It is in this fatal temper [of apathy] that men become sufficiently debased and embruted to wallow in placid and polluted servitude.[6]

The strength of feeling in such examples is undeniable; what is absent is a determination to be precise and fresh, to avoid

---

[1] *Vindiciae Gallicae*, p. 129. [2] Ibid., p. 311.
[3] Ibid., p. 206. [4] Ibid., p. 156.
[5] Ibid., p. 329. [6] Ibid., pp. 340-1.

the 'stock response' of the liberal writer to the shibboleths of his tradition. Control and discipline can, however, produce frigidity, and this, to some extent, is what happens. The evidence of Mackintosh's prose is that his imagination did not respond spontaneously except by means of commonplace metaphors; those which are not commonplace, on the other hand, show signs of careful pondering; they are apt but lack sparkle. When, for instance, Mackintosh denies the wisdom of gradual reformation of essentially despotic institutions, he comments: 'Power vegetates with more vigor after these gentle prunings.'[1] It is an apt, neat, and very controlled statement; how characteristic was the control is plain when this sentence is set beside another in which Mackintosh describes the results of monasticism:

> These short-lived phrenzies leave behind them an *inert* product, in the same manner as, when the fury and splendor of volcanic eruption is past for ages, there still remains a mass of *lava* to encumber the soil, and deform the aspect of the earth.[2]

Here the element of cerebration is obvious; the analogy provided is appropriate, but the imaginative expression of it is so firmly directed by the intellect that the result is wooden and the emotional intensity behind the writer's conviction has been sacrificed. Other examples could be quoted to confirm this impression of Mackintosh as a man in striking contrast with, say, Shelley: the first being one who relied on Coleridge's 'fancy' to produce emotive illustrations of an argument intellectually conceived; the second a writer whose thoughts naturally embodied themselves in fresh and memorable imagery.

This limitation on Mackintosh's powers being granted, his ability to argue well and to convey moral passion must also be emphasised. Here the intellectual discipline which restricted the working of his imagination becomes a source of great strength—of incisive irony, admirable terseness, and sustained argumentative writing of excellent quality. Commenting on Burke's description of the impoverished state of trade in post-revolutionary France, Mackintosh remarks:

---

[1] *Vindiciae Gallicae*, p. 106.   [2] Ibid., pp. 156–7.

The manufacturers of Lyons, the merchants of Bourdeaux and Marseilles, are silent amidst the lamentations of the Abbé Maury, M. Calonne, and Mr. Burke. Happy is that people whose commerce flourishes in *Ledgers*, while it is bewailed in orations, and remains untouched in *calculation*, while it expires in the pictures of eloquence.[1]

In a passage of this kind it is the precise working of the intellect which achieves the ironic pungency; there is an imaginative quality that produces the concrete images, but it is the intellect that balances 'flourishes' with 'bewailed', 'remains untouched' with 'expires', and controls the total effect of the passage. Similarly, the directing intelligence, supported by a Johnsonian sense of prose rhythm, realises the terse finality of the following three (from very many) examples:

Mean time the people of Paris revolted, the French soldiery felt that they were citizens, and the fabric of Despotism fell to the ground.[2]

Men will not long dwell in hovels, with the model of a palace before their eyes.[3]

[Burke and Judge Jeffries] indict the same crimes; they impute the same motives; they dread the same consequences.[4]

It is a stringent test of any of Burke's opponents to select for examination the manner in which they reply to his sensational description of the alleged atrocities in the early stages of the Revolution, and to his treatment of the English sympathisers. With both issues his opponents were deeply involved. The first called in question the humanity of men acting on principles they revered, the second their own integrity and patriotism. Both made severe demands on their self-control and literary abilities if they were satisfactorily to rebut Burke's charges and establish their own points of view.

As part of his reply to the first of these questions Mackintosh offers the exaggerated figure of 20,000 lives lost during the Revolution as a basis for argument. He then enquires whether, compared with parallel events in history, even this loss would cause 'a manly and enlightened humanity' to recoil.

Compare it with the blood spilt by England in the attempt to subjugate America, and if such be the guilt of the Revolutionists

[1] *Vindiciae Gallicae*, p. 172. [2] Ibid., p. 53.
[3] Ibid., p. 122. [4] Ibid., p. 328.

of France, for having, at the *hazard* of this evil, sought the establishment of freedom, what new name of obloquy shall be applied to the Minister of England, who with the *certainty* of a destruction so much greater, attempted the establishment of tyranny?[1]

There is no loss of control here in the face of Burke's inflammatory charges; with dignity Mackintosh compels his readers to measure an action for good which Burke has invited them to condemn against one for evil for which they, as a nation, were directly responsible. The long sentence, throwing its cumulative weight forward to the final question, carries the writer's own moral passion and offers the reader no chance of escape. Mackintosh then anticipates an objection to his question. He observes that the effect of the comparison given is blurred by an illusion:

> The massacres of war, and the murders committed by the sword of justice, are disguised by the solemnities which invest them. But the wild justice of the people has a naked and undisguised horror.

He does not try to minimise the horrors of revolutionary murders, but the words 'disguised', 'solemnities', and 'invest' compel us to reject any false illusions which may hinder our response to the comparison as a whole.

> Our sentiments are reconciled to them in this form [as acts of State], and we forget that the evils of anarchy must be short lived, while those of despotic government are fatally permanent.

There is a poise about this writing in the face of Burke's intense provocation and his own passionate feeling; Mackintosh forces the reader out beyond the single issue of revolutionary atrocities in order to obtain some sense of moral perspective; and he contrives to finish his paragraph on one of the central themes of *Vindiciae Gallicae*—the contrast between the temporary nature of evils resulting from the Revolution and the seemingly interminable tyranny it overthrew.

The merits of this prose stand out in sharper focus if we compare a portion of Mackintosh's reply to Burke's attack on the English sympathisers, with Mary Wollstonecraft's handling of

---

[1] *Vindicae Gallicae*, p. 174.

the same issue. Part of his opening paragraph in the chapter devoted to this topic runs as follows:

> For them [the English sympathisers] no contumely is too debasing, no invective is too intemperate, no imputation too foul. Joy at the downfall of despotism is the indelible crime, for which no virtue can compensate, and no punishment can atone.[1]

Mackintosh's moral indignation, carried in the Johnsonian triad of the first sentence, is stiffened by the bitter irony of the second, and together they indicate the approach he will make to the whole question. He then draws attention to the 'inconsistency' underlying Burke's denunciation and, incidentally, to the danger inherent in personal attacks whether in political controversy or in formal satire:

> [Burke] affects to despise those whom he appears to dread. His anger exalts those whom his ridicule would vilify; and on those whom at one moment he derides as too contemptible for resentment, he at another confers a criminal eminence, as too audacious for contempt. Their voice is now the importunate chink of the meagre shrivelled insects of the hour, now the hollow murmur, ominous of convulsions and earthquakes, that are to lay the fabric of society in ruins. To provoke against the doctrines and persons of these unfortunate Societies this storm of execration and derision, it was not sufficient that the French Revolution should be traduced, every record of English polity and law is to be distorted.

Mackintosh scores a palpable hit; one is reminded of Swift's warning to Pope at the time of the *Dunciad*:

> Take care the bad poets do not outwit you, as they have served the good ones in every Age, whom they have provoked to transmit their Names to posterity. Maevius is as well known as Virgil.[2]

The 'dunces' are remembered now chiefly because of Pope's poem; Richard Price's memory is kept alive by the prominence given him in the *Reflections*, and Mackintosh was shrewd enough to recognise the value of 'criminal eminence'. Moreover, he rightly stresses the mixture of fear and contempt that motivated Burke's attack on Price. But, most important,

[1] *Vindiciae Gallicae*, p. 293.
[2] Ed. G. Sherburn, *The Correspondence of Alexander Pope* (Oxford, 1956), II, 343.

Mackintosh directs his passionate feelings into vigorous, hard-hitting argument; he makes effective ironic use of Burke's 'shrivelled, meagre . . . insects of the hour'; and he castigates his opponent with restrained dignity.

Mary Wollstonecraft, facing the same problem, responds in a manner totally different.

> In reprobating Dr. Price's opinions you might have spared the man; and if you had had but half as much reverence for the grey hairs of virtue as for the accidental distinctions of rank, you would not have treated with such indecent familiarity and supercilious contempt, a member of the community whose talents and modest virtues place him high in the scale of moral excellence.[1]

She goes on to portray Price as benevolent, disinterested, ardent for the cause of liberty, and now on the point of death; and continues:

> I could almost fancy that I now see this respectable old man, in his pulpit, with hands clasped, and eyes devoutly fixed, praying with all the simple energy of unaffected piety.

It is evident, indeed, that Wollstonecraft's reply is presented solely in terms of the character of an individual; it is a narrow front on which to focus a defence, and it runs the risk of sentimentalising the central figure. In the passage from Mackintosh, Price, with his comrades, is associated in the reader's mind with disciplined thought and masculine feeling; whereas in the one from the *Vindication* he is linked with a flabby emotion; in the first the strenuousness of the writer's mind is evidenced by the firmness of his prose, in the second the validity of the writer's protest rests on the strength and quality of her feelings which her prose does not satisfactorily embody.

The same strenuousness of mind in Mackintosh's writing that is to be seen from this comparison is apparent when he assumes the part of literary critic. In order to undermine the appeal of the *Reflections*, to question the validity of Burke's claims, and to demonstrate their own intellectual superiority, Burke's opponents were compelled to examine his use of language. Since they remarked so frequently on what Wollstonecraft called 'the gorgeous drapery in which [he] enwrapped [his] tyrannic principles',[2] they were forced to act in the

---

[1] *Vindication of the Rights of Men*, p. 34. [2] Ibid., p. 88.

capacity of analytic critic. In the case of Mackintosh there is little need to add to the evidence already adduced to prove his competence both as critic and dialectician. As additional proof there is the literary awareness shown in his analysis of the 'privileges' Burke obtained by casting the *Reflections* in the form of a letter;[1] his alertness to Burke's persuasive use of the private moral character of the French nobility and clergy when only their political and collective character were at issue;[2] his comments on Burke's veneer of eloquence—his 'declamatory appendage'—to conceal his real meaning;[3] or his detection of the way in which Burke avoids the popular associations with the word 'Bastille' and prefers to speak of 'the King's Castles in Paris and at Marseilles'.[4] If, as is here assumed, the skill shown by a pamphleteer in his rôle as analytic critic has a direct correlation with his success as a controversialist, then Mackintosh's success cannot be doubted. Furthermore, his tone and style, his moral fervour and intellectual integrity, and his essential reasonableness convince Mackintosh's reader that he has been in touch with a reliable and authoritative writer of considerable distinction.

MARY WOLLSTONECRAFT: *A Vindication of the Rights of Men* (1790)

To apply the same critical criteria to the *Vindication* as to *Vindiciae Gallicae* is to obtain sharply contrasting results. More impulsive and spontaneous than Mackintosh, Wollstonecraft's feelings were obviously less under intellectual control than his, and she appears to have had no comparable understanding of the pitfalls to be avoided by the political pamphleteer. On the other hand, the emotional warmth which is largely played down in his pamphlet is a dominant feature of hers. It is possible that this fact proves in Mary Wollstonecraft a subtle understanding of the public temper within three weeks of the publication of the *Reflections*, a work which was then in the sale of its twelfth thousand[5] and which William Windham believed 'capable of overturning the National Assembly'.[6] It was

[1] *Vindiciae Gallicae*, pp. vi–vii.   [2] Ibid., p. 102.
[3] Ibid., p. 307.   [4] Ibid., p. 176.
[5] Ed. Countess of Minto, *Life and Letters of Sir Gilbert Elliot, 1st Earl of Minto*, I, 365–6.
[6] Ed. Mrs. H. Waring, *The Diary of the Rt. Hon. William Windham*, p. 213.

important quickly to make a spontaneous, almost 'off-the-cuff' retort to the acclamation with which Burke's work was being received; the 'eager warmth and positiveness' which *The Monthly Review*[1] detected in the *Vindication* were perhaps necessary qualities in a counterblast at this early stage in the controversy. When Mackintosh wrote nearly six months later a more considered and temperate manner was appropriate.

The *Vindication* gives the impression of having been dashed off in angry haste; it lacks the strict orderliness that marks the *Vindiciae Gallicae* and seems to have evolved under the writer's hand, subject to her strong feelings rather than to an organised plan. The vigour is refreshing, but the lack of organisation severely weakens Wollstonecraft's denunciation of the *Reflections* for the same defect. Consequently, her sneers at Burke's desultoriness and her contemptuous refusal to 'follow [him] through "horse-way and foot-path" '[2] are deprived of the authority with which Mackintosh supports similar criticisms by the ordered pattern of his own pamphlet. Similarly, the frustration she experiences in trying to counter Burke's persuasive tactics is made too clear and the superiority in argument that she would claim is not established.

> I glow with indignation when I attempt, methodically, to unravel your slavish paradoxes, in which I can find no fixed first principle to refute; I shall not, therefore, condescend to shew you where you affirm in one page what you deny in another; and how frequently you draw conclusions without any previous premises.[3]

The urgency of the writer's feelings is not in doubt, but her exasperation is too much in evidence; it is in danger of becoming a tribute to Burke's ability to prevent effective reply. And there is little to support the tacit claim that the reason and logic which Burke is said to lack are being deployed to destroy his 'romantic enthusiasm'.[4]

For it is here that Wollstonecraft makes her main attack. Burke is to be pilloried as an imaginative writer whose feelings are not controlled by his reason and who is out of his true *métier* when presuming to write on political theory; his gifts are undeniable, but they are out of place when directed to issues

---

[1] Op. cit. (January 1791), IV, 97. [2] *Vindication*, p. 7.
[3] Ibid., p. 9. [4] Ibid., p. 109.

such as are raised by the Revolution. In Wollstonecraft's view reason must always be the helmsman: 'She must hold the rudder, or, let the wind blow which way it list, the vessel will never advance smoothly to its destined port.'[1] The image makes one aware that Wollstonecraft's line of attack is Platonic; the imaginative writer is a dangerous deceiver and must be strictly confined to matters not affecting the commonwealth. On these grounds Burke's reliance on what he calls 'the moral constitution of the heart' is harshly dealt with:

> throughout your letter you frequently advert to a sentimental jargon, which has long been current in conversation, and even in books of morals, though it never received the *regal* stamp of reason. A kind of mysterious instinct is *supposed* to reside in the soul, that instantaneously discerns truth, without the tedious labours of ratiocination.[2]

Thus Burke may properly be compared with poets who 'must often cloud the understanding, whilst they move the heart by a kind of mechanical spring'.[3] Time and again Wollstonecraft repeats her rationalist assault on imagination and intuition in order to assert 'the sovereignty of reason' in opposition to Burke's belief in 'the happy effect of following nature, which is wisdom without reflection, and above it'.[4] This procedure commended by Burke is, in Wollstonecraft's view, out of place when a new constitution must be planned; 'understanding' is the essential guide in such circumstances and it would not look for models to earlier ages.

> If you had given the same advice to a young history painter of abilities, I should have admired your judgment and re-echoed your sentiments. Study, you might have said, the noble models of antiquity, till your imagination is inflamed; and, rising above the vulgar practice of the hour, you may imitate without copying those great originals.[5]

For a painter the advice would have been sound, but it has no relevance for the National Assembly, who required 'a higher model in view than the *imagined* virtues of their forefathers'. Wollstonecraft makes no attempt here to analyse and then

---

[1] *Vindication*, p. 73.   [2] Ibid., p. 68.
[3] Ibid., p. 70.   [4] *Reflections*, in *Works*, II, 307.
[5] *Vindication*, pp. 98–9.

demolish Burke's thesis; he is indicted as an aesthetician who has strayed into the field of political science, whose gifts and irrelevant principles may deceive the unsuspecting, and who must be shown as unequal to and unequipped for the task he has presumed to undertake.

Furthermore, not only is Burke out of his depth, his reverence for imagination and intuition indicates dangerous shortcomings in his moral philosophy.

> From observing several cold romantic characters I have been led to confine the term romantic to one definition—false, or rather artificial, feelings. . . . In modern poetry the understanding and memory often fabricate the pretended effusions of the heart, and romance destroys all simplicity; which, in works of taste, is but a synonymous word for truth. . . . The turgid bombast of some of your periods fully proves these assertions; for when the heart speaks we are seldom shocked by hyperbole, or dry raptures.[1]

In other words, Burke fabricated his emotions to provide himself with literary material, the expression of which betrayed its artificiality by its overcharged and ill-disciplined emotionalism. At bottom, then, this is a moral indictment which Wollstonecraft supports by evidence from Burke's career. She recalls his apparently heartless taunts about George III's insanity at the time of the Regency crisis: 'where was your sensibility when you could utter this cruel mockery, equally insulting to God and man?'[2] His feelings, she claims, are the servant of political expediency. The affected 'holy fervour' in the *Reflections* over Price's use of the *Nunc Dimittis* is another example: 'A rant to enable you to point your venomous dart, and round your period.' Moreover, Burke's sensibility is the dupe of his love of public prominence:

> There appears to be such a mixture of real sensibility and fondly cherished romance in your composition, that the present crisis carries you out of yourself; and since you could not be one of the grand movers, the next *best* thing that dazzled your imagination was to be a conspicuous opposer.[3]

The sensibility, then, which is claimed in the *Reflections* as a source of intuitive truth is not only irrelevant to political issues, it appears to Wollstonecraft as a mere source of emotive

---

[1] *Vindication*, pp. 65–6.   [2] Ibid., p. 56.   [3] Ibid., p. 108.

trickery in the cause of self-interest. And only because there is a contemporary vogue for compassion and sentiment are Burke's persuasive methods successful in the fashionable, upper-class world.

For Wollstonecraft herself, a desirable relation can exist between morality and a properly directed sensibility, but it will not do so in a man whose response to experience—as in Burke's case—is controlled by 'wit' rather than by 'judgment':

> great quickness of comprehension, and facile association of ideas, naturally preclude profundity of research. Wit is often a lucky hit; the result of a momentary inspiration. . . . The operations of judgment, on the contrary, are cool and circumspect; and coolness and deliberation are great enemies to enthusiasm.[1]

Nor will the relation exist in a man whose theory (as set out in Burke's *Enquiry into . . . the Sublime and Beautiful*) shows him to prefer weakness to the austere qualities of 'fortitude, justice, wisdom, and truth'.[2] Such a person is constitutionally incapable of appreciating the beauty of virtue; on the contrary he admires a 'spurious, sensual beauty, that has long debauched [his] imagination, under the specious form of natural feelings'.[3]

At the centre of this sustained attack—given a coherence in this summary which does not satisfactorily emerge from the pamphlet—is Wollstonecraft's assertion:

> We ought to beware of confounding mechanical instinctive sensations with emotions that reason deepens, and justly terms the feelings of *humanity*. This word discriminates the active exertions of virtue from the vague declamation of sensibility.[4]

The 'feelings of humanity', she implies by her general criticism of Burke as well as by her own positive humanitarianism, can be estimated by the stimuli to which they respond. Burke excites 'compassionate tears', but for the wrong objects. His 'respect for rank has swallowed up the common feelings of humanity';[5] he seems to consider the poor 'as only the live stock of an estate, the feather of hereditary nobility'; he responds acutely to the misery of kings and queens, but is blind to those who suffer from the press-gang;[6] and what he calls 'the final proportions

---

[1] *Vindication*, p. 139.   [2] Ibid., pp. 112–13.
[3] Ibid., p. 121.   [4] Ibid., p. 137.
[5] Ibid., p. 32.   [6] Ibid., p. 27.

of eternal justice' are sophistical and inadequate consolations for the poor whose sufferings are severe and immediate.[1]

These comprehensive criticisms of the *Reflections* give an invigorating and aggressive tone to the *Vindication*, and there is some validity in her strictures without doubt. The attentive reader of the pamphlet, however, also looks for evidence that the criticism is not merely captious, that the writer does not herself suffer from the same faults as she sees in Burke, and that her prose accurately embodies her positive beliefs.

Her own response to experience is undoubtedly consistent with the position she assumed for attacking Burke's alleged deficiencies. 'To labour to increase human happiness by extirpating error'; this, one feels, was the intention behind Wollstonecraft's moral, social, and political philosophy. Both moral and political indignation combine, for example, when she questions Burke's appeal to ancient precedents: 'Are we to seek for the rights of men in the ages when a few marks were the only penalty imposed for the life of a man, and death for death when the property of the rich was touched?'[2] A revolution which gave a new value and dignity to human life by its insistence on equality was passionately welcomed by a writer whose response to the past was in these terms. The same basic response is evident in all her critical remarks on the social state of England: there 'the man who lives by the sweat of his brow has no asylum from oppression';[3] men seized by the press-gang have not the necessary flexibility of mind to take up their old occupations on their return and 'consequently they fall into idleness, drunkenness, and the whole train of vices which you stigmatize as gross';[4] and the wealthy lavish attention on their estates merely 'as *objects* for the eye' instead of encouraging productive farms and caring for the poor 'with fatherly solicitude'.[5] Indeed, the *Vindication* abounds with evidence to prove the genuineness of Wollstonecraft's own 'feelings of humanity'. She is to be reckoned in the tradition of humanitarian reformers of her own and the following century. Her hope that the upper-class mother would come to 'think it necessary to superintend her family and suckle her children' instead of playing the

---

[1] *Vindication*, pp. 142–4.   [2] Ibid., p. 19.
[3] Ibid., p. 24.   [4] Ibid., p. 30.
[5] Ibid., p. 145.

'fine lady';[1] her concern about the slave-trade;[2] her proposals for economic changes to alleviate the lot of the poor—all such features place her unmistakably in that tradition.

In other words, there is convincing proof that Wollstonecraft's criticism of Burke was not indulged merely for the purpose of scoring points in a political controversy; it stemmed from strongly felt convictions. Her style, however, does not invariably constitute proof of her fervent belief in the 'sovereignty of reason', that reason which she insists must discipline otherwise merely instinctive emotions. 'Coolness and deliberation' are not the hallmarks of her writing. There are, for sure, passages firmly controlled by the intellect, in which energetic argument and what, in an excellent phrase, she calls 'the more playful bushfiring of ridicule'[3] move precisely towards the object in view. The passage in which Burke's pomposity is reduced to absurdity—'the mock dignity and haughty stalk, only reminds me of the ass in the lion's skin'[4]—is one such example. Another occurs when she challenges Burke's view on the position of clergy in noble households:

> It would be almost invidious to remark, that they sometimes are only modern substitutes for the jesters of Gothic memory, and serve as whetstones for the blunt wit of the noble peer who patronizes them; and what respect a boy can imbibe for a *butt*, at which the shaft of ridicule is daily glanced, I leave those to determine who can distinguish depravity of morals under the specious mask of refined manners.[5]

Without the qualifying word, 'sometimes', her account would be a loose generalisation, pleasing to the radical-agnostic but untrue in point of fact; the presence of the qualification indicates the thoughtful control she exercised without detriment to the vigour of the prose. And a third is provided by the skilful use of a Shakespearean allusion in the ironic quip:

> But you return to your old firm ground.—*Art thou there, Truepenny?* Must we swear to secure property, and make assurance doubly sure, to give your perturbed spirit rest?[6]

Such writing evidences powerful emotion directed by a strong intelligence; her style is itself proof of her philosophical position

---

[1] *Vindication*, p. 52. [2] Ibid., p. 129.
[3] Ibid., p. 98. [4] Ibid., p. 67.
[5] Ibid., pp. 90–1. [6] Ibid., p. 87.

regarding the desirable control by reason of otherwise wayward feelings. But this proof is not always available. All too frequently indignation or what, in saner moments, she would have dismissed as 'enthusiasm', becomes dominant, the prose is turgid and emotional, and the 'pomp of words' appears which she condemns in the *Reflections*. At such times Wollstonecraft relies on commonplace metaphors—the 'hot-bed of wealth', the senses are 'dazzled', and the mind is 'clouded';[1] the imagery becomes forced and portentous—'you must have seen the clogged wheels of corruption continually oiled by the sweat of the laborious poor';[2] or she uses diction and personifications which are drained of all freshness—'you mourn for the empty pageant of a name, when slavery flaps her wing, and the sick heart retires to die in lonely wilds, far from the abodes of men'.[3] Occasionally she abandons all pretence to disciplined writing and the result is a bogus kind of eloquence:

> That civilization, that the cultivation of the understanding, and refinements of the affections, naturally make a man religious, I am proud to acknowledge.—What else can fill the aching void in the heart, that human pleasures, human friendships can never fill? What else can render us resigned to live, though condemned to ignorance?—What but a profound reverence for the model of all perfection, and the mysterious tie which arises from a love of goodness? What can make us reverence ourselves, but a reverence for that Being, of whom we are a faint image? That mighty Spirit moves on the waters—confusion hears his voice, and the troubled heart ceases to beat with anguish, for trust in Him bade it be still.[4]

Here not only the writer's intellect but also the genuineness of her emotions are in question. The inflated idiom and rhetorical questions, the stock phrases ('aching void', 'profound reverence', 'troubled heart'), the commonplace metaphors and merely ornamental allusions to the Bible—all such features disastrously weaken Wollstonecraft's authority to deride Burke for 'rhetorical flourishes and infantine sensibility'.[5]

It is admittedly difficult for the ablest writer to give a convincing vision of his utopia; it is dangerous for a writer who

---

[1] *Vindication*, p. 52. [2] Ibid., p. 43.
[3] Ibid., p. 152. [4] Ibid., pp. 94-5.
[5] Ibid., p. 153.

possesses and wishes to communicate a boundless optimism in the future, particularly for one whose imaginative discipline is limited. Such a writer was Mary Wollstonecraft: she had a courageous and independent mind where social and political theories were concerned, but for her utopian vision she had to rely on the paradise-image which had become a commonplace in eighteenth-century literature. Rooted centuries deep in the pastoral tradition, it appears, for example, in Parnell's poem *The Hermit* and in Dyer's *The Fleece*, it lies behind Johnson's *London* and Goldsmith's *Deserted Village*, it suffices for Fielding when, through the Wilsons in *Joseph Andrews*, he wants to suggest how men lived in 'the golden age'—and it does duty again for Wollstonecraft. 'If men were more *enlightened*',

> A garden more inviting than Eden would then meet the eye, and springs of joy murmur on every side. The clergyman would superintend his own flock, the shepherd would then love the sheep he daily tended; the school might rear its decent head, and the buzzing tribe, let loose to play, impart a portion of their vivacious spirits to the heart that longed to open their minds, and lead them to taste the pleasures of men. Domestic comfort, the civilizing relations of husband, brother, and father, would soften labour, and render life contented.[1]

It would be difficult to find a better example in eighteenth-century political literature of what George Orwell calls the process of 'gumming together long strips of words which have already been set in order by someone else'.[2] It is doubtful whether there is a single original phrase in the whole passage; every one has its literary antecedents; and the writer has been content to let her vision be created for her by a string of associated clichés. The creative imagination, the critical intelligence —they are absent.

In the face of such writing it is clearly impossible to argue that the *Vindication* is a wholly satisfactory pamphlet. The total impression conveyed is of a writer whose views were strongly felt and vigorously communicated; many of the strictures she directs at the *Reflections* are valid and telling; but the chief weakness is Wollstonecraft's inability to embody at all times

[1] *Vindication*, p. 147.
[2] In 'Politics and the English Language', *Collected Essays* (1961), p. 345.

in her prose those qualities of intellectual honesty and emotional discipline which she claimed were of prime importance to a political philosopher. She condemns Burke and, by the same token, is herself condemned.

ARTHUR YOUNG: *'Travels in France'* (1792–94)

When the first volume of *Travels in France* was announced in *The London Chronicle* on 24 May 1792 pamphlets by Mackintosh, Paine, Wollstonecraft, Priestley, Christie, and others had already appeared; the *Reflections* was in its eleventh edition, and Burke's *Letter to a Member of the National Assembly, Appeal from the New to the Old Whigs*, and *Thoughts on French Affairs* were all in print. Young was chronologically, indeed, one of the last two major writers who can properly be related to the controversy, Godwin being the other.

This fact is important. The market had, by May 1792, been sated with pamphlets of every variety both in political colour and literary quality; even the politically conscious English public (to which Young is never tired of referring) must have suffered from some literary indigestion from over fifty works on the same subject; and those 'grocers, chandlers, drapers, and shoemakers of all the towns in England'[1] who were so alive to French affairs doubtless looked with some dismay on any new publication. Here Young was at a great advantage. His *Travels* was different in kind from the works of Burke, Mackintosh, or Paine; his reputation, unlike theirs, was founded on eleven volumes of *Tours* of England and Ireland, not on political writings; and while, almost accidentally, his book became regarded as a contribution to the debate on France, his appeal was not confined to the avid reader of political controversy.

By way of introduction a single extract will serve to substantiate some of these points:

[12 July 1789] Walking up a long hill, to ease my mare, I was joined by a poor woman, who complained of the times, and that it was a sad country; demanding her reasons, she said her husband had but a morsel of land, one cow, and a poor little horse, yet they had a *franchar* (42 lb) of wheat, and three chickens, to pay as a quit-rent to one Seigneur; and four *franchar* of oats, one chicken

[1] Ed. M. Betham-Edwards, *Travels in France*, p. 237.

and 1 *f* to pay to another, besides very heavy tailles and other taxes. She had seven children, and the cow's milk helped to make the soup. . . . It was said, at present, that *something was to be done by some great folks for such poor ones, but she did not know who nor how,* but God send us better, *car les tailles & les droits nous ecrasent.*— This woman, at no great distance, might have been taken for sixty or seventy, her figure was so bent, and her face so furrowed and hardened by labour,—but she said she was only twenty-eight. An Englishman who has not travelled, cannot imagine the figure made by infinitely the greater part of the countrywomen in France; it speaks, at the first sight, hard and severe labour: I am inclined to think, that they work harder than the men, and this, united with the more miserable labour of bringing a new race of slaves into the world, destroys absolutely all symmetry of person and every feminine appearance. To what are we to attribute this difference in the manners of the lower people in the two kingdoms?—TO GOVERNMENT.[1]

Here was a new voice in political controversy; not since Defoe had there been anything comparable before, and not for thirty years, till Cobbett's *Rural Rides*, was it to be matched. For readers who were possibly becoming 'punch-drunk' from the efforts of Burke and his opponents, such writing would be refreshing: it made new demands on them; it related observed and deeply felt experience; and it focused attention on real human beings engaged in the business of living. Young is concerned with the facts of life under the old régime, the principles of which Burke had defended and the liberals had attacked; his humane response to the facts is plain but not laboured; and his final deductions compel our attention to the wider political issues underlying the single incident. This is not the work of one of those writers (described in the Preface) 'whose political reveries are spun by their firesides, or caught flying as they are whirled through Europe in post-chaises';[2] only Paine and Butler indeed, among Burke's opponents—and they by different means—can at all approach Young in conveying the sense of speaking directly from experience of the situation about which they write.

This quality stems initially from the 'journal' method of presenting his material. Young says he rejected the idea of eliminating the 'variety of little circumstances relating to

[1] *Travels*, pp. 197–8.   [2] Ibid., p. lvi.

[himself] only' in favour of publishing his account 'just as it was written on the spot'.[1] The result is that, instead of reading a formal treatise on the state of French agriculture and society, we see Young as it were growing into a knowledge of French life, people, and institutions which is not rivalled for its intimacy by any participant in the controversy. There is a constant freshness about the discoveries he makes, whether they concern French inns or the peasantry, the follies of the Court or the pleasures of French cooking. And the immediacy with which these discoveries are recorded sets him aside from the other pamphleteers who, whatever the extent of their knowledge of France or their excited commitment to revolutionary principles, were compelled to reflect and ponder before communicating their knowledge and excitement; they were obliged to order their thoughts and fashion a coherent argument; and consequently, the freshness of their first engagement with the revolutionary philosophy inevitably lost some of its sparkle. Their enthusiasm is conveyed, but not the tangle of personal experiences which gave rise to it.

The journal form, however, has its own pitfalls. The danger of repetition and diffusiveness Young does not wholly escape. Features of French life which struck him as novel in 1787 often reappear in 1790, the place in which he finds them being their only distinguishing mark. Grammatical and syntactical errors creep in—they occur in the passage already quoted—when the discipline of writing continuous prose is withdrawn, and a slackness in the use of language is sometimes present. Indeed, *The Monthly Review*, in its enthusiastic notice of the *Travels*, is justified in asserting that some purification and compression of language were necessary if the work was to outrank 'any thing heretofore published of the kind'.[2]

The example of Boswell points to a further difficulty associated with publishing a journal: the impact made by the personality of the writer. No literary form brings us so directly into contact with the writer's personality, and while Young's lacks the fascinating complexity of Boswell's, it is also free from his less-attractive characteristics. Young is, for example, innocent of the desire to exploit a variety of *personae*; the range of literary experience that allows Boswell to develop the rôles he

---

[1] *Travels*, pp. 3–4.   [2] Op. cit. (March 1793), X, 290.

assumes with such finesse is beyond him. Young has only one *persona*: 'a man who travels for the plough.'[1] It is this character which gains him entry to French intellectual circles, brings him under the suspicion of alarmed peasants who interpret his enquiries about land and crops as those of a Court-agent, and makes him somewhat abashed in the presence of fashionable ladies. But this rôle is organic; it is not one, as are Boswell's various *personae* (the man-about-town or the penitent, the Restoration lover or the champion of Corsican liberty), assumed for particular occasions. With Young it is utterly consistent with his forthrightness on the wilful neglect of their land by many French noblemen or the stupidity of many agricultural theories held in France; it is all of a piece with his tenderness for the blind mare which had carried him 1,500 miles through France; and it conforms with his practical cast of mind, determination, and courage. There is something of John Bull about him; Young is sceptical about the Assembly's rejection of the idea of an upper chamber in France, and his veneration for the English constitution is immense. In fact, the test by which he intends to judge the sanity of the revolutionaries is whether they copy 'the constitution of England, freed from all its faults' or 'attempt, from theory, to frame something absolutely speculative'.[2] But he escapes chauvinism—the English constitution has its faults, especially inadequate representation—and his distrust of theory is not confined to politics, but embraces agriculture too. Furthermore, though Young is not accurate in every detail (as William Marshall had shown concerning his *Tours* in England); though he is not everywhere consistent in his ideas—on one occasion he decries reliance on theory where the liberty of a people is concerned, and on another he accepts unhesitatingly the necessity for experiment in government as in science;[3] nevertheless, it is a good-humoured, tolerant, sensitive personality that emerges. To use Fielding's word about himself, Young is 'companionable'.

These facts are central to any consideration of the nature of Young's contribution to the debate on the Revolution. The confidence between reader and writer that is necessary to the success of any piece of writing is, in the case of a journal,

[1] *Travels*, p. 212.
[2] Ibid., p. 206.   [3] Ibid., pp. 187, 344 n.2.

essentially a confidence in a personality, in the moral quality the writer displays by his response to and evaluation of experience without opportunity for extensive reflection. The habitual reader of political pamphlets in the 1790s was used to facing a discussion on the right way in which '25 millions of people in France should assert their right to liberty'; in Young's *Travels* he is brought face to face with the people themselves, their ragged clothes, stinking breath, or diseased bodies, or their elegance, sophistication, and alleged taciturnity. His confidence in Young's authority as an observer would turn largely on his estimate of the way Young assimilated a variety of recorded impressions and the value he put on them. For Young expressly says that his intention is not to provide 'memoirs of what passes' but to note feelings and opinions of real significance, a task which at once involves value-judgments. Elsewhere, justifying his inclusion of apparently trivial details, he remarks:

> To note such trifles may seem superfluous to many: but what is life when trifles are withdrawn? and they mark the temper of a nation better than objects of importance. In the moments of council, victory, flight, or death, mankind . . . are nearly the same. Trifles discriminate better. . . . It is everyday feelings that decide the colour of our lives.[1]

It is also by Young's own response to and proof of 'everyday feelings' in the face of ordinary and extraordinary events that he would establish an intimate relationship with his audience.

The variety of experience by which his moral fibre could be tested is endless. Young avoids, for example, any temptation to inflate the importance of his journey; although he is aware of the novelty of it and the seriousness of his enquiry, he is conscious that to many Frenchmen the idea of a Suffolk farmer 'travelling for agriculture' is as strange 'as if it had been like the antient philosopher's tour of the world on a cow's back, and living on the milk'.[2] But he is always on the alert to enlarge 'the sphere of [his] conceptions', to add 'to the stores of his knowledge', and to combine observation with judgment. He notices the French custom of dining at noon and is alive to its part in the neglect of agriculture by the upper classes:

[1] *Travels*, p. 89. [2] Ibid., p. 247.

What is a man good for after his silk breeches and stockings are on, his hat under his arm, and his head *bien poudré?*—Can he botanize in a watered meadow?—Can he clamber the rocks to mineralize?—Can he farm with the peasant and the plough-man?[1]

The custom is 'hostile to every view of science, to every spirited exertion, and to every useful pursuit in life'. The 'pompous folly' of courtly ceremonial earns his contempt, as do the 'nonsensical customs' governing the simplest royal activities.[2] On the other hand (in a way that reminds one of Cobbett), 'a beautiful [young] girl . . . smiling under such a bundle of rags . . . made [his] heart ache to see her',[3] and while he is full of praise for the best of French roads he cannot free his mind 'of the recollection of the unjust taxation which pays for them'.[4] Compassion, then, co-exists with a realistic appraisal of the facts, 'everyday feelings' with keen analysis, so that his response to the Revolution itself is not unexpected. Partly because his sympathies are aroused by the spectacle of human beings 'as the prey of tyrants',[5] and partly because of his belief that economic prosperity depends largely on free government, Young's reaction is ardent:

> The spectacle of the representatives of twenty-five millions of people, just emerging from the evils of 200 years of arbitrary power, and rising to the blessings of a freer constitution . . . was framed to call into animated feelings every latent spark, every emotion of a liberal bosom.[6]

This is not, however, the individual voice of the Suffolk farmer; personal emotion is hidden behind a stilted diction presumably chosen to accord with the great occasion. The genuineness of the feelings themselves is attested when one sees the passage in its context: on the previous day, in the midst of momentous events in Paris in June 1789, Young records his discovery of

> plants that promise greatly for the farmer, particularly the *lathyrus biennis*, and the *melilotus syberica*, which now make an immense figure for forage; both are biennial; but will last three or four years if not seeded;

[1] *Travels*, p. 38.   [2] Ibid., pp. 14, 15.
[3] Ibid., p. 125.   [4] Ibid., p. 49.
[5] Ibid., p. 60.   [6] Ibid., p. 163.

on the day following his visit to the Assembly, Young leaves Paris to meet 'the only practical farmer in the society of agriculture'. And, intense as is his pleasure at the liberation of the French people, there is no description more instinct with delight than that of the harvest-scene in Languedoc.

> The vintage itself can hardly be such a scene of activity and animation as this universal one of treading out the corn, with which all the towns and villages in Languedoc are now alive. . . . Every soul is employed, and with such an air of cheerfulness, that the people seem as well pleased with their labour, as the farmer himself with his great heaps of wheat. The scene is uncommonly animated and joyous.[1]

Energy, enjoyment, productive activity—these are the human characteristics which most vividly excite Young's response; in his view they flourish best under conditions of political liberty; hence his eagerness to see a free government established in France.

Contemporary readers, then, could be in no doubt as to the quality of Young's response to human experience and, in particular, to the political events in France. There was abundant evidence that his judgments and feelings were reliable. The public would not find, however, that he was wholly committed to one side or the other in the English debate on the Revolution; both sides would be encouraged and challenged, a fact which increased the significance of the *Travels*. Young is not blind to possible defects in the new French constitution; he seriously doubts the wisdom of the revolutionaries in taking extreme measures that might provoke civil war and endanger their positive gains;[2] he largely confirms Burke's description of the chaos that marked the meetings of the National Assembly;[3] and while in England he is eager for improvements in the constitution, in France he advises cautious action.[4] Nevertheless, although his own views for and against the Revolution are equally balanced, it was Burke's opponents who would obtain most support for their views in the *Travels*; frequently the reading public would find that claims advanced by Mackintosh, Paine, and the others were confirmed by Young's evidence. His cumulative picture of tyrannous oppression under the

[1] *Travels*, pp. 45–6.   [2] Ibid., p. 178.
[3] Ibid., p. 297.   [4] Ibid., p. 188.

ancien régime substantiates one of the most important assertions by such writers: that the Revolution was both expedient and inevitable. Mackintosh's claim that the word 'revolution' is capable of more than one interpretation is borne out by Young's personal experience in Paris; his argument that the revolutionary movement was largely leaderless and the work of a whole population in revolt finds support in the *Travels*; and his account of the sequence of events in 1789, along with the accounts of Paine, Christie, and others, is validated by Young's book. Burke's sneers at Rousseau are challenged by Young's praise for him, and on the other hand, Turgot, whom Mackintosh cites as a reliable authority, is for Young too a 'friend of mankind'.[1] But, as well as this and other detailed support, the factor which would most strengthen the liberal cause was Young's unfailing sympathy for the oppressed and those denied the constitutional liberty which promoted economic and social well-being.

It remains only to observe that, wide as would be the politically minded readership of the *Travels*, the book would be read, initially at any rate, for other than political reasons. His audience would include many who found their most absorbing reading among the voluminous travel literature of the period.[2] Their interest would first be caught not only by the detailed information about towns and villages, agriculture and architecture, but also by descriptions of natural scenes (for which Young adopts Burke's criteria of beauty and sublimity[3]), comments on gardening (for which Sir William Chambers and 'Capability' Brown are his standards of reference[4]), accounts of his visits to French theatres, and so forth. Young's appeal was not limited to the highly educated by esoteric allusions; rather he aimed at the moderately cultivated middle classes (among whom he believed, with Mackintosh, that 'knowledge, intelligence, information, learning, and wisdom . . . reside most'[5]) and these were precisely the people most in need of a balanced

[1] *Travels*, pp. 84–5, 87, 23.

[2] Paul Kaufman in *Borrowings from the Bristol Library, 1773–1784* (Charlottesville, 1960) provides statistical proof that, with the exception of *belles lettres*, travel literature was the most popular choice among library borrowers.

[3] Cf. *Travels*, pp. 40–1, 281.

[4] Ibid., pp. 101–2.   [5] Ibid., p. 336 n.1.

appraisal of the situation in France. From whatever motive this heterogeneous audience took up the *Travels*, they would not put it down without a clearer understanding of facts which, in Young's view, are the basis of 'real political knowledge'[1] and without in some measure coming under the influence of his liberal opinions.

[1] *Travels*, p. 149.

X

'TRUE MORALITY SHUNS NOT THE DAY': OTHER PAMPHLETEERS IN PROSE AND VERSE

T HE analysis of the more memorable contributions to the
debate on the Revolution has revealed some modes of
conducting political controversy, the readers to whom appeal
was made, and the degrees of success achieved. The remaining
pamphleteers are valuable in extending the scope of this enquiry. Their skill in using the language of politics varies enor-
mously, their failures are often as instructive as their successes,
but it would be tedious thoroughly to catalogue either. Consequently, at the risk of levelling the well-known writer like
Joseph Priestley with the completely ephemeral like Benjamin
Bousfield, or a man such as Capel Lofft who had some reputation in his own day with another such as John Butler who had
none, this chapter will deal more generally with, as it were, the
support-troops involved in the hostilities provoked by Burke's
Reflections. 'The more correct statement of one fact, or the more
successful illustration of one argument, will at least rescue a book
from the imputation of having been written in vain.'[1] Though
we can no longer view every pamphlet in the controversy with
Mackintosh's degree of seriousness, his statement briefly sums
up what each writer felt was the justification of his own efforts;

[1] *Vindiciae Gallicae*, advertisement.

185

it also goes some way to explain both the number and the ardour of the writers involved.

> Nineteen-twentieths of these productions are in favour of liberty, . . . but enquiring for such as had appeared on the other side of the question, to my astonishment I find there are but two or three that have merit enough to be known.[1]

The words are Arthur Young's and his location Paris; had he been commenting on London 1790–93, the same remark would have been appropriate, except that his 'two or three' would have been an exaggeration. There is no pamphlet supporting Burke that will now bear close scrutiny; the few which appeared are strident, vituperative, and small-minded. The anonymous *Vindication of Burke's Reflections* (1791) and the *Letters to Burke on Politics* (1791) by Dr. Edward Tatham (soon to be Rector of Lincoln College, Oxford) illustrate the language of politics addressed to the converted or to those who are to be cowed into agreement. Tatham appeals solely to Anglican supporters of the *status quo*. He describes the dissenters as a subversive 'phalanx of political literati'; he accuses them of using Sunday Schools to spread 'seditious doctrines'—a charge on a level with the Attorney-General's claim at Paine's trial that 'children's sweetmeats' were wrapped in sheets of the *Rights of Man*;[2] and he pleads hysterically for the extermination of these 'weeds' of dissent.[3] The vindicator of the *Reflections* insinuates that Wollstonecraft's anger against the press-gang is on account of her friendship with the 'honest mechanics' who have been pressed and with whom she was probably on intimate terms.[4] Or again, he clearly intends to frighten the English upper classes with the example of the French *tiers état* whose 'infectious yells of unglutted cruelty, horribly announced the envenomed gangrene of their souls' at the execution of the Marquis de Favras.[5] Any controversy is likely to throw up such writers who have no control over their own emotions and no respect for their readers' intelligence; it was Burke's misfortune that he was supported only by men of this kind.

'Railing stands where reason ought, and opprobrious epithets

---

[1] *Travels in France*, p. 153.
[2] *State Trials* (1817), XXII, 381. [3] Op. cit., pp. 92, 94, 100.
[4] Op. cit., pp. 5–6. [5] Ibid., p. 63.

supply the place of argument.'[1] This remark applies to Tatham's
Letters and to the *Vindication*; it applies equally to the pamphlet
in which it occurs, Robert Woolsey's *Reflections upon Reflections*.
Although, relative to their numbers, the amount of vituperation
indulged in by the pro-revolutionary writers is slight, they, too,
had their Thersites. Woolsey's diatribe, however, is worth a
passing glance, because it, like Tatham's, demonstrates the
danger, of an uncongenial personality making itself felt in a
political pamphlet. One certainly looks for vitality and intellectual energy in controversial writing, but Woolsey's lacks
decorum—of the kind that accompanies these qualities in *Vindiciae Gallicae*—as well as the sense of intense sympathy for the
oppressed classes which might justify some crude vigour as it
does with Paine. All we find in Woolsey is crudity without
justification. His reflections on Burke's work proceed in this
manner:

> Page 7 to 13. A great bundle of metaphysics and general stuff,
> full of your own uneasiness, solicitude, astonishment etc.[2]

> Page 13 to 16. Irrelevant farrago.[3]

> Page 50 to p. 99. A mighty jumble of general stuff, according to
> custom; full of groans, prophecies, etc.[4]

This is indeed vulgar in the normal pejorative sense; it is not
offset by the lively intellect and critical ability to be found in
Paine, nor does the idiom stand in an organic relation to the
views expressed as it does in his pamphlet. The sole end of such
writing is to be abusive, perhaps to be humorous, but certainly
not to persuade the reader into adopting new and positive
beliefs.

A conscientious attempt to persuade an audience to accept
views perhaps uncongenial hitherto is, of course, open to its own
problems. Capel Lofft is an example of a man whose genuine
determination to undertake a 'substantial discussion of the most
material points' exists alongside a suspicion of 'the charms of
style' and 'the graces of composition'.[5] He—like others in the
radical tradition—fails to understand that style provides the
writer's warranty for clarity of mind and incisiveness of

---

[1] R. Woolsey, *Reflections upon Reflections* (1790), p. 4.
[2] Ibid., p. 7.   [3] Ibid., p. 9.   [4] Ibid., p. 14.
[5] *Remarks on the Letter of Burke*, p. 78.

judgment; he does not recognise that satisfactorily to oppose 'the shield of Truth' to Burke's 'brilliant and dazzling arms' it is not enough merely to make a series of objections and counter-statements to Burke's claims. For instance, Lofft challenges Burke's assertion that men of eminence are the only persons competent to judge important issues:

> to say, that it is '*a question of state, not made for common occasions, nor to be agitated by common minds*', is to assert in the former clause of the sentence, what was too clear to require stating; and which seems only to have been introduced for the purpose of familiar-ising the doctrine in the close; a doctrine so alarmingly para-doxical, that it did indeed require preparation: it was necessary the mind should slide over it by aid of the smooth and insensible declivity offered it in the preceding proposition.[1]

This is bad prose: it is obtuse and long-winded, it lacks argu-mentative 'punch', and it does not support the implicit claim that Lofft is superior to Burke in judgment and mental clarity. A participant in political controversy can count on only one reading of his pamphlet, and he must convince his reader, by a lucid, nervous style, that an alert and critical mind is at work throughout. This Lofft fails to do.

He suffers from an inflated belief in the power of truth (as he conceives it) to triumph unaided over error. He imagines that to examine each of Burke's statements in the manner of the passage quoted will, in the end, destroy Burke's hold on his readers; he fails to reckon with the power of boredom. The fact is that Lofft lacks self-confidence: he cannot be sure that he has said enough until he has said all; he ends up by being merely instructive and tedious. The same lack of self-confidence is seen in his flaccid irony, his reluctance to commit himself decisively (the question of the French king's right to decide on war or peace 'ought not to be too hastily decided in the negative'[2]), and his pride when he finds himself agreeing with Burke.[3] It is, of course, meritorious to admit such agreement, but some decisive edge is necessary in political controversy; sharp distinctions are essential if vitality is not to be sacrificed.

At the end of his pamphlet Lofft gives twenty pages of

---

[1] *Remarks on the Letter of Burke*, p. 12.
[2] Ibid., p. 67.   [3] Cf. ibid., p. 70.

extracts from the proceedings of the Revolution and Constitutional Societies, the resolutions of other bodies, French reports,
and the like. The absence of any comments by Lofft on this
material demonstrates his almost Miltonic faith in his audience's
capacity to recognise and accept the truth with a minimum of
guidance on his part. He is not alone in this belief. Thomas
Christie, in his *Letters*, provides over 200 pages of similar
material. He, too, intends to oppose Burke's '*declamation* and
oratory' and his 'fine-turned periods' with 'a calm and dispassionate view of facts';[1] he believes that, if he states 'the facts
. . . as they really are', the public will discover

> that on the one hand the evils were not so great as [Burke]
> paints them, and on the other, that there was a great deal of
> good of which he says nothing, [and] they will begin to believe
> that he has led them into a deception; and the discovery of this
> will prejudice his opinion, more than all his arguments have
> served it.[2]

Without question this is an intelligent response to the *Reflections*,
a work which all Burke's opponents considered as 'little more
than the soaring flights of a boundless imagination, and the
effusions of an irritable and irritated mind'.[3] Nevertheless, they
still faced the problem of making the facts compulsive; they had
to reach a satisfactory compromise between trusting the reader's
intelligent search for truth and making sure that the truth could
not possibly escape him. And in this Christie is more successful
than Lofft.

The primary difference between them lies in Christie's faith
in his literary ability to sustain the cause in which they both
believe. Here is a man who can argue crisply and soberly, whose
style—by its lucidity, cogency, and logic—in general reflects his
reliance on the truth of factual information, and whose manner
is that of a man convinced of his own rightness. Like Lofft,
Christie admits that the French have made mistakes, but this is
not a matter for pride in agreeing with Burke: this is no more
than accepting the facts as they really are. Moreover, Christie
knows how to deploy his information to the best advantage. He

[1] *Letters on the Revolution of France*, pp. 7–8.
[2] Ibid., p. 49.
[3] B. Bousfield, *Observations on Burke's Pamphlet* (1791), p. 2.

destroys and creates simultaneously; he presents Burke's errors to full view and, at the same time, by evidence and quotation he builds up a true picture of the state of France and her constitution. Time and again he demonstrates Burke's unreliability: he uses M. Lally Tollendal, Burke's own authority, to show the extent of the confusion and corruption in pre-revolutionary France;[1] he condemns Burke's 'unaccountable negligence' and catalogues the resultant errors in discussing a '*project*' for the territorial division of France instead of 'the plan that was really adopted by the Assembly';[2] and (in a manner recalling George Orwell's account of the Spanish Civil War in *Homage to Catalonia*) he contrasts the sensational reports of events in Paris in English newspapers, on which Burke had relied, with his own personal experience of them.[3] Gradually Christie overwhelms the reader with proof either that Burke was dishonest or that his information was unreliable. Alongside this attack Christie constructs his own picture of France based on liberal quotation from primary sources. He even recommends particular French newspapers in which his readers can find accurate information.[4]

Christie is also aware, as Lofft is not, that his literary manner in itself provides evidence of his trustworthiness. Were his style throughout the pamphlet such as we meet in the early pages, this evidence would be missing.

> What avail [Burke's] brilliant colours, that only varnish the deformity of folly and oppression? With majestic grace, worthy of a nobler office, he conducts us to the Temple of Superstition, and the magic of his language soothes our hearts into holy reverence and sacred awe. But . . . we turn with disgust from the false splendor of the mansion of Idolatry, and hasten with chearful steps to the humble abode of unadorned Truth, to bow before her august presence, and receive from her the simple and salutary instructions of eternal wisdom.[5]

This is not the language which properly embodies 'unadorned Truth' and mercifully Christie's normal manner is one of unaffected directness:

> All I contend for is, not that there was not a great deal of happiness in France; but that that happiness was accidental, precarious,

[1] *Letters*, pp. 77–80. [2] Ibid., pp. 153–60.
[3] Ibid., p. 121. [4] Ibid., pp. 145–8.
[5] Ibid., pp. 6–7.

uncertain; and that the Government, at any rate, was not the cause of it.[1]

Both the idea and the expression of it (with the double negative) remind one strongly of the immediacy with which Arthur Young writes in his *Travels*. Christie can also convey the urgency and bewildering perplexity of a revolutionary situation:

> What was to be done in such a crisis? The executive power had yielded—the King removed the troops. Things had returned to the state of nature—all the springs of government were broken. There was but one way to prevent universal anarchy: that was for the States General to declare themselves a *National Assembly*—to assume the supreme power. . . .[2]

This is the writing of a man convinced, of a man, too, who had witnessed the events he describes and felt the urgency which compelled speedy, decisive action. Further, Christie's ability to control strong feeling and give it something of a cutting edge is apparent in his ironic passages. For example, he assures Burke that the Assembly will not issue a writ of libel against him—'His book was never noticed in the National Assembly, except once' —and continues:

> Indeed it could not be expected that his eloquence would do much in France, where it must be read in a translation. *Logic* is translatable. *Reason* is the same in all languages; but who can transfer *mere declamation* into a foreign tongue, without losing the spirit and consequently the *effect* of the original?[3]

This cannot match the irony of Junius; it lacks his sportive play of wit and lightness of touch, but it is the writing of a man who, almost because of the matter-of-fact cast of his mind, inspires our trust more than Junius. The analogies he uses elsewhere show him as a man whose imagination rarely, as it were, gets off the ground, and this quality (reminding one rather of Defoe) is again all of a piece with his reliance on 'unadorned Truth'. Christie scarcely ever provides memorable imagery; he lacks the fire and truculence of his friend Paine; but the discriminating public whom he addressed would find that his *Letters* expressed an honest and compelling belief founded on what seemed to him incontrovertible evidence.

In a footnote Christie refers to the pamphlet, *Thoughts on*

---

[1] *Letters*, p. 87.   [2] Ibid., pp. 110–11.   [3] Ibid., pp. 51–2.

Government (1790), by George Rous (who, along with Christie, received honorary French citizenship in 1792[1]): 'In point of candour and accuracy . . . In chaste elegance of language, and manly force of argument, it deserves to be held up as a model to political writers.'[2] It is not difficult to recognise, of course, from the account given of Christie's *Letters* that he is praising a work similar in character to his own. Like him, Rous declares that he will rely on 'deductions from reason, illustrating theory by a reference to historical facts', and that he addresses 'those sober understandings who . . . are willing to seek for truth, at the hazard of being reproached with cold hearts'.[3] Christie might well have made the same declaration; so might Joseph Towers in his *Thoughts on the Commencement of a New Parliament* (1790) or Joseph Priestley in his *Letters to Burke* (1791), or indeed any one of Burke's opponents whose appeal was largely intellectual. Rous's *Thoughts* is orderly in its arrangement, as befits a rationalist pamphleteer; the progress of the argument is lucid and shrewdly managed; the personality with which the reader makes contact is thoughtful, modest, and quietly assured; but like the other writers just mentioned, whose appeal is mainly carried by their patent honesty and serious-mindedness, Rous lacks sparkle and the kind of involvement one associates with Paine. Paine gives the impression of writing about a social system which matters to him as a normal person of loves and hates, anger and common sense, who has to live under it; his emotions as well as his intellect are engaged because it is out of deeply felt experience of life that he writes. Rous and Towers, on the other hand, are, relatively, men who stand on the touch-line of life; they have honest and just thoughts about it, but do not seem to live it with any robustness. Their detachment from the business of living is indicated by their infrequent imaginative use of details from life; they have nothing to match, for example, Paine's use of proverbs, colloquialisms, or snatches from ordinary conversation. He is asserting by the very style he employs the direct bearing of the controversy on the way men live, how it affects their conversation or the money in their pockets; Rous and Towers imply that its chief effect is on men's minds, that it pro-

[1] See M. Ray Adams, *Studies in the Literary Backgrounds of English Radicalism* (Lancaster, Pennsylvania, 1947), p. 49.
[2] *Letters*, p. 21 n.   [3] Op. cit. (4th edn., 1791), p. 6.

vides endless food for thought but has little to do with food for
the belly. Yet the audience addressed by Rous and the others
must not be underestimated; his *Thoughts* went into a fourth
edition in just over six months.

'I have . . . stated but little which I have not seen or experienced':[1] this is the sort of claim Paine might, but Rous would
not have advanced; it is made and justified in John Butler's
Brief Reflections. In this controversy Butler is *sui generis*. A shop-
keeper, 'a freeman of a great city'[2] (presumably Canterbury),
he is the local politician with all the strengths and weaknesses of
that type-figure, whose knowledge of local affairs provides him
with 'a picture in miniature of the whole external government of
the nation'.[3] We know nothing of him biographically, but to say
that a portrait of the man and his world could be drawn from
his pamphlet is to give some indication of the nature of his
writing.

Butler addresses himself to Burke, he constantly refers to the
Reflections by quotation and allusion, but his eyes are not on
France; they are on himself and his own kind in Canterbury or
similar provincial centres. It is one of the attractive features of
his pamphlet that this is so; he does not pretend to knowledge
or wisdom except as they stem from harsh personal experience;
he is, in fact, 'the emblematical figure of an obscure citizen,
labouring under every species of grievance here hinted at'.[4] He
applies to England Burke's objections to the administrative subdivisions in France; he denounces the petty, local tyrants who
flourished in this country, and remarks: 'What is Great Britain
. . . but a charter'd isle, and every city, town, borough, and
cinque port, have their charters also.'[5] (At almost exactly the
same time Blake, in his poem *London*, was denouncing 'the
charter'd Thames' and 'charter'd' streets of the capital.) At
every point Butler's illustrations spring from English common
life, from his experience of local justices, petty-session juries or
excise-men, or from the contrast between rich and poor. The
needy peasant does not dare to shoot game for food because of
the Game Laws—but:

[1] John Butler, *Brief Reflections upon the Liberty of the British Subject*, pp.
10–11.
[2] Ibid., p. 139. [3] Ibid., p. 135.
[4] Ibid., p. 143. [5] Ibid., p. 30.

There comes the esquire, mounted on his steed, overleaps the hedges, breaks down fences in pursuit of game; his spaniel and his pointer puts to flight the herdsmen's flock, regardless what depredations he commits while in pursuit of charming sport.[1]

Or again Butler translates into terms of real life the 'corporation' which, for Burke, is part of the structure of English government:

These self-conceited fribbles, placed at the head of destructive corporations, which are usually composed of the whole gang of raggamuffin gentry. . . . These petty rulers parade the streets, after the devotion of the church, with all the pomp of ancient pageantry, ornamented with their corporal robes, and preceded by a gilded bauble and sword of mockery.[2]

This is the writing of an unsubtle, unsophisticated citizen whose feelings of justice and propriety are outraged; his implicit assertion is that his sufferings at a local level and his response to the small-scale situation provide a valid commentary on the larger principles of the political system defended in the *Reflections*. Accordingly, in opposition to Burke, he declares:

I must dare be plain upon this part of the subject, and give it in as my opinion (which is not so much as the dust of the balance) that the corruption of the state ought not to be winked at, every defect in the manoeuvres of government should be as public as the noon-day sun.[3]

Such is Butler's personal style, with the tone of the speaking, colloquial voice; it recalls Paine's but notably lacks his defiance —the modesty parenthetically indicated here and more explicitly elsewhere one does not associate with the author of the *Rights of Man*. Butler is capable of a striking turn of phrase in homely terms, such as his comment that for years Parliament has 'clipped the wings of liberty, and left it as featherless as a trimmed game cock equipped for battle'.[4] He suffers, however, from the untrained writer's tendency to discursiveness; he lacks confidence in his ability to say something at once pungently and concisely. The worst sections of the *Brief Reflections* are those in which he does not trust his idiomatic English but tries to ape a supposed 'literary' style: 'Look yonder is the wandering bird that takes its flight, and wings its aerial way, promiscuously perches on the bare leafed tree . . .'[5] Fortunately such passages

---

[1] *Brief Reflections*, p. 71.   [2] Ibid., p. 91.   [3] Ibid., p. 33.
[4] Ibid., p. 36; see also p. 103.   [5] Ibid., p. 71.

are not normal. Butler is also at a disadvantage when he tries to counter Burke's analogical reasoning. For instance, he examines the analogy between the rebuilding of a state and of a ruined building, and concludes;

> At the same time I cannot be persuaded, that there is any similitude between the reparation of a state, and that of a mansion. It is true, both requires time and deliberation; and though there may be some kind of analogy between the two, I am confident no model can be drawn from the one as may be applicable to the reparation of the other.[1]

It is at points such as this that Butler requires Paine's vigorous recklessness. He is obviously suspicious of Burke's analogy; he feels he is being deceived, but cannot quite see how or where; and, hesitantly and without reason, he rejects it. There is an instinctive suspicion of rather than a rational objection to imaginative writing, and in this Butler provides an extreme example of a common failing among writers who 'seek no assistance but the light of Reason'.[2]

Nevertheless, the *Brief Reflections* remains a significant pamphlet in the controversy. Butler's political language at its best is an accurate embodiment of personal, deeply felt experience; even where the reader is not convinced intellectually, he does not despise the writer, but feels respect for a man who will not attempt more than his knowledge will allow. 'Common experience convinces us', 'experience convinces us', or, 'these are no chimerical notions, but founded upon the senses of sight and hearing';[3] these are the stylistic symptoms of a thoroughly pragmatic approach which abler writers than Butler would have done well to cultivate.

Butler illustrates, again as an extreme case, another tendency among Burke's opponents: to attack on a narrow front. To some extent this was forced upon them by the fact that they did not initiate the controversy. Burke had challenged, in their view, the justification for any kind of revolution; while condemning revolution in France, he had put up a case which would validate all arbitrary rule. 'You have attacked the fundamental principles of all reform,' says Sir Brooke Boothby to Burke.[4] And this was the Burke who, after his courageous efforts on behalf of

---

[1] *Brief Reflections*, p. 17.   [2] Ibid., p. 10.
[3] Ibid., pp. 49, 61, 48.   [4] *A Letter to Burke* (1791), p. 76.

the American rebels, the Irish Catholics, and economical reform, had a reputation as a defender of liberty. He seemed to have turned Judas in 1790. It was, then, a matter of urgency that Burke as an individual should be challenged lest his former reputation should strengthen the appeal of what seemed to be his new principles. The consequence was that, whereas in the *Reflections* Burke's language had invoked the authority of Christian civilisation and he had addressed the entire Western world, his opponents had a single focal point: Burke himself. The contrast comes out most strikingly in those pamphlets which, like Burke's, took the form of a letter: in the *Reflections* the recipient is not named and every reader feels as if the letter is addressed to him personally; in the replies by Priestley, Boothby, Scott, or Christie (to name a few) the writers address Burke and the reader is cast in the rôle of an onlooker, sympathetic perhaps, but not directly involved. These writers draw on their own political and moral wisdom, of course, but one is always aware of the narrow front on which their campagn is being conducted. Some, like Priestley, Francis Stone, and David Williams, narrow their scope even more by selecting for particular attention the relevance of Burke's theory to the position of English dissenters. This, too, was inevitable. Not only were many remarks in the *Reflections* offensive to religious nonconformists, but also Richard Price, an eminent dissenter, was Burke's whipping-boy; moreover, some of his ablest opponents were either dissenters or unsympathetic to the established Church. But whatever the reason and however cogent their arguments (as is certainly the case with Priestley), their pamphlets lack the comprehensive vision that is a mark of the *Reflections*.

Again, a sustained attempt is made to discredit Burke personally. His opponents question his factual honesty and emphasise the apparent inconsistency between his present and former attitudes to reform.

> There is not, in short, Sir, an opinion you have held, a doctrine that you have supported through a long political life, which your present pamphlet does not contradict; and there never was a politician to whom the *Argumentum ad Hominem* can be applied, so strongly as to yourself.[1]

[1] [John Scott], *A Letter to Burke . . . By a Member of the Revolution Society,* p. 39.

As a variant, Burke is charged with applying to politics the highly personal theory of aesthetics he had presented in his *Enquiry into . . . the Sublime and Beautiful*; his supposed intention is inferred in David Williams's remark: 'An opinion is never so effectually impressed on the public, as when accompanied by terror and astonishment'.[1] Yet however subtly managed and temporarily effective, the *argumentum ad hominem* has the drawback of putting the reader on his guard, endangering the writer's freedom of movement and often seeming to reduce him to the level of a quibbler or backbiter. The frequent use of this mode of argument is one of the most powerful reasons for rendering ephemeral so many pamphlets by Burke's opponents.

Intelligent understanding of Burke's character was, of course, important to his opponents. It may well have prompted the frequent use of ridicule as a method of attack. Burke was well known for his over-sensitiveness to criticism and for the emotional intensity which marked his behaviour in the Commons and led one speaker to urge restraint on Burke if he wanted to avoid imprisonment as a madman.[2] The dramatic use of a dagger in a parliamentary debate or the renunciation of his friendship with Fox in the famous debate of 6 May 1791 also testify to the obsessive seriousness which could be played upon by the anti-Burke writers.

Virtually every reply to the *Reflections* makes use of ridicule as a persuasive method, though with varying degrees of success. The indignant writing at the opening of Wollstonecraft's *Vindication* lacks the necessary pointed indirectness; the incessant irony and banter in Williams's *Lessons to a Young Prince* eventually become wearisome; but, on the other hand, there are examples of considerable ironic skill. The anonymous *Short Observations on Burke's Reflections* (1790) contains many. The author sets his discussion in a humorous context by reference to a commercial treaty between England and France from which one 'species of manufacture' had been forgotten: political systems. Now, however, 'political adventurers have opened warehouses with systems at all prices, and adapted to all constitutions'.[3] Among the 'venders of political specifics' are, of course, Burke

[1] *Lessons to a Young Prince* (2nd edn., 1791), p. 136.
[2] See T. W. Copeland, *Edmund Burke—Six Essays* (1950), p. 76.
[3] Op. cit., p. 2.

and Price; the latter wishes to import the French Revolution, and the former, 'instead of the hard-ware of Birmingham and the stuffs of Manchester, zealously proposes to export across the channel the English Constitution'. The author proceeds to ridicule various aspects of the *Reflections* and, for example, traces Burke's alarm at the possibility of revolution in all countries to 'a pair of colours presented by a patriotic society at Nantz' to the English Revolution Society.

> I confess the fears of Mr. Burke reminded me of the hopes of Sir Epicure Mammon in the Alchymist; he was promised the philosopher's stone, that was to procure him immortal youth and inexhaustible riches; but all ended in some little thing for curing the itch.[1]

This level of irony, enforced by literary allusions, indignation, and common sense is maintained to the final destructive remark:

> I will not dispute the resemblance of the portrait [the self-portrait at the end of the *Reflections*], but when I behold the Champion of American Freedom, the avenger of Asiatic oppression, dwindled into the captious antagonist of Dr. Richard Price, it reminds me of the Giant Loupgarou, whose body was used by Pantagruel to discomfit whole squadrons and battalions; and at last, thrown over the walls of the city, killed a She-Cat and a lame Duck![2]

It is noticeable that the *Vindication of Burke's Reflections* finds it impossible, except by cavilling at two minor points, to answer this type of writing.[3]

The anonymous author of *Short Observations* intends to undermine Burke's appeal largely by demonstrating that, if properly regarded, the *Reflections* is really a source of humour. But his dialectical skill is slight; he lacks a convincing argument which can be invigorated by means of irony. Francis Stone, on the other hand, can argue more capably and has more of a case to put; consequently, his occasional satiric passage strikes the reader with the force of novelty and the pamphlet avoids that tedious seriousness which, for example, befalls Lofft's. To take one instance, Stone gives a fanciful account of a vision induced by Burke's apostrophe to Marie Antoinette in 'a young maiden

[1] Ibid., p. 24. (In August 1790 the Jacobin Society of Nantes presented to the Revolution Society a drawing of a tricoloured banner which had been used at the Anglo-Gallic festival in the same month. See G. S. Veitch, *Genesis of Parliamentary Reform* (1913), p. 156.)

[2] Ibid., pp. 41–2.   [3] Op. cit., pp. 23–4.

lady who shall be nameless'[1] (though she appears to be related to Samuel Richardson's Pamela). She is alleged to say:

> You may be sure a girl of my insatiable curiosity could not rest, till she became one of the 20,000 purchasers of Mr. Burke's Reflections. . . . I at once dropped all my light airs, and prepared myself with much mental gravity for the slow, quiet perusal of a work, which I apprehended would abound with much close reasoning, and deep philosophic theory. But, to my astonishment, I no sooner entered on the perusal, than I found it to be a mere romance, a poem in prose, or an undefinable whip-syllabub declamation, which amused my imagination instead of informing and improving my judgment.

The girl falls asleep while reading the apostrophe and imagines herself carried to the heaven of Greek mythology, where she is fêted by Venus and offered Pegasus for her return to earth, only to find that he has been borrowed by 'a privy counsellor of the king of [her] isle'. She is allowed to see this man, Burke, soaring on Pegasus to 'Phosphorus, or the morning star'; she is then adorned by Venus to resemble 'the fair Dauphiness' and, in this guise, she deceives even 'her Platonic paramour'. The account of the vision suffers from Stone's faulty sense of selection; he is too eager to fill it with detail; but at least it is given point by the charge Stone argues more formally elsewhere—that Burke should have written as a rational philosopher and moralist, whereas he preferred to rely on deluding his readers with highly charged emotionalism.

Forcefully to state this charge—the most common in pamphlets attacking the *Reflections*—and openly to ridicule 'a poem in prose', verse was inevitably chosen by some of Burke's antagonists. The mere choice of verse is ironic: it proclaims that only a highly wrought medium is appropriate for recording the response Burke set out to achieve. Moreover, in varying degrees, the verse writers—Courtenay, Sharpe, and one who is anonymous—recognise that the formal structure of their medium gives to ridicule a thrust that is missing in prose. The difference between these writers is that Courtenay and the anonymous poet are capable of some ironic detachment, whereas Sharpe is merely angry.

In his *Rhapsody to E—— B——* (1792) Sharpe shows some

---

[1] *An Examination of Burke's Reflections* (1792), pp. 139–52.

facility in managing his octosyllabic couplets but the subtlety
Swift had shown to be possible in this form is beyond him.

> when penetrating sages
> Expect to read polemic pages,
> And find no argument appears,
> But every janty passage wears
> The tinsel'd garb that fancy wrought,
> And from her fairy regions brought,
> To deck romance her darling guest,
> And rival fact when simply drest;
> The insult sense disdains to brook,
> And to the shelf consigns the book.[1]

The contempt is too much on the surface and Sharpe's whole
attention is given to sustaining (as best he can) the octosyllabic
formula. One suspects that, like Butler in prose, Sharpe had
little literary education; he held his Painite ideas fervently, but
lacked sufficient ease of manner to write successfully in verse.

The bantering tone employed by the anonymous author of
Reflections on Reflections (1791?) is more effective; one feels here
an urbane man impudently mocking what he considers is Burke's
uncontrolled response to the Revolution:

> But why this mighty thundering, whence
> This wasteful blaze of eloquence?
> Could he not say, what mischief's brewing,
> Without this hideous cry of ruin?[2]

The deliberate flouting of the octosyllabic form with the final
unaccented syllable in the second couplet indicates the easy
assurance this writer feels in writing verse. Later he shows the
efficacy with which a parodist can extract a significant feature of
his opponent's philosophy—Burke's insistence on the importance of natural feelings—and give it special prominence so as to
criticise through ridicule. Burke is presented as saying:

> 'That dreadful morning in October':
> (Who can speak of it and be sober?)
> 'O that some artist would engage
> To bring that story on the stage,
> That I might give my tears to flow
> O'er the dire scene of royal woe!

[1] Op. cit., p. 4.
[2] Op. cit., in *An Asylum for Fugitive Pieces, in Prose and Verse* (New edn.,
1798), IV, 40.

> There would I sit and shew the world
> How I can weep when kings are hurl'd,
> Hurl'd by misfortune from their throne—
> (I'm not *now* speaking of our own.)
> But let not Dr. Price appear
> Nor any of his flock come near;
> I know they do not feel as I;
> No: 'these sour-natur'd dogs' can't cry.
> I'd be asham'd to show my face,
> If 't did not cry at such distress.
> Why, I have cried, when Siddons late
> Presented the sad turns of fate,
> In the frail, beauteous, humbled Shore;
> I cried, when Garrick long before
> Acted a 'fond and foolish' King;
> And shan't I, when the very thing—
> I would say, when the story's real?
> 'Tis *natural* that one should feel.'[1]

The references and criticisms here are many and complex. One of the central features of Burke's philosophy is effectively satirised by dint of ridiculing his own lachrymose nature; he is not content with a natural response, but will weep indiscriminately at any time whether in the theatre or on a political occasion which his imagination has made theatrical; he glories in his ability to weep and welcomes an opportunity for public display. It is the exaggeration introduced by the poet that carries his criticism: he does not condemn natural feelings, but the conscious parade of them, the pride Burke reveals in a sensibility which responds equally to human distresses and the imaginative portrayal of them by a Rowe or a Shakespeare. Furthermore, the second parenthesis contains a stricture which would not be lost on the public of the 1790s. Many writers contrast Burke's inhumanity in his remarks on George III's insanity at the time of the Regency crisis with his exploitation of the sufferings of the French royal family. The anonymous poet implies in one line what Mary Wollstonecraft, for example, takes several paragraphs to convey. And, finally, the whole passage is packed with allusions for the attentive reader of the *Reflections*.

The writer continues to exhibit Burke's fondness for parading

---

[1] Op. cit., IV, 44–6. (One of Mrs. Siddons' most successful parts was as Jane Shore in Nicholas Rowe's play by that name (1714).)

his emotional facility by recalling, as a footnote has it, 'Mr. Burke's *great history-piece of the massacre of the innocents*'[1] at the Hastings trial in his description of the barbarities committed by Devi Sing. The 'tragedy' of 6 October in France 'surpasses all /That [he] imported from Bengal'. This, too, is interesting. Like Benjamin Bousfield,[2] the anonymous poet is linking Burke with the sublime-school of painters; he is suggesting that Burke works on a vast canvas with the kind of theatrical grandeur one associates with a painter such as James Barry or, later, James Martin. He proposes, in other words, that Burke's aim is not to achieve truth but grandiloquent art.

The heroic couplet is the form chosen by the same writer for his *Heroic Epistle to Burke* (1791) in which, he claims, 'there is scarcely a single image . . . which is not extracted from Mr. Burke's celebrated *Reflections*'. His claim is borne out in a passage such as this:

> So awful grandeur guards the Gothic hall,
> And crests and mantles dignify the wall;
> Ensigns armorial, pedigrees sublime,
> And wax and parchment half as old as time:
> The sombrous list succeeding years extend,
> And sacred lumber bids the rafters bend.
> 'Mid frowning forms in coronets and cowls,
> The bat engenders, and the tempest howls:
> When lo! awakes from monumental rest,
> With fees and fines, and mortgages opprest,
> The beggar'd heir. Prince, bishop, marquis, knight,
> To foreign garrets wing their solemn flight.
> The cumbrous ruin falls, no more to rise,
> And simplest masonry the place supplies.[3]

Combining satire on emotive prose—so like poetry that it can easily be versified—with criticism of obscurantism and the useless lumber of antiquity, the author subtly uses Burke's own diction to mock his views. Quite clearly 'the beggar'd heir' represents contemporary man newly alive to the fact that his heritage is worthless; it is superficially imposing but inwardly corrupt; and it must be rejected in favour of the 'simplest

---

[1] Op. cit., IV, 47 n.
[2] Cf. *Observations on Burke's Pamphlet*, p. 28.
[3] In *Asylum for Fugitive Pieces*, IV, 33–4.

masonry' which implies a constitution formed in accordance with the unrestricted light of reason. The whole poem (of 110 lines) is managed in this way, subtly and ironically; the writer neatly turns some of Burke's phrases inside out and takes others to absurd conclusions; and the bantering tone is itself a persuasive method, dispelling the aura of dedicated seriousness with which, it is implied, Burke masks invidious principles.

Assured as the anonymous writer is, John Courtenay, M.P. for Tamworth and well known in the Commons for his irony, shows a greater satiric skill in his *Poetical and Philosophical Essay on the French Revolution* (1793). He is both destructive and constructive: he ridicules Burke and denounces the proposed military intervention in France, but also pleads with the French for mercy towards Louis. This positive element is absent from the other verse pamphlets. Moreover, Courtenay is aware of readers who require some literary pleasure as well as controversial vitality; he assumes an audience which will recognise his allusions to established poets.

The poem opens with a mock-invocation to 'Ye Nuns and Capuchins' whose 'ravish'd joys' the apostate Whig, Burke, 'now labours to restore'. Having linked his opponent with the symbol of obscuranticism and political oppression, Courtenay attacks him on by now familiar lines:

> To sooth vain sorrows, your Knight-Errant flies,
> With real grief he scorns to sympathise;
> Dramatic woe in splendid fiction's dress,
> He bodies forth—to weep at the distress!
> Of pomps and vanities bewails the loss,
> Cries o'er the Ribband, and adores the Cross.
> Ye poor and wretched, suffer and be dumb,
> And wait for happiness in worlds to come;
> With meekness, patience, your sad duties fill,
> What's cold and hunger to ideal ill?
> When vice is gross, he owns 'tis mean and base,
> But polish'd vice assumes bright Virtue's grace;
> By Dovey's art, as spurious diamonds shine,
> And boast the splendour of Golconda's mine.
> Vice decks a Lord, but ill becomes a Swain;
> Charming at Court, but odious on the Plain.[1]

[1] Op. cit., pp. 3–4.

This denunciation of Burke's luxuriating in imagined and ignoring actual distress is not new, but there is a greater indignation on behalf of despised poverty than appears in the other poems. The sympathy for the poor which Wollstonecraft rather extravagantly expresses is here restrained, but it comes through with ironic bitterness. Courtenay also, by his allusion to Pope's *Epistle to a Lady*[1] in the last lines, subtly identifies Burke with the aristocratic world of that poem. The choice of words—'Swain', 'Charming', 'odious'—admirably catches the attitudes of that world, with its distance from the life of the poor and its pastoral pretensions. A further Popeian allusion confirms the subtlety with which Courtenay writes. He comments after the passage above:

> Such Edmund's logic, such his moral page,
> Fit for the bar, the pulpit, and the stage.

Pope's famous line from the *Epilogue to the Satires* is slightly modified, but the changes are in harmony with the overriding intention to degrade Burke's logic and morality and to show that both are the servants of his desire to make an affecting public spectacle. But the reader who recognised the allusion would also know the whole of Pope's couplet:

> Safe from the Bar, the Pulpit, and the Throne,
> Yet touch'd and sham'd by Ridicule alone.

There can be little doubt that Courtenay allowed the second line to make its own impact: it conveys precisely his own attitude to Burke. It expresses, too, the hope of all the ironists mentioned here.

After further writing of this kind, with more allusions to Pope, Milton, and perhaps Johnson, and more ironic sallies against 'the dazzling Sophist':

> Soaring in mystic prose, 'bove flights in rhyme,
> Th' obscure he proves one source of the sublime[2]

Courtenay turns to the achievement of France where liberty shines 'in splendid triumph':

> No slaves in arms now shield a despot's throne,
> Man's sacred claims her generous soldiers own.

---

[1] Cf. ll. 37–40. [2] Op. cit., p. 7.

He looks forward to the spread of liberty throughout Europe, including England, and trusts that, recognising the sanctity of human life, the French will extend mercy to Louis.

There is a finish and completeness about this poem which set it above the others: a finish in that the verse is competently handled with a recognition of the complex pleasure as well as the lively irony which it can convey; and a completeness in that Courtenay not only satirises Burke but also contrives to set the Revolution in the context of a European desire for liberty.

Finally, the verse-writers serve especially to focus our attention on perhaps the main problem facing all Burke's opponents. Their genuine object was to proclaim what they considered the truth about the French Revolution and its fundamental principles, to rely on 'fact when simply drest', and to use 'the plain English garb of language'.

> I believe your paradoxes may be safely entrusted to the ordinary sense of mankind notwithstanding the authority of your name and the splendid oratory with which they are introduced.[1]

But no single pamphleteer acted wholly on this belief, not even Boothby whose words these are: indeed he follows this very statement with a ten-page attempt to counter one of Burke's 'paradoxes'. The verse-writers make great play with the overpitched writing in the *Reflections*:

> Choice stories these, when finely penn'd!
> For what?—To set the hair on end;
> To blanch with horror ladies' cheeks;
> To call forth groans and piteous shrieks:
> To make men stare, and children cry;—
> What pity 'tis they're all—[2]

It is admirable ridicule, but no writing could be further from the 'sober reasoning' that Priestley thought essential; the very choice of verse is an implicit avowal that emotive means are central to the problem of persuasion, and that when 'choice stories' are 'finely penn'd' no dispassionate display of facts will undo their effect. The liberal pamphleteers did not, of course, try to rival Burke in his field of eloquence (or when they did, failure invariably resulted). The best of them rely on firm, lucid, vigorous

[1] Boothby, *Letter to Burke*, p. 43.
[2] *Reflections on Reflections*, in *Asylum for Fugitive Pieces*, IV, 48.

writing which conveys not only their conviction that the Revolution was necessary and highly significant but also the fervour with which they held that conviction. It is when they encounter what they allege to be Burke's attempts 'to persuade men to believe something more than we are willing to assert in plain terms or can prove by plain argument',[1] that mere expressions of a contrary belief, however fervent, are inadequate. Then 'arduous efforts of critical skill' (as Mackintosh called them) are required; Burke's emotive and imaginative appeal has to be analysed—as Mackintosh does it on occasions or like Paine when he exposes Burke's dramatic techniques—and a viewpoint which is intellectually more acceptable and emotionally of at least equal compulsion substituted. Though many writers attempt this difficult task, only a few—Paine, Mackintosh, Christie, and perhaps Wollstonecraft—succeed. Nevertheless, Burke's opponents collectively subjected the *Reflections* to more scrutiny and attack than has perhaps ever converged on any other single work; they exposed his weaknesses and subterfuges with extraordinary care; and though the existence of their writings and the urgency of their tone are an implicit tribute to the persuasive force of the *Reflections*, they were all imbued with the confidence suggested in the title of this chapter and reiterated in Priestley's words:

> Prejudice and error is only a *mist*, which the sun, which has now risen, will effectually disperse. Keep them about you as tight as the countryman in the fable did his cloak; the same sun, without any more violence than the warmth of his beams, will compel you to throw it aside, unless you chuse to sweat under it, and bear all the ridicule of your cooler and less encumbered companions.[2]

[1] Boothby, op. cit., p. 56.   [2] *Letters to Burke*, p. 111.

XI

WILLIAM GODWIN, PHILOSOPHER AND NOVELIST

I

Priestley's confidence, expressed in the quotation at the end of the last chapter, was fully shared by Godwin; indeed, the faith that prompted the writing of *Political Justice* (1793) may well be summed up by another of Priestley's statements:

> *to follow truth wherever it leads you,* confident that the interests of truth will ever be inseparable from those of virtue and happiness, and equally so to states, as to individuals.[1]

Though, then, their political beliefs diverged—democracy, so highly esteemed by Priestley, did not have Godwin's unqualified approval—their fundamental conviction of the inevitable triumph of truth to be secured by the exercise of unfettered reason was identical. It was, of course, a conviction Godwin shared with all the radical pamphleteers—and yet his *Political Justice* from the standpoint of literary criticism as well as political theory was *sui generis*. If in nothing else, in its comprehensiveness and thoroughgoing determination 'to follow truth' wherever it led him, Godwin's work stood alone.

It may seem at first sight, however, that Godwin does not strictly belong in a study of political controversy, that in *Political Justice* he almost defiantly remains aloof from the furore over Burke's *Reflections*, examining all sides but taking

---

[1] *Letters to Burke*, p. 112.

none. He was certainly not involved as were Paine, Mackintosh, Wollstonecraft, or the others previously discussed; his scope and freedom of action were not restricted by an intention to attack the case advanced by an eminent individual in one book. It would be ludicrous, of course, to doubt his keen awareness of the controversy—his allusion to it in the preface to *Caleb Williams*[1] as well as his references to Burke and Paine in *Political Justice* make this explicit—but it is true that he was more alert to the ultimate issues it raised than to the particular merits of the *Reflections*. Godwin was concerned with nothing less than the whole question of man's moral nature, and hence the nature of the political society appropriate to the human condition. Yet the fact that *Political Justice* coincided with the effective end of the controversy, that it made a major contribution to political philosophy, and that in it Godwin made a bold attempt to employ the language of speculative reason that the radical pamphleteers claimed to use but failed to sustain, makes its relevance to this study unquestionable.

Moreover, Godwin's novels were written with an avowed didactic intention; just as much as any political pamphlet, they were conceived as part of a campaign to secure popular assent to a certain view of political morality. Indeed, it will be argued subsequently that the novels were more intimately connected with the controversy over Burke's *Reflections* than has been recognised hitherto; they undoubtedly belong in a study of the language of politics connected with that controversy. They also make possible a comparative study of writing addressed to an audience capable of following 'abtruse speculations',[2] and works designed to carry the same message to less philosophically capable readers. Godwin's dual purpose is explicitly stated in the preface to *Caleb Williams* (1794), where he asserts that the truth conveyed by the novel is 'highly worthy to be communicated to persons whom books of philosophy and science are never likely to reach';[3] the people who would read such books had been reached by *Political Justice* in the previous year. And if we may take Hazlitt's estimate as at all

[1] Op. cit. (1831 edn.), p. xix.
[2] Ed. F. E. L. Priestley, *Enquiry concerning Political Justice* (Toronto, 1946), I, 363 n.
[3] Op. cit., p. xix.

accurate—'Truth, moral truth, it was supposed had here [in *Political Justice*] taken up its abode'; '*Caleb Williams* and *St. Leon* are two of the most splendid and impressive works of the imagination that have appeared in our times'[1]—then in Godwin we are dealing with a man who, on contemporary evidence, successfully reached both kinds of audience.

II. POLITICAL JUSTICE

Sound reasoning and truth, when adequately communicated, must always be victorious over error: sound reasoning and truth are capable of being so communicated.[2]

The twin beliefs expressed here—faith in the victory of truth and in the possibility of communicating truth so that the victory is realised—are central both to the philosophical system expounded in *Political Justice* and to the literary methods used to communicate it. Indeed, as has been demonstrated in earlier chapters, style is not only a means of conveying ideas, it is at the same time an incarnation of their validity and reasonableness; the qualities of Godwin's style—lucidity, logic, directness, plainness and so on—are themselves witnesses to the philosophical position he maintains on the level of formal argument. For example, he argues that openness and complete honesty are essential in human relationships, that 'reason and conviction' are proper and sufficient 'for regulating the actions of mankind',[3] that justice—'the true standard of the conduct of one man towards another'—requires the individual to be 'an impartial spectator of human concerns, and divest [himself] of retrospect to [his] own predilections',[4] or that man's most desirable state is one of 'high civilisation'.[5] Such and other philosophical claims are sustained by complex and lengthy argument, but what is being asserted at this point is that their validity is mirrored in qualities of style. To take one characteristic paragraph (from the chapter on 'Promises');

The foundation of morality is justice. The principle of virtue is an irresistible deduction from the wants of one man, and the ability of another to relieve them. It is not because I have promised, that I am bound to do that for my neighbour, which

[1] *Works*, XI, 17, 24. [2] *Political Justice* (hereafter *P.J.*), I, 86.
[3] Ibid., I, 70. [4] Ibid., I. xxv. [5] Ibid., I. xxiii.

will be beneficial to him, and not injurious to me. This is an obligation which arises out of no compact, direct or understood; and would still remain, though it were impossible that I should experience a return, either from him or any other human being. It is not on account of any promise or previous engagement, that I am bound to tell my neighbour the truth. Undoubtedly one of the reasons why I should do so, is, because the obvious use of the faculty of speech is to inform, and not to mislead. But it is an absurd account of this motive, to say, that my having recourse to the faculty of speech, amounts to a tacit engagement that I will use it for its genuine purposes. The true ground of confidence between man and man, is the knowledge we have of the motives by which the human mind is influenced; our perception, that the motives to deceive can but rarely occur, while the motives to veracity will govern the stream of human actions.[1]

Such is Godwin's normal level of writing—and this should be remembered when critical reservations are stated later—and the qualities it exhibits are precisely those of honesty and openness, confidence and disinterestedness that were mentioned above. The movement of the writing is leisurely but controlled; the writer is determined not to sidestep difficulties, but rigorously to follow where his argument leads him; he writes as 'an impartial spectator of human concerns', and since he communicates his ideas lucidly and logically, his style is doing its job of acting as a warranty for the proposition being presented. Burke's style, for example, would defeat Godwin's purpose: Burke is not open and direct, he is not disinterested, and his writing evidences the importance of feeling not of reason.

Stated in this way the point is obvious, but what is perhaps less immediately evident is the extent to which the principle is at once a source of liberation and of restriction to the writer in question. Godwin had to establish an image of himself as an honest, scrupulous enquirer for whom truth, plain and unadorned, was the absolute objective. His method of presentation —which directly influences the structure of his sentences and paragraphs as well as choice of language—had to demonstrate that no by-ways of argument were too troublesome, no possible objection too minute to be ignored. It was almost inevitable, then, that his writing would be loose-limbed; it could not have

[1] *P.J.*, I, 195.

the kind of precision, economy, and pungency that contribute
to the Swiftian type of clarity, but was more likely to resemble
Johnson's. Godwin's writing in fact comes much closer to
achieving the sort of lucidity and fullness one associates with the
Rambler style, whose movement and scope are comprehensive
enough to embrace nuances of argument and shades of philosophical discrimination. Stylistic amplitude of this kind was
permissible, but, on the other hand, many rhetorical devices
would have been inappropriate. Godwin could not indulge, for
instance, an apostrophe even to Truth on the lines of Burke's to
the French Queen; exaggeration and over-statement were not
for him; and frequent emotive heightening of language would
be out of place. Such devices might make his integrity suspect,
they would certainly mar the image it was essential to create.
Irony too would be a dangerous weapon: irony puts a reader
on his guard against deception and inhibits his response to the
surface meaning of words. Godwin had to avoid possible mis-
interpretation, and since his task was (to use Mary Wollstonecraft's words) 'to labour to increase human happiness by
extirpating error', his own style could run no risks such as
Defoe ran with *The Shortest Way with the Dissenters*.

One section of *Political Justice*—'Of Political Associations'—
makes clear Godwin's strong suspicion of rhetorical devices in
political speeches; these suspicions were carried over into his
own philosophical writing. 'Harangue and declamation' are
decried because they 'lead to passion, and not to knowledge';
they fill the mind with 'pompous nothings' or with mere
'images', whereas it is with 'argument' that the memory should
be stored.[1] Godwin acts on the principles stated here in two
ways: he eschews the methods denounced, but also, more
subtly, he frequently uses an imaginary objector to test the
theory advanced in *Political Justice* and allows him to indulge in
'pompous nothings' and trite metaphors.

> Democracy is a monstrous and unwieldy vessel, launched upon
> the sea of human passions, without ballast. Liberty, in this
> unlimited form, is in danger to be lost, almost as soon as it is
> obtained.[2]

Here the objector is given the high-flown language of a political
orator; there is a false buoyancy about the rhythm and a

[1] *P.J.*, I, 290.   [2] Ibid., II, 116.

flabby cocksureness about the thought. Such pitfalls Godwin himself normally avoids; he usually achieves that 'accuracy of language' that he considers 'the indispensible prerequisite of sound knowledge',[1] but again restrictions follow. Burke and Paine provide obvious examples for reference. They do not deny themselves the freedom to exploit language to achieve an impassioned response; they both present argument, but the reader remembers it not as an abstraction but as vividly attached to images, descriptions, people, or events. Burke and Paine do not assume that 'a plain and direct appeal to [the] understanding'[2] of their readers will achieve the complete persuasion they intend; Godwin must assume it, or his philosophical position is falsified. The consequence, however, seems to be that Godwin is so concerned with accuracy of language, with primary, dictionary meaning, that his use of words is wooden; he is frequently unadventurous in expression, so occupied with careful analysis of ideas that he fails to carry the truth and relevance of them alive to his readers. A brief example will serve temporarily to make the point. Mary Wollstonecraft had berated Burke for considering the poor 'as only the live stock of an estate, the feather of hereditary nobility'[3]; Godwin is content to observe that a vassal 'was regarded as a sort of live stock upon the estate'.[4] The difference is small but typical. Wollstonecraft's object is to enforce her meaning by vivid, emotive means, Godwin's to communicate an idea; the metaphorical elaboration she indulges is irrelevant to him, and any such superfluity is rigorously excluded. From Godwin's standpoint he is completely justified; the philosophical need for accurate, plain language imposes restraint on him; but we should note the price he pays in expressional timidity.

'Truth dwells with contemplation' is an admirable belief for a closet-philosopher but it can enfeeble the effectiveness of writing which aims—as Godwin's so obviously does—at influencing human conduct. 'Whatever can be adequately brought home to the conviction of the understanding, may be depended upon as affording a secure hold upon the conduct.'[5] There is truth here—if complete conviction is achieved we may well expect appropriate action to follow—but conviction de-

[1] *P.J.*, I, 385.   [2] Ibid., I, 297.   [3] See above, p. 171.
[4] *P.J.*, I, 23.   [5] Ibid., I, 79.

pends partly at least on our recognising the relevance of abstract principles to a real-life situation. Godwin's language, however, frequently suggests that he is remote from the specific details of life. A man who adduces an illustration from billiards, for example, and writes about 'the impinging of one ball of matter upon another and its consequences',[1] may fairly be charged with being remote from the world in which the conduct he hopes to influence is to operate.

Nevertheless, it would be wrong to infer that Godwin does not feel strongly about the principles he advances or that the feeling is kept out of his writing. As one sample paragraph, the following comes from the section on the 'General Features of Democracy':

> Supposing that we should even be obliged to take democracy with all the disadvantages that were ever annexed to it, and that no remedy could be discovered for any of its defects, it would still be preferable to the exclusive system of other forms. Let us take Athens, with all its turbulence and instability; with the popular and temperate usurpations of Pisistratus and Pericles; with its monstrous ostracism, by which, with undisguised injustice, they were accustomed periodically to banish some eminent citizen, without the imputation of a crime; with the imprisonment of Miltiades, the exile of Aristides, and the murder of Phocion:— with all these errors on its head, it is incontrovertible that Athens exhibited a more illustrious and enviable spectacle, than all the monarchies and aristocracies that ever existed. Who would reject their gallant love of virtue and independence, because it was accompanied with irregularities? Who would pass an unreserved condemnation upon their penetrating mind, their quick discernment, and their ardent feeling, because they were subject occasionally to be intemperate and impetuous? Shall we compare a people of such incredible achievements, such exquisite refinement, gay without insensibility, and splendid without intemperance, . . . shall we compare this chosen seat of patriotism, independence and generous virtue, with the torpid and selfish realms of monarchy and aristocracy? All is not happiness that looks tranquillity. Better were a portion of turbulence and fluctuation, than that unwholsome calm in which all the best faculties of the human mind are turned to putrescence and poison.[2]

[1] *P.J.*, I, 373. [2] Ibid., II, 117–19.

Here relevant emotion comes vigorously through; Godwin is showing, as a philosopher may legitimately be required to do, the excitement and urgency he experienced during the act of contemplating his subject; and his emotions are related to the facts as well as to the abstract qualities of Athenian democracy. The emotion produces the brief allusion to the older Hamlet—the symbol of perfection to his son—'sent to [his] account/With all [his] imperfections on [his] head'; the allusion is timely in view of Godwin's argument and, further, it intensifies as well as giving the measure of his own feelings. The questions are more than mere rhetorical tricks; they convey not only summary judgments but also Godwin's genuine astonishment at the extent of Athenian achievements within the severe limitations of their democratic system. Nor is the feeling out of hand: it is channelled, with just a hint of Johnsonian phrasing in 'gay without insensibility, and splendid without intemperance', and moves inevitably forward to the aphorism—'all is not happiness that looks tranquillity'—which might itself have come from *Rasselas*, and finally to a biting, alliterative close. This is what De Quincey might have called literature of knowledge becoming literature of power; the significance of the facts Godwin is contemplating is carried along by his emotional response to them, and the felt experience of the contemplation becomes the persuasive factor.

To return to Godwin's philosophical principles, it might be thought that they were of a kind to demand concrete illustration to show their relevance to actual human existence. The individual living his moral life in society is the focal point of Godwin's deliberations: 'individuals are everything, and society, abstracted from the individuals of which it is composed, nothing'.[1] Yet he is often more concerned to demonstrate how abstract principles operate on Man than on men. For example, when he is discussing the necessity for equality he contrasts a possible state of material well-being with the poverty afflicting many of his contemporaries:

Every man would have a frugal, yet wholsome diet; every man would go forth to that moderate exercise of his corporal functions, that would give hilarity to the spirits; none would be made torpid with fatigue, but all would have leisure to cultivate the

[1] *P.J.*, II, 176.

kindly and philanthropical affections, and to let loose his faculties in the search of intellectual improvement. What a contrast does this scene present, to the present state of society, where the peasant and the labourer work, till their understandings are benumbed with toil, their sinews contracted and made callous by being for ever on the stretch, and their bodies invaded with infirmities, and surrendered to an untimely grave? What is the fruit they obtain from this disproportioned and unceasing toil? In the evening they return to a family, famished with hunger, exposed half naked to the inclemencies of the sky, hardly sheltered, and denied the slenderest instruction. . . .[1]

There are parts of this extract that are almost parodies of Augustan periphrasis and generalities; from the evidence of this language there is no sign that Godwin knew more of poverty than he could learn, say, from Lear's speech on the heath or some of Cowper's poems; it smacks of the second-hand and diminishes Godwin's authority to discuss the subject. As a contrast, to read Swift's *Short View of the State of Ireland* is to be in touch with a writer whose authority to speak about poverty is established by the language he uses:

. . . The Families of Farmers, who pay great Rents, living in Filth and Nastiness upon Butter-milk and Potatoes, without a Shoe or Stocking to their Feet; or a House so convenient as an *English* Hog-sty to receive them. . . . The Rise of our Rents is squeezed out of the very Blood, and Vitals and Cloaths, and Dwellings of the Tenants; who live worse then *English* Beggars.[2]

Here, where Swift has explicitly abandoned his favourite irony, he is speaking from the kind of felt experience of poverty that we look for in vain in *Political Justice*.

If it be argued that Godwin is at an unfair disadvantage in a comparison with the pamphleteer Swift, the point can be made through a comparison with Johnson whose penchant for general wisdom needs no emphasis. Towards the end of *Political Justice* Godwin considers 'the received system of marriage' and describes the way that people in 'European countries' come to marry:

The method is, for a thoughtless and romantic youth of each sex, to come together, to see each other, for a few times, and under

[1] *P.J.*, II, 460–1.
[2] Ed. H. Davis, *Irish Tracts 1728–1733* (Oxford, 1955), pp. 10–11.

circumstances full of delusion, and then to vow eternal attachment.[1]

Such a description is so generalised as to be worthless; there were, it is true, the Lydia Bennetts, but there were also the Emma Woodhouses of Godwin's day; but more crippling is the fact that the language is out of touch with the situation it is supposed to describe. Johnson, putting precisely the same view, gives Rasselas this to say:

> A youth and maiden, meeting by chance, or brought together by artifice, exchange glances, reciprocate civilities, go home, and dream of one another. Having little to divert attention, or diversify thought, they find themselves uneasy, when they are apart, and therefore conclude that they shall be happy together. They marry. . . .[2]

This, too, is a generalised account; it, too, can be indicted for the same bias as shown by Godwin; but the language establishes Johnson's implicit claim that he is providing a general view of actual experience. 'Meeting by chance', 'exchange glances', 'go home', 'dream of one another', 'uneasy': such terms spring from the facts of human existence. Moreover, Johnson reinforces his case by stylistic means, by witty antithesis, where Godwin's is presented plain.

A further comparison between the same two writers is at hand in their respective attacks on the optimistic philosophers and the view of evil as universal good. Godwin announces that he wishes to avoid 'a pompous and delusive survey of the whole'; he wants to break down the total picture of 'pain and calamity' and 'examine parts severally and individually'.[3] This seems to promise the kind of specificity we have charged Godwin with omitting, but the promise is not fulfilled. He does not, it is true, write about human ills in the mass; instead he subdivides the total pain and discusses kinds—the sufferings resulting from poverty, illness, mental anguish, punishment, and the like—but speaks of each in the abstract. We read of the poor 'tormented with injustice, or chilled into lethargy'; we 'plunge into the depths of dungeons [to] observe youth languishing in hopeless despair'; or we 'view man writhing under the pangs of disease'. Language is here keeping life at arm's length;

[1] *P.J.*, II, 507.   [2] *Works*, I, 260.   [3] *P.J.*, I, 455.

we cannot doubt Godwin's genuineness of emotion, but the facts that cause him distress scarcely even peep through the blanket of abstraction. In contrast, Johnson not only writes with greater vivacity—having the specific case of Soame Jenyns in view—but also with greater particularity. Jenyns had suggested that 'the beings above us' perhaps torment us for 'their own pleasure or utility'; Johnson translates these activities into terms of human existence, and the facts of suffering are presented at every turn:

> As we shoot a bird flying, they take a man in the midst of his business or pleasure, and knock him down with an apoplexy. . . . To swell a man with a tympany is as good sport as to blow a frog . . . good sport it is to see a man tumble with an epilepsy, and revive and tumble again, and all this he knows not why . . . the paroxysms of the gout and stone, which, undoubtedly, must make high mirth.[1]

It must be allowed, of course, that Johnson is scoring debating points—though they add up to a considered view of human life—and he is not out to contemplate truth in Godwin's manner, but there can be little doubt which writer more effectively establishes his claim in the reader's mind. To observe that Godwin throughout speaks of 'man' whereas Johnson on every occasion is concerned with 'a man' is merely to underline the cardinal difference between them.

That there is some similarity of phrasing and rhythm between the two writers is evident; it comes out in a sentence such as the following (when Godwin is announcing at the beginning of Book V how he intends to proceed):

> Under each of these heads it will be our business, in proportion as we adhere to the great and comprehensive principles already established rather to clear away abuses, than to recommend further and more precise regulations, rather to simplify, than to complicate.[2]

There is a Johnsonian amplitude of phrasing and feeling for prose rhythm here. The two writers also show a similar interest in universal principles, in fine shades of moral distinctions, and

[1] 'Review of a Free Enquiry into the Nature and Origin of Evil', in *Works*, VI, 65.
[2] *P.J.*, II, 2.

a comparable ability to conduct an argument by analysis and accumulation. What Godwin lacks, as has been shown, is Johnson's range of real and imaginative experience to illuminate discussion of universals. When Godwin says that noblemen are 'gratified with baubles and splendour'[1] he does not clinch his point either with Johnsonian vigour or with the bite of a writer like Paine. In *The Vanity of Human Wishes* the famous couplets on Wolsey speak of

> the pride of aweful State,
> The golden Canopy, the glitt'ring Plate,
> The regal Palace, the luxurious Board,
> The liv'ried Army, and the menial Lord.

The nouns are generic as they are in Godwin's phrase, but they gain vitality from the generalised adjectives; there is colour, sparkle, life, and human attitudes in Johnson's lines, where Godwin's words draw what emotive force they possess from pejorative associations. Paine's method of expressing his contempt for aristocratic love of ostentatious show is first to dehumanise the people concerned—aristocrats and their 'foppery' become 'it'—and then to translate the folly into terms of childish behaviour: 'it talks about its fine blue *ribbon* like a girl, and shows its new *garter* like a child'.[2] Paine's scorn is thus dramatised and comes alive with great pungency.

There is, however, a quality in Paine's scorn that is absent from Godwin's writing: an element of self-gratification, a sense of enjoyment in his own ability to express his contempt. The sense of power over words, and thence over the object of attack, is, of course, commonly found among ironists. Now Godwin is free of any such emotion; he appears to feel that his intention to communicate truth through 'sound reasoning' would be incompatible with a delight in style for its own sake or a self-gratifying enjoyment of the power to manipulate language. Language for Godwin is a tool to achieve full and clear communication; any aesthetic pleasure it affords is a by-product of secondary importance. Indeed, he gives a clue to his view of the relationship between truth and the emotion which accompanies its discovery or communication:

---

[1] *P.J.*, II, 8.
[2] Ed. P. S. Foner, *Complete Writings*, I, 286.

No one is ignorant of the pleasures of knowledge. . . . Sublime and expansive ideas produce delicious emotions. The acquisition of truth, the perception of the regularity with which proposition flows out of proposition, and one step of science leads to another, has never failed to reward the man who engaged in this species of employment. . . . When we are engaged in promoting [man's] benefit, we are indeed engaged in a sublime and ravishing employment.[1]

This, Godwin would persuade us, is the reward of thinking profoundly, creatively, and altruistically, but it is important to recognise with what care and precision his words are used in describing the reward. He does not rely on emotive associations: 'sublime' does not carry the overtones which were commonly associated with it in the late eighteenth century; it means, as Johnson's dictionary defines it, 'grand' or 'elevated', and similarly 'delicious' means 'agreeable', and 'ravishing', 'rapturous'. Godwin is not trying to excite in his readers an intense feeling of rapture; his sole object is to communicate an experience whose causes he has carefully analysed. The kind of emotional pleasure he describes is analogous to that experienced by a scientist as he contemplates the evolution of a carefully ordered experiment; it is an aesthetic regard for the beauty of relevant and logical form or pattern. Godwin refers above to the regularity with which 'one step of science leads to another' and it is in this sense that he claims 'politics is a science'.[2] Indeed, it is significant that, having associated the 'progress of science' with 'intellectual cultivation', he compares both with 'the taking to pieces a disordered machine, with a purpose, by reconstructing it, of enhancing its value'.[3]

Godwin is here describing his own practice: when writing *Political Justice* he was dismantling and analysing traditional systems of political morality and simultaneously building up his own; the aesthetic pleasure resulting from a contemplation of a logically evolving whole was one of his rewards. But this was essentially a disinterested pleasure, since he acted in literary matters according to his own moral principle that 'the interest of him who is corrected' is of far greater importance than 'the triumph of the corrector'.[4] A brief comparison with Burke will

[1] *P.J.*, I, 308, 309. [2] Ibid., I, 272.
[3] Ibid., II, 243. [4] Ibid., I, 341.

reinforce this claim. In the *Reflections* Burke scornfully dismisses the radical societies:

> Because half a dozen grasshoppers under a fern make the field ring with their importunate chink, whilst thousands of great cattle, reposed beneath the shadow of the British oak, chew the cud and are silent, pray do not imagine that those who make the noise are the only inhabitants of the field; that, of course, they are many in number; or that, after all, they are other than the little, shrivelled, meagre, hopping, though loud and troublesome, insects of the hour.[1]

Godwin, looking to a future when human relationships could be conducted on the basis of 'plain dealing' and honest speech, remarks that his contemporaries were enfeebled by not being used to hearing the truth about themselves. He continues:

> How then can we be justified in thus subverting the nature of things, and the system of the universe, in breeding a set of summer insects, upon which the breeze of sincerity may never blow, and the tempest of misfortune never beat?[2]

The two passages are highly characteristic of their authors. Burke likes to explore the detail of a metaphor, whereas Godwin leaves his metaphors brief, undeveloped, almost casual. Both authors use their images as a means of developing an argument, but Burke is obviously much more intent on mounting an emotional attack and derives a keen delight in his verbal advantage over his opponents. Godwin was entitled to feel as much contempt for men who could not endure plain speaking as was Burke for the radicals, but his expression of it is restrained. He is content to allow the force of the argument, to which this sentence is the conclusion, to make his attitude clear; to exploit an opportunity for irony and bitterness would destroy the effect of calm ratiocination and falsify his moral position. Burke, on the other hand, employs a fund of detail to create a distinct imaginative landscape; the rhythm is manipulated to enforce the contempt contained in the final phrase; and the contrast between the din caused by the insects and their essential insignificance conveys his personal scorn for his adversaries. Burke is indeed more concerned with scoring a literary triumph than with correcting the alleged evil he attacks; the reverse is true of Godwin.

[1] Op. cit., *Works*, II, 357.   [2] *P.J.*, I, 332.

His philosophical tenets required this of him. Godwin maintains that although the present state of society does not promote the capacity of every man to listen 'with sobriety to the dictates of reason',[1] this is no excuse for acting on the assumption that the capacity is non-existent. Men must be treated as intelligent reasonable beings, they will then act as such. From a literary viewpoint this seems to have suggested to him that a clear, level-headed, emotionally subdued and logically conducted prose is generally necessary; it seems also to have inspired the belief that his readers would regard his words in much the same way as biblical language—as all equally inspired and worthy of close attention. At any rate, while he takes great pains to argue with enormous care and propriety—the massive proportions of the book, the cumulative weight of argument, the innumerable subdivisions, definitions of terms, and the like all evidence this—he is not equally sensitive to the constant necessity for vivid, fresh, and compelling prose.

Occasionally Godwin is guilty of undistinguished, even commonplace writing in which words are mere counters. In the section on 'Limited Monarchy', for example, he is discussing the degrading habit of venerating a king, an imperfect being like any other:

> Such is the idol that monarchy worships, in lieu of the divinity of truth, and the sacred obligation of public good. It is of little consequence whether we vow fidelity to the king and the nation, or to the nation and the king, so long as the king intrudes himself to tarnish and undermine the true simplicity, the altar of virtue.[2]

'Idol', 'shrine', 'sacred', 'altar' (and 'shrine' occurs in the next paragraph) show a flabby imagination which is not actively searching out its own fresh terminology but is content to draw on the capital of clichés amassed by radical thinkers. A quotation from the Bible in the succeeding paragraph—'we cannot "bow the head in the temple of Rimmon" '—highlights his own imaginative paucity; there is a sharp contrast between Godwin and the biblical writer whose idiom derived from an actual situation and was appropriate to it as well as to his own cast of mind. Godwin's phrase in the same paragraph, 'bend the knee before the shrine of vanity and folly', may have some

---

[1] *P.J.*, I, 181.   [2] Ibid., II, 77.

reference to courtly manners (though this is not clear), but it has no actuality, none of the vivid concreteness that comes from genuinely felt experience. The phrase is an easy way out and relieves Godwin of the responsibility of thinking freshly and creatively about his language.

It is noticeable too that when Godwin quotes from another author he rarely shows himself aware of the value of a quotation to intensify the impact of his own ideas; the few occasions when this awareness is revealed emphasise his failure on others. When he is describing the ubiquitous parade of kingly pomp in a limited monarchy, he comments: 'We find him like Pharaoh's frogs, "in our houses, and upon our beds, in our ovens, and our kneading troughs".'[1] The quotation is excellently used here; his own contempt and irritation are admirably focused by the biblical words. On the other hand, writing about the relative inadequacy of sensual pleasures, Godwin instances a man sitting alone at a splendid feast, ' "taste after taste upheld with kindliest change" '.[2] The Miltonic quotation adds no compelling vividness to the pleasures of the table and might just as well have been omitted. Or again, he remarks that 'it has been the perpetual complaint of despotism, that "the restive knaves are overrun with ease, and plenty ever is the nurse of faction" '.[3] Here Rowe's play *Jane Shore* is the source, but to what purpose? Neither vividness nor pungency are added. Clearly the choice of quotations is dictated solely by their surface usefulness to an argument but without the recognition—such as we find in Matthew Arnold, for example—of the extra contribution they can make to the energy with which an argument is stated. One is reminded of Godwin's observation that if a man aspires to be a poet or historian, so far as he is influenced by reason his object is to be 'useful to mankind'.[4] A similar limited sense of utility directs his own use of quotation.

Indeed, the more one looks critically at Godwin's language the more one becomes aware of his utilitarian view of it. This is, of course, not to denigrate such a view—every writer must be guided by a sense of utility—but to suggest its limitations. On a strict utilitarian basis a cliché can be useful; it is meaningful and may be relevant; only a developed critical sense of

---

[1] *P.J.*, II, 70–1. [2] Ibid., I, 72.
[3] Ibid., II, 28–9. [4] Ibid., II, 179.

language will reject the cliché on the grounds that, like an old joke, it will fail to evoke a spirited response. Probably no writer has ever been more aware of the utility of language than Swift, but a quotation from *Gulliver's Travels* which Godwin introduces early in *Political Justice* serves to underline the marked differences between the two writers. The passage lists the causes of war as Gulliver relates them to the Master Houhyhnhnm, and a single glance reveals its satiric purpose:

> Sometimes the quarrel between two princes is to decide which of them shall dispossess a third of his dominions, where neither of them pretends to any right. . . . It is a very justifiable cause of war to invade a country after the people have been wasted by famine, destroyed by pestilence, or embroiled by factions among themselves. It is justifiable to enter into a war against our nearest ally, when one of his towns lies convenient for us, or a territory of land that would render our dominions round and compact. If a prince sends forces into a nation where the people are poor and ignorant, he may lawfully put the half of them to death, and make slaves of the rest, in order to civilise and reduce them from their barbarous way of living. . . .[1]

Here words are used with great precision so that the tone of honest confession on Gulliver's part is sustained, but without any cost to the irony which pervades the passage; characterisation and exposure are simultaneously achieved. The prose is not, like Godwin's, loose-limbed; it is economical, moves rapidly, and has a cumulative purpose—after reading the passage one might be (wrongly) tempted into thinking that this is an exhaustive list of the causes of war. From Godwin's viewpoint its surface statement is useful; he remarks that in it 'the usual causes of war are excellently described' but does not comment on the irony of the passage, nor, at the end, does he make any further reference to it; he switches immediately to an analysis of domestic policy in established societies. Its usefulness is at an end. Later, in Book V of *Political Justice*, Godwin returns to the subject of war, examining and rejecting the reasons normally given for making war. One paragraph from this analysis will illustrate what is implied by calling his language utilitarian.

---

[1] *P.J.*, I, 11–12.

'The vindication of national honour', is a very insufficient reason for hostilities. True honour is to be found only in integrity and justice. It has been doubted, how far a view to reputation, ought, in matters of inferior moment, to be permitted to influence the conduct of individuals; but, let the case of individuals be decided as it may, reputation, considered as a separate motive in the instance of nations, can perhaps never be justifiable. In individuals, it seems as if I might, consistently with the utmost real integrity, be so misconstrued and misrepresented by others, as to render my efforts at usefulness almost necessarily abortive. But this reason does not apply to the case of nations. Their real story cannot easily be suppressed. Usefulness and public spirit, in relation to them, chiefly belong to the transactions of their members among themselves; and their influence in the transactions of neighbouring nations, is a consideration evidently subordinate.—The question which respects the justifiable causes of war, would be liable to few difficulties, if we were accustomed, along with the word, strongly to call up to our minds the thing which that word is intended to represent.[1]

Compared with the Swiftian extract, the movement of this prose is lumbering; in an effort to comprehend the ramifications of the argument Godwin intentionally moves slowly, almost meanders to the end of his paragraph. Economy of language is not important to him; as in the novels, so here rapid transitions are not aimed at. Hazlitt's assertion that 'no style is worth a farthing that is not calculated to be read out, or that is not allied to spirited conversation'[2] is ludicrously inappropriate to a style where punctuation and subordinate clauses proliferate and clog its motion. Nor is Godwin consistently alive to the way in which syntax controls rhythm and emphasis; his brief sentences are cogent but in the third sentence, for example, the main proposition is obscured by qualifications, modifications, and exceptions. And to observe that at no point in the paragraph is the abstract thought vivified by metaphor or imaginative reference to the world in which wars are fought or 'the conduct of individuals' takes place, is to stress the obvious. Yet concentrated attention undoubtedly reveals Godwin's meaning; the words are useful in conveying ideas from him to us, and to object that the reader's labour could have been less arduous, that language can be at

[1] Ibid., II, 151.   [2] *Works*, XII, 7.

once meaningful and aesthetically rewarding, would be to introduce premises of no concern to Godwin.

For, ultimately, meaning, 'truth and sober reasoning' are his prime objects. Even when Godwin contemplates the highest reaches of human happiness—those enjoyed by the man who disinterestedly tries to promote the well-being of others—his idiom prevents any full communication of the joy he speaks about. 'No man so truly promotes his own interest, as he that forgets it. No man reaps so copious a harvest of pleasure, as he who thinks only of the pleasures of other men.'[1] The concept obviously means a great deal to Godwin; it is expressed with clarity, even with urgency, despite the commonplace metaphor; but the richness of the pleasure itself does not come across to us. Godwin does not exclude the relevant emotion that the idea stirs in him, but it is allowed to come through only by means of argument and affirmation. The force of the argument provides the objective correlative of the emotion. Godwin's is a rhetoric of statement which, at its best, makes a distinctive impact through tight logic and urgent affirmation and through its tone of personal conviction; at times it carries an almost messianic fervour. Such are the qualities displayed in this paragraph where, midway through his chapter on 'Good and Evil', he contemplates the improvement of mankind:

> The inference from this survey of human life, is, that he who is fully persuaded that pleasure is the only good, ought by no means to leave every man to enjoy his peculiar pleasure according to his own peculiar humour. Seeing the great disparity there is between different conditions of human life, he ought constantly to endeavour to raise each class, and every individual of each class, to a class above it. This is the true equalisation of mankind. Not to pull down those who are exalted, and reduce all to a naked and savage equality. But to raise those who are abased; to communicate to every man all genuine pleasures, to elevate every man to all true wisdom, and to make all men participators of a liberal and comprehensive benevolence. This is the path in which the reformers of mankind ought to travel. This is the prize they should pursue. Do you tell me, 'that human society can never arrive at this improvement?' I do not stay to dispute that point with you. We can come nearer it than we are. We can come nearer and nearer yet. This will not be the first time that persons, engaged in

[1] *P.J.*, I, 447–8.

the indefatigable pursuit of some accomplishment, have arrived at an excellence that surpassed their most sanguine expectations.[1]

The biblical rhythms and phrasing in mid-paragraph, the repetitions later, the onward flow of the prose, the overt evidence in 'I do not stay to dispute . . .', all emphasise the powerful feeling lying behind this writing. The emotion does not excite Godwin to fresh metaphors; he continues to rely on the traditional—'not to pull down those who are exalted', 'the path' men should 'travel', 'the prize they should pursue'; yet the vigorous affirmations evidencing unshakeable conviction remain both impressive and persuasive.

III. GODWIN AND BURKE

It is a commonplace in Godwin-criticism to cite the novels as demonstrating the working of his ideas on society in human situations. D. H. Monro remarks, for example, in his enlightening book, *Godwin's Moral Philosophy*: 'Indeed [the novels] show, more clearly than his avowedly political writing, exactly how he thought of his principles as working out in practice.'[2] Monro goes on to argue that in *Caleb Williams* not only is the country squire, Falkland, able to persecute Caleb because of his superior social position—and thus illustrate the claim of *Political Justice* that a tyrannous social organisation gives its character to the individuals who comprise it—but also that in Falkland Godwin symbolises 'the whole idea of Honour'. 'He is the spirit of Monarchy made visible.'[3] A similar argument is advanced by P. N. Furbank, though he detects a more complex symbolism working in Caleb's curiosity to discover the secrets hidden in Falkland's trunk, a discovery that leads to Caleb's persecution:

> In this plot Caleb Williams is clearly Godwin himself, Falkland the *ancien régime*, and the opening of the trunk is the writing of *Political Justice*. The secret of the trunk is the secret which Godwin brings to the light of day in *Political Justice*, the guilty secret of government: and in describing Caleb's fierce glee and terror at making the discovery he is describing his own emotion at conceiving the theories of that work.[4]

[1] *P.J.*, I, 448.   [2] Op. cit. (1953), p. 87.   [3] Ibid., p. 88.
[4] 'Godwin's Novels', *Essays in Criticism* (1955), V, 215–16.

Both Monro and Furbank are justified in their claims, but neither pushes his argument far enough; they see the relationship between the novels and *Political Justice*, but fail to recognise that the former have a further point of reference in the controversy over Burke's *Reflections*. Burke is a key figure in a very real sense.

The clue appears in a passage within a few pages of the end of *Political Justice*—and it is well to remember Godwin's statement that *Caleb Williams* was 'the offspring of that temper of mind in which the composition of *Political Justice* left [him]'.[1] In this passage Godwin addresses himself to 'the *enlightened* and *accomplished* advocates of aristocracy':

> 'We know', I would say, 'that truth will be triumphant, even though you refuse to be her ally. We do not fear your enmity. But our hearts bleed to see such gallantry, talents and virtue employed in perpetuating the calamities of mankind. We recollect with grief, that when the lustre of your merits shall fill distant generations with astonishment, they will not be less astonished, that you could be made the dupes of prejudice, and deliberately surrender the larger portion of the good you might have achieved, and the unqualified affection that might have pursued your memory.'[2]

The tone of respectful regret, admiration for talents mixed with sorrow at their application, is enough in itself to remind one of Caleb's attitude to Falkland. Despite the relentless persecution he had suffered from the intrinsically noble Falkland, and despite the murder Falkland had committed to preserve his chivalric sense of honour, Caleb considers him 'worthy of reverence . . . he was endowed with qualities that partook of divine'.[3]

> Mr. Falkland is of a noble nature. Yes; in spite of the catastrophe of Tyrrel [whom he murdered], of the miserable end of the Hawkinses [wrongly executed for the murder], and of all that I have myself suffered, I affirm that he has qualities of the most admirable kind.[4]

In both novel and philosophical treatise, then, the tone is the same: profound admiration for certain qualities and regret

[1] C. Kegan Paul, *William Godwin* (1876), I, 78.
[2] *P.J.*, II, 545 (my italics).
[3] *Caleb Williams* (hereafter *C.W.*), p. 445.   [4] Ibid., p. 448.

for their misuse. This, as has been remarked, is enough to stimulate interest in the passage from *Political Justice*; the interest is intensified by a note added in the 1796 edition: 'In this passage Mr. Burke was particularly in the mind of the author.' Then one recalls not only Godwin's continued veneration for Burke—which outlasted political differences—but also Falkland's dominant characteristics: his intense 'love of chivalry and romance'. 'He believed that nothing was so well calculated to make men delicate, gallant, and humane, as a temper perpetually alive to the sentiments of birth and honour.'[1] If there were no further evidence one would be justified in suspecting that *Caleb Williams* provides a sympathetic but none the less searching analysis of an attachment to notions of 'the age of chivalry', translated into human actions in contemporary society. But further evidence does exist.

In 1797 when Godwin was revising *Political Justice* for its third edition he heard of Burke's death, whereupon he enlarged the footnote mentioned above to include an assessment of the statesman's career and character. Several statements in it are significant for the present purpose:

> In all that is most exalted in talents, I regard him as the inferior of no man that ever adorned the face of the earth; and, in the long record of human genius, I can find for him very few equals. In subtlety of discrimination, in magnitude of conception, in sagacity and profoundness of judgment, he was never surpassed. . . . No impartial man can recal Burke to his mind, without confessing the grandeur and integrity of his feelings of morality, and being convinced that he was eminently both the patriot and the philanthropist. . . . But his principal defect consisted in this; that the false estimate as to the things entitled to our deference and admiration, which could alone render the aristocracy with whom he lived, unjust to his worth, in some degree infected his own mind. . . . He has unfortunately left us a memorable example, of the power of a corrupt system of government, to undermine and divert from their genuine purposes, the noblest faculties that have yet been exhibited to the observation of the world.

The central features of this assessment are these: Godwin's fervent admiration for Burke's essential greatness; his regret for Burke's false scale of values involving an unjustified reverence

---

[1] *C.W.*, p. 11.

for things aristocratic; and his linking this defect, in terms of cause and effect, with the existing system of government. Exactly the same features occur in Caleb's estimate of Falkland. Falkland's obsessive veneration of chivalry, birth, and honour has already been demonstrated; part of Caleb's final tribute to him will complete the parallel:

> A nobler spirit lived not among the sons of men. Thy intellectual powers were truly sublime, and thy bosom burned with a godlike ambition. But of what use are talents and sentiments in the corrupt wilderness of human society? It is a rank and rotten soil, from which every finer shrub draws poison as it grows.[1]

The same features are present, then, in the assessments of both Burke and Falkland; there can be little doubt that Godwin's conception of the one directly influenced his creation of the other. The footnote also contains a comment on Burke's 'boundless wealth of imagination' which manifested itself in a too lavish 'exuberance' of imagery, and on his 'vein of dark and saturnine temper' that strangely contrasted with his 'urbanity and susceptibility of the kinder affections'. Falkland also possessed 'the creative fancy of the poet' which, when one of his poems is read, succeeds 'at one time [in] overwhelming the soul with superstitious awe, and at another transporting it with luxuriant beauty'.[2] His 'disposition', too, is 'extremely unequal'; he, too, is 'hasty' and 'peevish'; 'sometimes he entirely [loses] his self-possession, and his behaviour [is] changed into frenzy'; while at other times he acts with kindliness and 'inflexible integrity'.[3]

The upshot of this argument is not to dispute the interpretations put forward by Monro and Furbank, but to allow the evidence to give further precision to them. In Falkland Godwin was not only presenting the ideal of honour, of the *ancien régime*, or of the aristocratic type at its best; he was providing an imaginative presentation and assessment of the supreme advocate of these ideals, Edmund Burke, and demonstrating—according to principles in *Political Justice*—how this man (to use Godwin's words about Falkland) 'originally endowed with a mighty store of amiable dispositions and virtues'[4] could be

[1] *C.W.*, p. 451.
[2] Ibid., p. 33.
[3] Ibid., pp. 6, 7.
[4] *Fleetwood* (1832 edn.), p. viii.

contaminated by his own genuine convictions. For the whole story of Falkland has this central irony. The same beliefs that gave him 'such dignity, such affability, so perpetual an attention to the happiness of others, such delicacy of sentiment and expression',[1] also made him

> the fool of honour and fame: a man whom, in the pursuit of reputation, nothing could divert; who would have purchased the character of a true, gallant, and undaunted hero, at the expense of worlds, and who thought every calamity nominal but a stain upon his honour.[2]

It can scarcely be questioned that in Falkland who believed 'honour, and not law, [should] be the dictator of mankind' and 'vice' should 'shrink before the resistless might of inborn dignity',[3] we have a man who held to

> that sensibility of principle, that chastity of honour, which felt a stain like a wound . . . and under which vice itself lost half its evil, by losing all its grossness.[4]

Falkland is motivated by an over-sensitive honour which is threatened if he is exposed as a murderer, and yet, ironically, when the crime is finally revealed vice does indeed lose its grossness: Caleb, having exposed his master and thus dishonoured him and caused his death, feels that it is he who is the 'cool, deliberate, unfeeling murderer'.[5] This presumably was Godwin's own reaction: despite his veneration for Burke he had exposed him to public scrutiny in the novel, and had employed the same determination—sympathetic but unwavering—as is found in *Political Justice*.

It is superfluous to provide further evidence from *Caleb Williams*, but it is worth noting that Godwin's second novel, *St. Leon*, bears some marks of a similar (though now less insistent) symbolic purpose. St. Leon's early story is set in the sixteenth century; he is fifteen in 1520, the year of the Field of the Cloth of Gold, a scene he remembers for 'all that was graceful and humane in the age of chivalry';[6] and he is twenty at Pavia, where Francis I suffers defeat by the Emperor Charles:

> and the defeat of Pavia may perhaps be considered as having given a deadly wound to the reign of chivalry, and a secure

---

[1] *C.W.*, pp. 25–6.
[2] Ibid., p. 140.
[3] Ibid., p. 241.
[4] *Reflections*, in *Works*, II, 348.
[5] *C.W.*, p. 449.
[6] Op. cit. (1799), I, 16.

foundation to that of craft, dissimulation, corruption and commerce.[1]

(The words are too clearly reminiscent of Burke to be accidental: 'The age of chivalry is gone. That of sophisters, economists, and calculators has succeeded; and the glory of Europe is extinguished for ever.'[2]) St. Leon suffers hardships and poverty, but prides himself on remembering the lesson learned 'in the halls of chivalry' to despise 'every thing disgraceful'.[3] When he secures the philosopher's stone, and consequently unlimited wealth, he finds himself isolated from his family and society; he becomes an exile and a wanderer, driven on by the search for status and acclaim; he is driven out of society because he has no equals, and, as Monro observes, St. Leon's wife Marguerite points the moral:

> Equality is the soul of all real and cordial society. A man of rank indeed does not live upon equal terms with the whole of his species; but his heart also can exult; for he has his equals. How unhappy the wretch, the monster rather let me say, that is without an equal; . . . and that is therefore cut off for ever from all cordiality and confidence, can never unbend himself, but lives the solitary, joyless tenant of a prison whose materials are rubies and emeralds![4]

Here is 'the ideal of Honour defeating itself', the obsession with rank and splendour taken to its ultimate extremity.

Finally, it is instructive to discover that, in some respects, Godwin's imaginative indictment of Burke is similar to the charges made by Mary Wollstonecraft in her *Vindication of the Rights of Men*. Monro argues that Falkland is presented as 'the man of taste' described by Godwin in *Political Justice*, one who has a keen enjoyment of aesthetic pleasures—'He enters, with a true relish, into the sublime and pathetic'[5]—and the pleasures of learning, but who lacks the self-denying, altruistic purpose of 'the man of benevolence'. Now, in view of the previous argument, we can go further than Monro and claim that Godwin has Burke in mind when presenting Falkland in this light, a claim that receives support from Wollstonecraft's denunciation

[1] *St. Leon*, I, 67.   [2] *Reflections*, in *Works*, II, 348.
[3] *St. Leon*, II, 163.   [4] Ibid., II, 234–5. (Cf. Monro, op. cit., p. 99.)
[5] *P.J.*, I, 446. (Cf. Monro, op. cit., p. 92.)

of Burke on precisely similar lines. A sentence from *Political Justice*—'The sublime and pathetic are barren, unless it be the sublime of true virtue, and the pathos of true sympathy'[1]— takes on new force when we recall Wollstonecraft's charge that Burke lacks the 'feelings of humanity', that he excites 'compassionate tears' for undeserving objects, and that his 'respect for rank has swallowed up the common feelings of humanity'.[2] This last remark in particular could be applied without alteration to Falkland, whose care for his prestige leads him to murder his local adversary, Tyrrel, allow a tenant-farmer, Hawkins, to be charged and executed for the murder, and persecute Caleb Williams unmercifully for discovering the truth. Despite his unquestioned virtues and abilities Falkland is motivated by no genuine feelings for humanity at large. Like St. Leon, his egotistical pride distorts his view of mankind; neither man sees people as they really are, because they appear to him as a means to obtain respect and status for himself. Indeed, although Godwin wants to show how a society that encourages deception, that takes refuge behind plausible notions of property rights, marriage, artificial modes of behaviour, and the like will produce individuals who are morally distorted; although he rigorously develops his thesis by demonstrating that individuals with position and power in such a society will become inflexible tyrants; although, then, Godwin goes beyond the radical pamphleteers in his moral scrutiny, fundamentally he adopts a similar viewpoint. He accuses Burke of trying to perpetuate a social organisation which is based on insincerity and on false values of rank and honour. As Paine had said of Burke, so Godwin is saying of Falkland and St. Leon—and he goes on saying it of Fleetwood and Mandeville—that they care for the plumage but forget the dying bird.

IV. GODWIN'S EARLY NOVELS

A useful point of departure for a discussion of the early novels is supplied by a significant analogy used by Caleb Williams during his relation of his own history:

> I do not pretend to warrant the authenticity of any part of these memoirs, except so far as fell under my own knowledge, and that

[1] *P.J.*, I, 447.   [2] See above, p. 171.

part shall be given with the same simplicity and accuracy, that I would observe towards a court which was to decide in the last resort upon everything dear to me.[1]

Procedure in a law-court with its insistence on hypothesis, evidence, argument, and thorough proof (as well as the tedium occasionally involved) has a peculiar relevance to Godwin's manner as a novelist and clearly it provides common ground with the method of argument in *Political Justice*. In essence it is related ultimately to the doctrine of necessity, the belief that

> the man who is acquainted with all the circumstances under which a living or intelligent being is placed upon any given occasion, is qualified to predict the conduct he will hold, with as much certainty, as he can predict any of the phenomena of inanimate nature.[2]

In his novels Godwin wished to possess his readers of 'all the circumstances' bearing on an individual in any given situation, the circumstances being both material and psychological. Psychological analysis was his *forté* as he realised:

> the thing in which my imagination revelled the most freely, was the analysis of the private and internal operations of the mind, employing my metaphysical dissecting knife in tracing and laying bare the involutions of motive, and recording the gradually accumulating impulses, which led the personages I had to describe primarily to adopt the particular way of proceeding in which they afterwards embarked.[3]

The novelist's 'dissecting knife' is both a valuable and a dangerous tool: it can lay bare motive with great vividness and clarity, it can be used to demonstrate the connection between impulse and action, and so on, but if its use becomes an end in itself the patient is reduced to the level of an 'object' and ceases to be a living creature. When Godwin uses the dissecting knife at his most skilful he is brilliant because he is fascinated by his own findings—he is making the 'moral discovery' that Conrad says 'should be the object of every tale'[4]—but when the sense of discovery flags he ceases to create and merely *reports* on the 'personages [he] had to describe'. For it is well to remember that Godwin was, as his prefaces make clear, a didactic novelist; at his best he surmounts the obstacles this title suggests,

---

[1] *C.W.*, p. 145.   [2] *P.J.*, I, 363.
[3] *Fleetwood*, p. xi.   [4] *Under Western Eyes* (1911), Pt. I, Sec. III.

but at other times he was obstructed by them. 'We will en-lighten you', he remarks in *Political Justice*[1] and it is when this determination takes hold of the novelist—whether the en-lightenment be moral or intellectual, through an exhaustive examination of motive and intention or through the giving of information—that he becomes tedious. And even if our final judgment emphasises his creative success in, say, *Caleb Williams* or the final volume of *Fleetwood*, the first two volumes of that novel and many wearying passages in *St. Leon* among others must not be left out of account.

The experience of writing *Political Justice* must not of course be held responsible only for Godwin's failures; it also contrib-uted significantly to his success. As in that work, so in the novels, the essence of his manner is an inexorable deliberate-ness; 'the chain and combination of events, that proceeds *systematically* from link to link'[2] is what fascinates him and gives a distinctive comprehensiveness to his novels. It is this which lends to the pursuit of Caleb by the seemingly omnipresent Falkland, or to the endless frustrations of St. Leon, or the gradual and inevitable oncoming of jealousy in Fleetwood, an almost nightmarish dimension of relentless inevitability. All Godwin's chief characters suffer the agony described by St. Leon—'the snare, woven and drawing close round me on all sides for my destruction'[3]—and if this experience is to be agonising it must be slow but not ponderous; there must be a high degree of inwardness in the presentation of characters and not mere psychological 'information' given about them; and general truths deriving from specific situations should seem to arise inevitably rather than being a principal objective.

To take an example: the following passage records Caleb's decision to watch Falkland in order to discover his apparently guilty secret:

The instant I had chosen this employment for myself, I found a strange sort of pleasure in it. To do what is forbidden always has its charms, because we have an indistinct apprehension of some-thing arbitrary and tyrannical in the prohibition. To be a spy upon Mr. Falkland! That there was danger in the employment, served to give an alluring pungency to the choice. I remembered the stern reprimand I had received, and his terrible looks; and

[1] Op. cit., I, 241.   [2] *St. Leon*, II, 280 (my italics).   [3] Ibid., III, 166.

the recollection gave a kind of tingling sensation, not altogether unallied to enjoyment. The further I advanced, the more the sensation was irresistible. I seemed to myself perpetually upon the brink of being countermined, and perpetually roused to guard my designs. The more impenetrable Mr. Falkland was determined to be, the more uncontrollable was my curiosity. Through the whole, my alarm and apprehension of personal danger had a large mixture of frankness and simplicity, conscious of meaning no ill, that made me continually ready to say every thing that was upon my mind, and would not suffer me to believe that, when things were brought to the test, any one could be seriously angry with me.[1]

Here Godwin's slow, deliberate analysis is at its best. His concentration is on the movement of Caleb's mind, but his own fascination in the amalgam of a curious terror and pleasure, and in the attraction of 'brinkmanship' to a mentality which is at once alert and naïve, comes strongly through. In other words, though the record of this mental state is Caleb's, the zest with which it is communicated arises from the creative pleasure Godwin experienced while writing it. His tendency to generalise is kept subservient to the interest in Caleb's state of mind; the second sentence is a general statement, but it is valid, pertinent, and so placed that we cannot forget the specific situation that gives rise to it. And, finally, there is nothing static about the prose; the analysis is not an academic exercise, but is justified because it advances the plot and records, at a significant moment, the psychological condition of a central figure.

In such a passage—and the mental torment Fleetwood suffers after his marriage provides further examples[2]—the psychological insights are first-rate and the deliberate slowness with which they are revealed largely accounts for Godwin's success: one feels that this *is* the way in which a man's mind motivated by both honesty and self-justification would work. But when urgency and creative excitement are absent the slowness develops into tedium, pleasurable discovery into laborious informativeness; habits of thinking and writing formed while composing *Political Justice* then become deleterious. Unfortunately such occasions are numerous, particularly in the first two volumes of *Fleetwood* and especially there in the story

---

[1] *C.W.*, pp. 147–8.   [2] See *Fleetwood*, pp. 240–1.

of Ruffigny, the hero's elderly adviser. This story occupies over sixty pages and gives Godwin the opportunity to discourse on topics such as factory conditions and child labour; the writing for the most part is in a low key and the psychological analysis becomes a tedious habit. When, for example, Ruffigny is describing for Fleetwood the numbing effect of repetitive work in a factory, he remarks:

> Another law which governs the sensorium in a man is the law of association. In contemplation and reverie, one thought introduces another perpetually; and it is by similarity, or the hooking of one upon another, that the process of thinking is carried on. In books and in living discourse the case is the same; there is a constant connection and transition, leading on the chain of the argument. Try the experiment of reading for half an hour a parcel of words thrown together at random, which reflect no light on each other, and produce no combined meaning; and you will have some, though an inadequate, image of the sort of industry to which I was condemned. Numbness and vacancy of mind are the fruits of such an employment. It ultimately transforms the being who is subjected to it, into quite a different class or species of animal.[1]

In the main this is a potted lecture on Hartley's theory; it is conceived in no mood of excitement, and thus becomes merely an informative explanation rather than a dramatic discovery. The idiom is academic, fitted for a textbook, but not for a novel; the writer is the Godwin of *Political Justice* and not of *Caleb Williams*.

Between these two qualitative extremes is a mid-way level of writing which might be described as analytic 'statement'; it lacks the dramatic immediacy and inwardness of the first passage and relies on first-person statements *about* a psychological condition. It is the equivalent in Godwin's novels of the descriptive method used in *Political Justice* to disprove the optimistic philosophers;[2] in both analysis is present but the language keeps the felt experience at arm's length. St. Leon, for example, relates his 'dark night of the soul' after he has gambled away the money needed to support his family:

> How every malignant and insufferable passion seemed to rush upon my soul! What nights of dreadful solitude and despair did I

---

[1] *Fleetwood*, p. 105.   [2] See above, p. 216.

repeatedly pass during the progress of my ruin! . . . My eyelids seemed to press downward with an invincible burthen! My eye-balls were ready to start and crack their sockets! I lay motionless the victim of ineffable horror! The whole endless night seemed to be filled with one vast, appalling, immoveable idea! It was a stupour, more insupportable and tremendous, than the utmost whirl of pain, or the fiercest agony of exquisite perception![1]

Godwin is on the edge of penetrating a state of mind here, but he fails; St. Leon relates his feelings, but does not manage to make them live. The prose itself reveals the flaw: it lacks the sort of fluency that marks Caleb's self-analysis quoted earlier; we are faced with a series of consecutive descriptive features which remain separate and are not synthesised. We recognise the *idée fixe*, we are in no doubt about the strong sense of guilt, but the ecstatic idiom compels us to contemplate rather than experience it.

We are reminded of the statement in *Political Justice* that 'truth dwells with contemplation' and also of St. Leon's determination 'to relate the simple, unaltered truth'.[2] But Godwin frequently fails to distinguish between conceptual truth arrived at through argument and logical exposition such as is appropriate in *Political Justice*, and the imaginative truth of a novel which is embodied in the facts of a created situation and validated by the intensity and completeness of our response to it. In this connection, Godwin's generalising mode, necessary in *Political Justice*, often proves deleterious in the novels. Appropriately used, as noted already in the passage from *Caleb Williams*, the general statement helps to involve the reader intellectually as well as emotionally in the dramatic moment described; used to excess it can effectively put up a barrier between the reader and the imaginative experience. *St. Leon* frequently suffers from this defect. Having modified his views about 'the culture of the heart' by 1799, Godwin takes every opportunity in this novel to speak of sexual attachment with 'the warmest eulogium',[3] but he does so in general terms more appropriate to *Political Justice*.

To feel that we are loved by one whose love we have deserved, to be employed in mutual interchange of the marks of this love, habitually to study the happiness of one by whom our happiness

[1] *St. Leon*, I, 150.　　　[2] Ibid., I, 80.　　　[3] Ibid., I, viii–ix.

is studied in return, this is the most desirable, as it is the genuine and unadulterated condition of human nature. . . . In every state we long for some fond bosom on which to rest our weary head, some speaking eye with which to exchange the glances of intelligence and affection. Then the soul warms and expands itself; then it shuns the observation of every other beholder; then it melts with feelings that are inexpressible . . .[1]

and so on. To read such a passage in its entirety effectively nullifies our involvement in the love between St. Leon and Marguerite; we are being invited to contemplate *the* truth, not experience *a* truth. The two-page generalised comment on the joys of parenthood, and on friendship, in the same novel are two of several other examples.[2]

A similarly uneven awareness of the difference between philosophical treatise and imaginative literature accounts for Godwin's variable success in handling dialogue. There are many occasions when—as Furbank claims[3]—his 'aptitude for short, intense exchanges' is powerfully used; many of the conversations between Falkland and Caleb are of that order, but not all. Occasionally they address each other as if they were both philosophers—for instance, when they have a Godwinian debate on the kind of greatness that is built on tyranny[4]—though for the most part Godwin's imagination is actively engaged in creating characters whose speech idiom is alive and appropriate. Particularly in this novel does he score with the many low-life characters; the very fact that they lack the philosophical sophistication that Godwin was accustomed to meet with in his personal life, the fact that they live intellectually in a recognisably different world compelled him to think creatively about their idiom. This was not invariably the case. In *St. Leon*, where a negro character appears, the narrator disdains 'the mimic toil of inventing a jargon . . . suitable to the lowness of his condition'.[5] In *Caleb Williams*, however, Godwin does not sidestep the problem in this way, nor do we feel that he has invented a 'jargon'; consequently, characters like Tyrrel and Grimes live through their spoken language. Without a

[1] *St. Leon*, I, 103–4.   [2] Ibid., II, 27–9, 81–3.
[3] *Essays in Criticism*, V, 222.
[4] *C.W.*, pp. 150–4. (See also Marguerite's moral lecture in *St. Leon*, II, 134–41.)
[5] Op. cit., II, 299.

living idiom they would be nothing better than properties in a horror novel. Tyrrel, the local bully and despot who is Falkland's rival, is a boorish, selfish Squire Western with something of the calculating brutality of Heathcliff; Grimes, to whom he tries to marry his dependent cousin Emily Melville, is a grotesque lout: both are given a coarse but valid animal vigour. For example, Grimes, uncouth and clumsily humorous, having pretended to rescue Emily from Tyrrel (at his instigation), threatens to rape her:

> Did you think I were such a goose, to take all this trouble merely to gratify your whim? I' faith, nobody shall find me a pack-horse, to go of other folks' errands, without knowing a reason why. I cannot say that I much minded to have you at first; but your ways are enough to stir the blood of my grand-dad. Far-fetched and dear-bought is always relishing. . . . Nay, none of your airs; no tricks upon travellers! I have you here as safe as a horse in a pound; there is not a house nor a shed within a mile of us; and, if I miss the opportunity, call me spade.'[1]

Or again, when Caleb is in jail and spurns the offer of certain privileges by the jailer he is rebuffed by this man:

> Well done, my cock! You have not had your learning for nothing, I see. You are set upon not dying dunghill. But that is to come, lad.[2]

And, finally, a brief speech in which Caleb overhears himself discussed by a farm labourer shows Godwin's imagination faltering. The labourer is answering one of his fellows who scorns to earn a reward for Caleb's capture and subsequent execution:

> Poh, that is all my granny! Some folks must be hanged, to keep the wheels of our state-folks a-going. Besides, I could forgive the fellow all his other robberies, but that he should have been so hardened as to break the house of his own master at last, that is too bad.[3]

Clearly the idiom and rhythm of the last sentence are inappropriate to the speaker of the first two; sophistication creeps in and the illusion is destroyed. But for the most part jailers and thieves, boors and labourers in *Caleb Williams* are made convincing by means of their idiom; they, too, form part of a

[1] *C.W.*, p. 86.   [2] Ibid., pp. 263–4.   [3] Ibid., p. 325.

society organised on one central principle of tyranny which affects the behaviour of all classes—and it was the recognition of this fact that stimulated Godwin's creative imagination.

When this compulsion is inoperative he lapses too easily into an undistinguished style which responds neither to the speaker nor to the occasion; it is solely a vehicle for the communication of ideas. To give proof of this claim would be tedious; suffice it to say that Godwin is capable merely of turning into direct speech the kind of meditation already quoted (on marriage) from *St Leon*.[1] At such times he notably lacks what can be called a common, workaday level of style which will crisply and effectively carry him over stretches of ordinary narrative; instead he often has recourse to a clumsy version of the language he had been accustomed to using in *Political Justice*. The passage of generalised comment quoted above is proof both in manner and content.[2] It is more instructive at this point, however, to examine an extract representing Godwin's narrative at an average level of competence.

> I was so alarmed at this instance of diligence on the part of the enemy, that, for some time, I scarcely ventured to proceed an inch from my place of concealment, or almost to change my posture. The morning, which had been bleak and drizzly, was succeeded by a day of heavy and incessant rain; and the gloomy state of the air and surrounding objects, together with the extreme nearness of my prison, and a total want of food, caused me to pass the hours in no very agreeable sensations. This inclemency of the weather however, which generated a feeling of stillness and solitude, encouraged me by degrees to change my retreat, for another of the same nature, but of somewhat greater security. I hovered with little variation about a single spot, as long as the sun continued above the horizon.[3]

Now this is not a crucial moment in the story; Caleb is on the run, a state in which he spends a great deal of his time, but Godwin occupies a paragraph in telling us that Caleb did not move. Indeed, a further paragraph is required to inform us that he had to wait until the moon went down—'I was therefore obliged to wait for the setting of this luminary'—before progress was possible. Granted that an undue pace in the writing would slacken the tension Godwin has successfully built up, the slow-

[1] Cf. *St. Leon*, I, 248.   [2] See above, pp. 237–8.   [3] *C.W.*, p. 287.

ness which has been noted as a feature of his novel-writing is excessive here. The idiom, too, is worth noting—'I scarcely ventured to proceed', 'caused me to pass the hours in no very agreeable sensations', 'another of the same nature, but of somewhat greater security': there is a flabby verbosity about such phrases; though we appear to be learning something, we are being kept at a distance from real experience. The slow pace of the writing in fact turns into mere verbal desultoriness; it is obvious too that the circumlocutions, brief and incidental here, are capable of developing into those of major proportions to be found, say, in *St. Leon*.

Another test of Godwin's sensitivity to appropriate style is to examine the echoes of other writers—principally Shakespeare and Johnson—that one frequently comes across in the novels. Johnson's manner, it was remarked earlier, provided some advantages (amplitude, comprehensiveness, attention to nuances and distinctions, and the like) as a model for the writing of *Political Justice*; it is a handicap as a *general* guide for writing a novel. Its deliberate, considered pace is, of course, valuable for subtle and detailed psychological analysis, but the paragraph just quoted reveals its drawbacks when it becomes an habitual mode. And the more obvious echoes indicate to what extent it had become habitual. 'Learned without ostentation, refined without foppery, elegant without effeminacy.'[1] This description of Falkland exactly reproduces the rhythm and balance of Johnson's remarks on Addison's prose style,[2] and it is not out of place—but St. Leon's memory of his mother's affection is less appropriately cast in a Johnsonian mould:

> I was her darling and her pride, her waking study, and her nightly dream. Yet I was not pampered into corporeal imbecility, or suffered to rust in inactivity of mind.[3]

Once Godwin drops into the Johnsonian triad of the first sentence he is, as it were, led into the pseudo-Johnsonian pomposity of the second. 'The face of nature around it was agreeably diversified, being partly wild and romantic, and partly rich and abundant in production'[4]—the Johnson of the Scottish *Journey* was capable of giving rise to this kind of vague

[1] *C.W.*, p. 26.   [2] See *Works*, VII, 472–3.
[3] *St. Leon*, I, 8–9.   [4] *C.W.*, p. 401.

wordiness. And it is this accumulation of verbal weight that is one of Godwin's chief failings.[1]

But it is Shakespeare on whom Godwin most often leans. In *Caleb Williams*, where Godwin's imagination works most effectively, the source-play for the majority of his allusions is *Macbeth*, the Shakespearean tragedy that is undoubtedly closest in mood and story to his own novel. Macbeth and Falkland are both pursued and pursuing, both are inexorably caught in the net of their own making, and both are the victims of ambition. To be reminded, therefore, of the play by 'curses, deep, not loud', 'misfortune comes so thick upon me', ' "sleep no more" ', or 'the milk of human kindness',[2] might be regarded as valid and purposeful. But one's conviction is weakened by looking at the contexts of these allusions. The first relates to the social reaction to Tyrrel's brutal treatment of Emily, the second is spoken by the dispossessed tenant-farmer Hawkins, the third has reference to the suffering Caleb endured from the discovery of Falkland's secret, and the last is applied to the grotesque female who cooks for the band of thieves which befriends Caleb. There is indeed no thematic consistency about the use of these allusions; Godwin does not introduce them with a full understanding of their value, but indiscriminately as they occur to him by simple association. The extreme example of an allusion used as a cliché occurs in *St. Leon*, where the hero considers the advantages of wealth: 'I contemplated the honour, love, obedience, troops of friends, which are so apt to attend upon wealth.'[3] The words are mere counters which happen to have been strung together and remain as a unit in Godwin's mind; the fact that Macbeth was lamenting the absence of these things and that the allusion inevitably evokes a sense of tragic decline and loss does not perturb Godwin in the least. As was noticed about his use of quotations in *Political Justice*, Godwin appears to be insensitive to the emotive connotations of other men's words; their surface meaning is his sole concern.

[1] *Rasselas* may have acted to some extent as a model for *St. Leon*. St. Leon learns too late the 'lesson' of 'the emptiness and futility of human wishes' (II, 290), he despairs of ever finding unalloyed content, and even the achievement of happiness through altruism is denied him. He discovers in fact that human life contains much to be endured and little to be enjoyed.

[2] *C.W.*, pp. 126, 156, 190, 295.

[3] Op. cit., II, 36.

In the final volume of *Fleetwood* Godwin blatantly exploits the Othello–Iago–Desdemona situation: Fleetwood is driven insane with jealousy because of his wife's supposed infidelity with his nephew, the soldier Kenrick, through the machinations of Gifford, also his nephew. The reliance on Shakespeare is in itself no disgrace, and it must be said that the device produces some of Godwin's most powerful writing. He relies on a detailed memory of *Othello*: Gifford's techniques were all learnt from Iago; Fleetwood is given a letter by Gifford which seems fully to incriminate Mary; he visits her bedroom, finds her asleep, disbelieves the affectionate words she speaks to him in a dream, and steals a kiss from her; and finally he denounces her. And yet, not only does Godwin allude, not to Iago but to Hamlet when describing Gifford—'thus did this damnable calumniator lead me on, with broken sentences, and "ambiguous givings-out" '—but when Fleetwood imagines Mary to be set on calming his misgivings he remarks:

> It was thus that Cleopatra inveigled Mark Antony to his ruin, when she had determined to play him false with his confident Dolabella. As my wife left the room, I saw her apply her handkerchief to her eyes. . . .[1]

Such evidence of insensibility is scarcely credible.

Yet this kind of literary and verbal insensitivity is frequently found. In *Caleb Williams* even Falkland at times almost degenerates into the conventional figure of a horror novel, the man who gnashes his teeth and stamps in rage, who bids Caleb, 'Begone, devil! . . . Quit the room, or I will trample you into atoms'[2] (he later threatens to 'grind [him] into atoms'[3]), and who is capable of chivalric courtesies such as his apology to an Italian count: 'Will you allow me to retract the precipitate haughtiness into which I was betrayed?'[4] The young Emily Melville feels a 'teen-age' infatuation for Falkland, but Godwin's version is that she experiences 'the wildest chimeras in her deluded imagination',[5] and although he speaks of her 'vivacity', he can also describe her as 'a delicate valetudinarian'.[6] A similar imprecision occurs in *Fleetwood*. In the account of the hero's early amours we learn that a countess 'reminded

[1] Op. cit., p. 320. [2] Op. cit., p. 8. [3] Ibid., p. 394.
[4] Ibid., p. 17. [5] Ibid., p. 55. [6] Ibid., pp. 110, 111.

her admirer of the most delicate flower of the parterre';[1] the analogy is valid, since she is a blend of beauty with thorough-going artificiality. Later, however, Fleetwood's wife-to-be, Mary, is also found to remind him of 'one of the beauties of her own parterre'.[2] The contrast between Mary and the countess is sharp—Mary is above all 'ingenuous' and 'artless'—but Godwin can apply precisely the same descriptive terms to both women. Again, Godwin periodically seems unaware of the intrusion of irrelevant ideas or emotions as a result of linguistic carelessness. Caleb on one occasion is lost, but he does not say so; his words are:

> I surveyed the horizon round me; but I could observe nothing with which my organ was previously acquainted.[3]

Generic terms are important—as the eighteenth century well knew—for drawing attention to general ideas, but here 'organ' is distracting; we are interested only in the individual Caleb and what his eye saw or failed to see. Similarly, St. Leon contrasts his own eternal youth with the lament of an old man:

> My weather-beaten trunk shall at no time clothe itself with a smoother rind. A recruited marrow shall never fill these bones, nor a more vigorous sap circulate through my unstrung limbs.[4]

Irrelevant emotions are certainly aroused; our attention is diverted by the insensibility of the language which meta-phorically and clumsily identifies the speaker with a tree.

On the other hand, it is vital to note occasions when God-win's choice of language and metaphor is precise and effective. Three examples must suffice. The first is a brief one from *Caleb Williams*; it occurs when Caleb establishes his initially idyllic relationship with Laura Denison:

> While our familiarity gained in duration, it equally gained in that subtlety of communication by which it seemed to shoot forth its roots in every direction.[5]

The metaphor is unobtrusive, almost casual, but it acts exactly as it should, stressing the living yet invisible growth of a developing acquaintance. The second comes from the point at which St. Leon experiences immortality as distinct from merely

---

[1] Op. cit., pp. 58–9.   [2] Ibid., p. 207.   [3] *C.W.*, p. 201.
[4] *St. Leon*, III, 282.   [5] Op. cit., pp. 405–6.

contemplating the idea of it. Godwin tries to capture the sensation vividly, and does so through an exploration of the difference between the Christian, who believes in 'eternal bliss' but has only a 'faint and indistinct picture' of it in his mind, and

> the feelings of the celebrated apostles, who had been taken up into the third heaven, and had beheld the new Jerusalem with all its jaspers, its chrysolites, its emeralds, and its sapphires.[1]

The parallel is just, it is worked out with care, and one can feel the writer's determination to think concretely about the abstract issue: 'It is so different a thing to conceive a proposition theoretically, and to experience it in practice.' And the final example, from *Fleetwood*, involves a discrimination between the man of 'simple perception' (Sir Charles Gleed) and the man of 'imagination' (Fleetwood himself).[2] The distinction is made by contrasting the responses to a landscape of a farmer and a poet, the former seeing the detail of soil, weather, and crops, the latter seeing 'a living scene, animated by a mysterious power, whose operations he contemplated with admiration and reverence'. 'The farmer's were perceptions; his were feelings.' That the distinction was a commonplace in the late eighteenth and early nineteenth centuries is immaterial; it is important that it should be made, and Godwin makes it with great care and vividness.

This is to take only one illustration from each of three novels, but the common factor in all is significant. Each example— and they were not initially chosen with this in mind—involves an attempt by Godwin to think precisely about a feature of human character, to assess and capture imaginatively some moral perception. Behind each lies an abstract issue which had stimulated the philosopher in him—the nature of human relationships, the difference between theory and practice, or the nature of perception; the intellectual stimulus excited clear, creative thought about the characters and situations which embodied these abstractions; and the result is fresh, lucid, and fluent prose. The same characteristics are invariably found in the various trial scenes which occur in the novels: a trial is a formal embodiment of argument, discussion, elucidation of principles, and the like, and in these scenes Godwin is not only

---

[1] *St. Leon*, IV, 7.　　　　[2] Op. cit., pp. 55–6.

contemplating the moral issues that arise but is also creating active figures who justify or question them. On the other hand, where Godwin is not intellectually as well as emotionally involved the outcome is unconvincing. He is not so involved for most of the first two volumes of *Fleetwood*, for example, hence their tediousness for long stretches. The rakes and mistresses with whom Fleetwood associates do not come alive, they are merely verbal forms without body; consequently when we learn that Fleetwood had 'passed the Rubicon of vice' and had become 'hardened and brutalised'[1] we note them as statements that mean nothing on our pulses. Indeed, at one point Godwin implicitly confesses his lack of involvement. Fleetwood visits the court of Louis XV and Godwin remarks that it would be 'superfluous' for him to describe the depravity of a court which 'the reader may find in so many volumes amply and ambitiously detailed'.[2] In thus avoiding his responsibility he may have had in mind those 'innocent and inexperienced readers' for whose safety he is scrupulous in *St. Leon*,[3] but the truth is that he is writing as an observer and not as a man imaginatively involved in human actions. (Where 'research' material is essential and is creatively integrated into the narrative—as it is in Caleb Williams' prison experiences—Godwin eagerly calls attention to its accuracy in footnotes.[4])

The conclusions to be drawn from this accumulated evidence take us back to the beginning of this section and to the two preceding, because, as has been demonstrated, there is much common ground between the novels and *Political Justice*—and not only on the level of ideas. All writers on Godwin draw attention to the principles elaborated in that work, the kinds of tyranny, the deficiencies of society, the need for sincerity, and so forth, which are exemplified in the novels, so repetition is superfluous—but something more is required to account for the relative failure of *St. Leon* and the early volumes of *Fleetwood*, and the success of *Caleb Williams*. It is certain that Godwin needed the intellectual stimulus of abstract ideas; it is equally true that in *Caleb Williams* this stimulus is more pervasive than in any other novel. Fresh from writing *Political Justice*, in that novel Godwin's intellectual excitement was at its height and

---

[1] Op. cit., pp. 48, 54.   [2] Ibid., p. 47.
[3] Op. cit., I, 85.   [4] *C.W.*, pp. 247 n., 248 n., 277 n.

the determination to convey his ideas to a different audience focused his attention on living figures in the kind of society he had so recently analysed. Hence his strenuous thinking, his emotional intensity, and his punctiliousness as a psychologist. But the form of the novel and the symbolic person of Burke must also be taken into account.

A major reason for the failure of *St. Leon* lies in Godwin's design: to ' "mix human feelings and passions with incredible situations, and thus render them impressive and interesting" '.[1] *St. Leon*, in other words, is Godwin's *Ancient Mariner*. The story was to be of 'the miraculous class', necessitating the constant invention of novel and surprising situations; Godwin's ingenuity is kept at full stretch, but the reader becomes wearied by an incredible sequence of events, each of which increases the hero's misfortunes. There are incidental successes within the novel; even in the improbable happenings centring on the giant, Bethlem Gabor, Godwin's amazement at the resilience of the human mind brings St. Leon alive and momentarily saves him from being a puppet of circumstance;[2] but as a whole the novel is insufficiently pervaded by intellectual vigour and, because of its design, Godwin is too intent on manipulating events. If, however, *St. Leon* is Coleridgean, *Caleb Williams* and *Fleetwood* are Wordsworthian. In them he is concerned with '*things as they are*';[3] his purpose is to give the charm of novelty to things of every day. The first is a story of 'uncommon events' but 'entirely within the laws and established course of nature'; the second, even more Wordsworthian, is to give 'a certain kind of novelty' to 'common and ordinary adventures'.[4] Thus, although inventive ingenuity was still called for, it was working on the material of ordinary life and—equally important—within a society in which operated the moral forces Godwin had examined in *Political Justice*. That *Fleetwood* does not make a forceful impact on the reader until the final volume is significant. At the end of the second volume Fleetwood learns that the woman he is to marry has lost the fortune she was entitled

---

[1] *Fleetwood*, p. xiv.   [2] Cf. op. cit., IV, 189 ff.
[3] *C.W.*, p. xix (my italics).
[4] *Fleetwood*, pp. xiv, xv. (For the views of other eighteenth-century writers on the relation of the everyday and the uncommon in the novel, see Miriam Allott, *Novelists on the Novel* (1959), pp. 45–8.)

to expect; he does not love her the less for that, but—and it is a crucial moment:

> I am formed like all other corporeal essences, and am affected by the adventitious and unmeriting circumstances of rank or riches with which my fellow-being is surrounded. Had Mary entered into my alliance a distinguished heiress, this, in spite of my philosophy, would have commanded from me a certain deference and homage.[1]

From this moment Fleetwood catches himself addressing Mary 'with the condescension of a superior'; he no longer regarded her as 'an independent being' but rather as someone to be pitied and patronised. When, in volume three, Mary asserts her independence as a being with individual rights and emotions, Fleetwood's prestige is challenged, and the stage is set for the disintegrating effect of jealousy. In other words, the novel comes to life with dramatic suddenness when a false estimate of rank and wealth distorts the moral perception of the central character, a man—as Godwin said of Burke—who was a strange mixture of 'dark and saturnine temper' with 'urbanity and a susceptibility of the kinder affections'.

This final volume of *Fleetwood* is the nearest approach both in mood and successful achievement to Godwin's best novel, *Caleb Williams*. And what most distinguishes these two among his other novels—besides a more intelligent choice of form, the stimulus of intellectual excitement, and the concentration on 'things as they are'—is the presence in both of a powerful central figure driven to near insanity by a regard for rank and social eminence, a veneration for the values of aristocracy. He is a man in both cases whose moral vision is distorted by this obsessive veneration; he earns of the other characters and of the reader sympathy and admiration mixed with regret for misused talents; he excites a response, indeed, such as Burke aroused in Godwin. Godwin might truly have remarked about Burke as Boswell about Paoli: 'The contemplation of such a character *really existing* was of more service to me than all I had been able to draw from books . . . or from the exertions of my own mind.'[2] For here was the most fearful evidence of the

[1] Op. cit., p. 223.
[2] Ed. F. Brady and F. A. Pottle, *Boswell on the Grand Tour: Italy, Corsica and France 1765-1766*, (1955), p. 188 (my italics).

power of a traditional social morality to corrupt even the best human qualities, and the creative results, above all in *Caleb Williams*, are manifest. Instead of characters dissected as mere objects (as in *St. Leon* or the early volumes of *Fleetwood*), we are presented with an excited series of discoveries about the springs of human action; instead of the language of abstract speculation habitually used in *Political Justice*, we have an idiom that is generally alive and flexible; and instead of a writer who is a kind of bemused schoolmaster, we have Godwin imaginatively resolving the problem raised by a contemporary situation. Edmund Burke was for him 'the inferior of no man that ever adorned the face of the earth'; simultaneously he was

> a memorable example, of the power of a corrupt system of government, to undermine and divert from their genuine purposes, the noblest faculties that have yet been exhibited to the observation of the world.[1]

Under the impetus of the intense admiration and remorse released by the contemplation of a situation well-nigh tragic in the Aristotelian mode, Godwin created his most disturbing character, Falkland, and, in *Caleb Williams*, the finest piece of imaginative literature to emerge from the controversy over the *Reflections*.

[1] *P.J.*, II, 545–6 n.

CONCLUSION

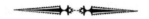

'G ENTLEMEN, . . . you will be pleased to take into your consideration the phrase and the manner as well as the matter.'[1] This valuable advice was given to the jury by the Attorney-General at Paine's trial for seditious libel—and it remains valid. The 'matter' of the works examined in the foregoing chapters has been analysed with varying degrees of thoroughness by historians of politics and ideas, but it is the contention of this book that such analysis is incomplete without an accompanying examination of 'the phrase and the manner'. To see a political controversy as a whole—particularly when it is of the magnitude of that over the *Reflections*—is to recognise the truth of this contention contained in the experience of, say, Johnson confronted with a pamphlet by Junius, or Paine with one by Burke. Their response is obviously too complex to be accounted for merely by considering the 'matter', and if we are accurately to gauge that response (and thus accumulate evidence of public reactions) we must estimate the challenge of the 'manner', the felt experience brought home to the reader in the texture of the style, or the emotional impact. All such features form part of the total literary experience (more especially when this takes place in the highly charged atmosphere of a controversy), and because the response is a total thing, not merely an abstract, intellectual one, the critical evaluation of pamphlet literature is necessarily incomplete if attention is given only to the content of ideas. In that case the 'imaginative understanding' that E. H. Carr claims the historian must possess 'for the minds of the people with whom he is dealing'[2]

---

[1] Ed. T. B. Howell, *State Trials* (1817), XXII, col. 383.
[2] *What is History?* (1961), p. 18.

CONCLUSION

cannot properly exist. Such understanding must show itself not only in a sympathetic appraisal of a man's system of ideas but also of the imaginative material used in communicating those ideas, the rhythm of his prose and the build of his sentences which image his attitude to his task and to his readers, the choice of idiom and the like. Furthermore, when the document under consideration is part of a political controversy, the response to it of an articulate audience requires a further extension of the imaginative understanding we are discussing. For, if we may adapt some words of Richard Pares, each writer 'creates or changes the conditions in which all the other [writers] have to act and, by so doing, modifies their action or, at least, the results of their action'.[1] For a reader who had no knowledge of other pamphlets the *Reflections* was clearly quite a different document from that remembered by another reader whose mind had been acted upon, say, by Paine, Mackintosh, or Arthur Young. And this fact imposes yet another requirement on our view of a controversy: we should try to see it as a whole, to measure the interaction of one mind or pamphlet on another, the interplay of influences exerted on the reading public, and the kind of residual pressures which remain after the furore of the controversy has played itself out.

The complexity of the problem is enormous, but at least its existence should be recognised. Some aspects of it have been explored on the basis of particular texts in the previous chapters —though it is not assumed that it has been fully resolved; it is the business of the present chapter to deal with certain general issues and to underline the contribution which the literary-critical approach can make towards reaching the goal just described.

To begin with there are some quite specific ways in which literary analysis reinforces and extends the conclusions reached by modern historians. Two examples from the Wilkes controversy will serve to make the point. In her Creighton Lecture for 1959, *The City of London and the Opposition to Government, 1768–1774*, Dr. L. S. Sutherland is concerned with the movement of public opinion in the late 1760s, and though she does not mention Junius, she points to the influence of the Press on the fortunes of metropolitan radicalism. Critically to examine

[1] *The Historian's Business and other Essays* (Oxford, 1961), p. 37.

Junius's writings is to go some way towards explaining *why* the Press had an important influence and in what directions it was exerted. It was not merely that Junius handled ideas of a particular kind that enabled him to stir the minds of his readers; the literary-historical 'fact' that he wrote in a satiric tradition to which his century had grown accustomed and which readers of Defoe and the *Craftsman*, of Pope, Swift, and Churchill took delight in is probably of equal weight in any assessment of the reasons for his influence. We learn, too, many things about the people for whom the Press catered— what an astute writer like Junius could assume was common knowledge, or would be readily believed, what kind of literary sensitivity he could rely on in his readers, or what their prejudices were. By these means we come closer to the temper of the times, to the clamour of a vociferous opposition group, and to the kind of emotions which were currently accessible to a shrewd propagandist.

Miss Sutherland also demonstrates the reluctance on the part of the upper classes to involve themselves with a movement associated with Wilkes and metropolitan radicalism; she quotes William Dowdeswell (the leader of the Rockingham Whigs in the Commons) as saying that in most places 'people of rank and fortune' shrink from signing petitions organised by the Opposition.[1] These were precisely the people—'of higher rank and more enlightened mind'—for whom Johnson wrote, and to analyse his *False Alarm* is to arrive, by another route, at Miss Sutherland's conclusion. This other, literary-critical route, moreover, tells us more about the classes to which she refers, about their culture, education, prejudices, and literary training, and consequently provides some further reasons for their reluctance to commit themselves in the way Miss Sutherland describes. Her contention that the Wilkes affair most strongly aroused the sympathies of the lower middle class is also supported by an analysis of *The False Alarm*. Johnson's scorn for sympathisers of inferior social rank—particularly those associated with the world of trade—bears out Miss Sutherland's contention; it shows, too, how alive Johnson was to the value of such scorn to reinforce the natural hesitancy of the enjoying classes.

[1] Op. cit., p. 30. (Also printed in Burke, *Correspondence*, II, 70.)

As a second example, Richard Pares, in his excellent work *George III and the Politicians*, pointed out that the most permanent opposition to the king was aristocratic, a body of men convinced of their monopoly of political responsibility and appropriating the title of Whig.[1] A literary-critical examination of Burke's *Present Discontents* would not challenge this claim, but would add to it an important rider. It would add that when Burke, the spokesman for the 'pure' Whigs, urged his case against George III and appealed both to his own associates and to the wider audience of the aristocracy as a whole, he was addressing not simply a political but also a cultural aristocracy. He could assume that this body was bound together not solely by social ties or political expediency but also by the shared experience of literature which linked a *'novus homo'* (as Burke described himself[2]) with men of the so-called great Revolution families. He appealed to the aristocracy's sense of common purpose, therefore, not only on the basis of common political interests but just as much on the basis of a shared cultural tradition, on an alertness in his audience to subtleties of style, on their ready response to an imaginative evocation of certain areas of human experience—and so on. These are 'facts' about the political aristocracy which had an importance for Burke and his age, and which the historian frequently neglects. Thus, when Professor Pares maintains that Burke's *Present Discontents* did more than anything else to clean the word 'party' from the stigma of 'faction' and to consecrate the opinion that party alignment was the only guarantee of an elevated political morality,[3] we should want to ask why and how Burke was the one to achieve this. The answer will only partly be in terms of political ideas; it will also be in terms of literary astuteness and persuasive methods. And it will not be enough to argue, as Mr. Romney Sedgwick does, that Burke merely repeats the 'stock catchwords' associated with Opposition charges since the days when Frederick, Prince of Wales, led the Opposition to George II.[4] This does not account for either the continuing readability or the relevance of Burke's pamphlet.

[1] Op. cit. (Oxford, 1953), pp. 59–60.
[2] Burke, *Correspondence*, II, 128.
[3] Op. cit., p. 84.
[4] *Letters from George III to Lord Bute*, p. xviii.

At least part of the explanation lies in the presence of those literary qualities that were revealed by analysis. Moreover, even if Burke's notions about the value of 'party' in political life have contributed to the continuing interest taken in the *Present Discontents*, and even though these notions were not realised in practice until the nineteenth century, it should be recognised that the climate of opinion which eventually brought them to fruition was at any rate partly the result of his verbal skills.

In ways such as these examples reveal, the findings of literary criticism provide an essential factor which has to be reckoned with before a final judgment is made on political writings. They may also prevent our looking for the wrong things in the first place or claiming that one facet of a writer's achievement is the whole. The earlier analysis of the *Reflections*, for instance, brings out clearly that Burke's form of expression is pre-eminently a fusion of thought and emotion, and that both require simultaneous critical study. Thus, the search by political philosophers for Burke's abstract 'political thought' emphasises one element at the expense of, or to the detriment of, the other and gives a picture that is essentially one-sided. To compare Godwin's use of language in *Political Justice* with Burke's in the *Reflections* is to recognise the sharp difference between a man who was an abstract philosopher and one who was not; consequently, to treat Burke as if he offers the kind of speculative thought to be found in Godwin is seriously to misapprehend the nature of his thinking.

To take a specific example, it is argued by political theorists that the philosophical centre of the *Reflections* is the famous passage beginning, 'Society is indeed a contract'.[1] From any point of view this is a fine passage, the ideas it contains are significant, and if we were looking for a schematic expression of Burke's *abstract* view of society and polity as a whole, this might well be the paragraph we should choose. But the *Reflections* was not written to act as a source-book for Burke's political theory; it is not a kind of Burkean *Political Justice*, and while theorists have every right to treat it as such and create Burke in their own image, we must recognise that they are making out of the book something different from what its author intended it to be.

---

[1] *Reflections*, in *Works*, II, 368–9.

He wished to expound a theory of society and government, but he was also determined to persuade a body of readers to adopt it. For this reason he chose a particular literary form in which to communicate his views, a form which was designed to ensure their acceptance. If, then, we are adequately to assess both his purpose and his achievement we must regard Burke as at once a thinker and a rhetorician. We are compelled to enquire, therefore, not only which passage is philosophically central but also which passage combines that kind of significance with the highest persuasive efficiency. And if we use the evidence provided by the controversy—which is the immediate context for the *Reflections*—there is little doubt that this combination is found pre-eminently in the apostrophe. Both the admiration it evoked from his supporters and the sustained effort of virtually the whole Opposition to decry it amply confirm this judgment.

Leaving Burke's book in order to take a view of the controversy it provoked, it is interesting to bear in mind the approach of what may be called without any disrespect the conventional political historian—in this case G. S. Veitch, whose *Genesis of Parliamentary Reform* (1913) still gives one of the fullest accounts of the controversy. One of his principal objectives is to chart the ebb and flow of opinion, and to achieve this he insists that 'the more important pamphlets' require close examination.[1] In this category of 'the more important' Veitch puts such works as Wollstonecraft's *Vindication*, Mackintosh's *Vindiciae Gallicae*, and Paine's *Rights of Man*. From the standpoint of political philosophy, of course, such categorising is valid, but to restrict our view by these standards is to miss an important feature of a controversy—the cumulative excitement built up as it runs its course, the compulsion which interested readers feel to follow it through and explore even those writings that time proves ephemeral. William Windham, for example, records in his diary for 2 April 1791:

> Instead of joining the party to the Opera I came home and employed myself reading the absurd work of Dr. Cooper in answer to Priestley. Such a compound of dulness and self-sufficiency I could not have expected even from him.[2]

[1] Op. cit., p. 159.
[2] Ed. Mrs. H. Baring, *The Diary of the Rt. Hon. William Windham*, p. 221.

This judgment on Cooper's *First Principles of Civil and Ecclesiastical Government Delineated* is perfectly just, but the fact remains that Windham deprived himself of an entertaining evening to read it. Or again, the attitude of many readers may well have been that suggested in the remark by the anonymous author of *A Short Letter to Burke* (by a Member of Parliament, 1791): 'Answer upon Answer has been published to [the *Reflections*], and the last is generally thought the best'[1]; undiscriminating enthusiasm is implied, but we must not overlook the enthusiasm in a search only for ideas which seem permanently significant in a context of political history.

Moreover, in addition to the Windhams and people of his class whose diaries record their response to particular pamphlets, there were innumerable other readers who did not keep diaries, who responded differently but no less vigorously to the controversy. These were the members of the popular constitutional societies, or those nameless spinners and weavers for whom, as John Galt observes, a bookseller in 1790 used to buy a newspaper to keep them informed of events in France.[2] Their reading habits disturbed the governing classes. They were reported, for example, by an anonymous informer to the Rev. Henry Zouch, a Wakefield J.P., who interested himself in the activities of the Sheffield Association for Constitutional Information and passed on his findings to Lord Fitzwilliam. The informer described the Association's members as

> of the lower order of manufacturers and amount to several hundreds, and . . . they profess to be admirers of the dangerous Doctrine of Mr. Payne whose pamphlet they distribute with Industry and support his Dogmas with zeal.[3]

This is the 'industry' and the 'zeal' which may be overlooked in a concentration on the matter of the philosophically significant pamphlets. But this kind of response was widely prevalent among these readers; it caused Archdeacon William Paley to make one of his rare incursions into national politics and to issue his *Reasons for Contentment*. A general search made by 'masters of families' in Cumberland led to the discovery that cheap

---

[1] Op. cit., p. 13.
[2] *Annals of the Parish*, in *Works* (Edinburgh, 1936), I, 190.
[3] Papers, Correspondence etc. of 2nd Earl Fitzwilliam (F 44 a).

publications, such as Paine's *Rights of Man*, 'were much in circulation' and prompted Paley to publish his sermon (preached in 1790) as a pamphlet.[1]

To account for this popular enthusiasm solely in terms of the ideas purveyed by Paine, or to give economic and social reasons for it, is to ignore facts of another order but of comparable significance provided by literary analysis. After all, the attention of Paine's audience was held by literary means and to examine his literary techniques leads to a deeper imaginative understanding of his readers. Analysis of these techniques points to the nature of the sensibility that Paine assumed to exist among 'the lower orders'—and the sales and influence of the *Rights of Man* proved him right; it reveals a great deal about their ways of thinking and feeling, their attachment to folk literature, the prominence of a certain kind of dramatic element in their imaginative life, or the importance of a feeling of shared humanity with other oppressed peoples rather than a sophisticated attention to political principles. Awareness of principles was present; it was perhaps naïve, though clear and fundamental; and, as Butler's *Brief Reflections* shows, for many it was articulated in terms of personal and local rather than of national issues. And the language in which Paine or Butler appropriately expressed their views illuminates by contrast the sagacity of William Pitt when he refused to take legal action against Godwin's *Political Justice*. Language such as Godwin used, remote from the life lived by the mass of people who might have been potentially dangerous radicals, was unlikely to be a subversive factor. Paine's was another matter. The Sheffield Association obtained his permission to print about 2,000 copies of the *Rights of Man*, approximately a copy for each member, and one member is recorded as saying that 'they had received more knowledge and information from the works of Mr. Payne (part 1st and 2nd) than from any other author on the subject of government'.[2] This man was expressing approval of Paine's ideas; he was also paying tribute to his literary manner. That word 'received' is important: from George Rous or Thomas Christie, for example, they would 'receive' little,

[1] *Works* (1838), I, cxxiii–cxxiv.
[2] Papers, Correspondence etc. of 2nd Earl Fitzwilliam (F 44 a). Abstract of the proceedings of the Association, 26 March 1792.

because such writers would affect their pulses scarcely at all; Paine's writing, on the other hand, could be felt, it stemmed from lived experience which they recognised as their own, and it was conveyed in a tone which they found congenial. As Charles Knight said later of William Cobbett, Paine's manner was effective because it contained 'no fine words or inverted sentences'[1]; his language and style were all of a piece with his political philosophy. 'Fine words' and 'inverted sentences' bespoke a culture that was aristocratic, of the past, and identified with the *status quo*; Paine's manner was radical in both literary and political terms.

What the approach of an historian like Veitch demonstrates —and his book is instanced because in so many ways it is admirable—is the lack of attention to the persuasive force of words in a given situation. For example, he considers Wollstonecraft's *Vindication* 'in some ways the best of the replies' to the *Reflections*; it is 'the only one which is adequate on the emotional side'.[2] There is some truth in this second claim, but, as the earlier analysis has perhaps established, Wollstonecraft was unable to exercise the necessary control over her emotional intensity so as to provide a disciplined prose which would, in turn, give evidence for the reliability of her ideas. On the other hand, Veitch finds Mackintosh's *Vindiciae Gallicae* 'almost unreadable'; he believes that Mackintosh 'never' abandons 'the cool and persuasive language of reason'; and claims that what *Vindiciae Gallicae* gains in argument it loses in 'literary merit'.[3] Again, if the earlier analysis is valid, Veitch's claims are false. In any case it should have been clear that in the midst of a fierce controversy a work that relied solely on the 'language of reason' would not arouse the response which contemporary evidence (quoted by Veitch) shows it to have stirred. Fundamentally, what Veitch fails to do is to see Mackintosh (or any other participant) as responding and contributing to a complex verbal situation. It is obviously important to decide whether the ideas expounded by a controversialist are permanently valid or not, but in the first place he must be seen as a man speaking to men of his time, using their words in a fresh or

---

[1] *Passages of a Working Life* (1864), I, 188.
[2] *The Genesis of Parliamentary Reform*, p. 167.
[3] Ibid., p. 170.

CONCLUSION

commonplace way, exploiting their emotions which those words connote, and strenuously or feebly urging his ideas upon them. Furthermore, once his pamphlet is published it becomes part of a highly fluid situation; its words may be pillaged and distorted or, owing to some new factor, it may be necessary to redirect the pamphlet to an audience for which it was not originally intended (as happened to the *Reflections* as a result of Paine's influence). Both such developments offer further scope for attentive analysis.

The first can be illustrated by looking at the treatment accorded to one of the best-known phrases from the *Reflections*: 'a swinish multitude'.[1] It was used by Burke to denote the unthinking, uncultivated masses, the irresponsible elements in society whose lack of involvement in sustaining the cultural heritage would lead them to destroy it. Despite the distinctly political and social overtones in Burke's prediction that this catastrophe would be linked with the overthrow of the nobility and clergy, the 'natural guardians' of culture, it must be stressed that at this point he is concerned with the danger from the multitude to 'learning'. But, as on other occasions, the author's intentions counted for little; the phrase was taken by the left wing as summing up the attitude of the 'establishment' towards the electorally insignificant majority; and frequent usage allowed it to accrue significances and nuances until it became one of the most emotive catch-phrases through the last century. The process started early; the satiric illustrations to Sharpe's *Rhapsody to E—— B—— Esq.* show how far it had gone by 1792. A parson, shown sitting astride a pig, holds in his hand a paper inscribed 'Church and State' and facing him is Burke also mounted on a pig and offering to the parson a paper inscribed 'Tithes'; under the first figure is a pig saying, 'I eat the Straw, who gets the Peas?', and beneath the second, another pig, named 'Sinking Fund', is forced to its knees by a burden marked 'Budget'. A whole complex of attitudes—political, religious, social, and fiscal—which the enjoying classes are alleged to hold towards the poor, has already been attached to Burke's phrase. The longer the controversy continued, the more currency was given to it. It is obviously present in the title and certainly in the content of Daniel Isaac Eaton's

[1] Op. cit., in *Works*, II, 351.

259

compilation (selling for 2d.), *Hog's Wash, or, A Salmagundy for Swine* (1st number, 29 September 1793); *Pearls cast before Swine* (1793?) by 'Old Hubert' (James Parkinson); *Burke's Address to the 'Swinish Multitude'* (1793?), a verse composition probably by Thomas Spence; and *One Pennyworth of Pig's Meat* [later, *Pig's Meat*]; *or, Lessons for the Swinish Multitude* (1793–95), a weekly publication at one penny by Spence. The exploitation suffered by Burke's words is made clear by the first of the twelve stanzas from *Burke's Address* (reprinted in *Pig's Meat*), to be sung to the tune, 'Derry, down, down':

> Ye vile Swinish Herd, in the Sty of Taxation,
> What would ye be after?—disturbing the Nation?
> Give over your grunting—Be off—To your Sty!
> Nor dare to look out—if a King passes by:
> Get ye down! down! down!—Keep ye down![1]

The phrase has now become a set formula for arousing any number of age-old complaints by the poor against the rich and privileged classes. It recurs time and again in popular writings of the 1790s, but it is interesting to find it reappearing in the next outburst of cheap political literature, at about the time of the first Reform Bill. In the *Poor Man's Guardian*, one of the numerous cheap journals to appear in the early 1830s, there is a letter to the editor in the issue for 8 September 1831 signed by 'One of the Swinish Multitude'. The response by readers of this penny journal to that pseudonym was doubtless expected to be immediate. And still later, in Samuel Bamford's *Passages in the Life of a Radical* (1844) where Burke is described as 'the great orator and political apostate', the famous phrase recurs.[2]

This mass of evidence—and there is undoubtedly more of it—provides a striking illustration of literary behaviour that we recognise as habitual in a controversy; the purpose of including it here is to underline the assertion that to concentrate principally on the abstract principles contained in controversial literature is to miss half the significance of such writing. Much more attention should be given to the behaviour of words to which human emotions and attitudes have become indissolubly attached. Burke did not intend by 'a swinish multitude'

---

[1] Op. cit., I, 250.　　　　　[2] Op. cit., (new edn. 1859), p. 408.

a fraction of the meanings appropriated to his words, but generations of men believed that he did; men who had not read the *Reflections* and (like Samuel Bamford's wife) did not know who Burke was would regard the phrase as summing up the attitude of the rich to the poor. Only by careful attention to development of meaning and accumulation of overtones can we explore such evidence and assess its bearing, for example, on the growth of the problem stated by Disraeli in *Sybil*—that of the 'Two nations; between whom there is no intercourse and no sympathy; who are as ignorant of each other's habits, thoughts, and feelings, as if they were dwellers in different zones, or inhabitants of different planets.'[1]

The redirection of a pamphlet to an audience for which it was not originally intended further illustrates the unexpected repercussions of a developing controversy; once the pamphlet is published, the writer as it were loses the initiative and it passes into the hands of other writers who follow. Particularly is this the case with the man, like Burke, whose work triggers off the controversy. The appearance of an influential reply in the shape of the *Rights of Man*, aimed at an audience not catered for by the *Reflections*, meant that Burke's pamphlet had to be rearranged for this new audience if it was to meet the challenge. The abridgement by 'S.J.' (published in 1793 at one shilling) enabled it to do so.[2] S.J. explains in his Advertisement that his object is to counter the effect of Paine's writing—which was 'published in a manner peculiarly suited to the pockets of the lower class of people'—by encouraging the study of the *Reflections* 'among the lower (though certainly not therefore less valuable) orders of his fellow-countrymen'. He has, he claims, 'pruned some little exuberances of genius and effusions of fancy into which [Burke's] lively imagination . . . had sometimes betrayed him' and 'only retrenched such passages as he conceived Mr. Burke himself' would have omitted if he had produced a cheaper version of his own work. The result from our point of view is valuable. The very existence of S.J.'s

---

[1] Op. cit. (1845), I, v.

[2] There had been an earlier abridgement (1791), probably by Thomas Percy, nephew of Dr. Percy, Bishop of Dromore. It was intended, as Percy says in a letter to Burke, 28 February 1791 (Fitzwilliam MSS. (Sheffield)), to put the book within the reach of the poorer classes. Its price was 6*d*.

version is a strong reminder that in the *Reflections* Burke had been addressing a particular section of the reading public; the pruning of the work (not only in the interest of cheapness) lays bare the elements in it that were recognised as being persuasive for his primary audience but would antagonise some other.

A brief glance at the editor's selection of material emphasises more than anything else the extent to which the *Reflections* is a piece of 'class' literature written for people of gentlemanly education and tastes. One of the longest sections omitted by S.J., for example, is that following immediately after the apostrophe (which, significantly enough, is itself retained).[1] In it Burke expounds the consequences of abandoning the 'mixed system of opinion and sentiment' which originated in 'the ancient chivalry'. He foresees that the 'noble equality' extending through 'all gradations of life' will be lost along with the dignity and grace he associates with the ritual of chivalric manners and values; rank will forfeit its traditional respect; citizens will no longer love their country but concern themselves only with their private interests; and 'a swinish multitude' in its brute ignorance will extinguish the learning fostered by 'the spirit of a gentleman, and the spirit of religion'. The persuasiveness of such writing for Burke's primary audience is undeniable; it would prove either repugnant or unintelligible to poorer readers, and S.J. sensibly left it out. Similar considerations dictated the omission of passages with particular cultural implications: Burke's reference to the acting of Garrick and Siddons, coupled with argument based on knowledge of the Greek theatre and theory of tragedy;[2] his discussion of aristocratic education, the 'grand tour', and the tribute to the continuing tradition of monastic education;[3] many classical quotations and the extract from Denham's *Cooper's Hill*.[4] There is other similar evidence, but this is enough to demonstrate in what cultural terms Burke conceived his original audience, and thus what problems faced an editor preparing the text for readers with a totally different educational background. S.J. was also keenly aware of religious feeling other than that Burke assumed in his readers when he was writing the *Reflections*.

[1] *Reflections*, in *Works*, II, 348 l. 41–352 l. 36.
[2] Ibid., II, 353 l. 12–354 l. 19.   [3] Ibid., II, 371 l. 23–372 l. 17.
[4] Ibid., II, 388, 388–389 n.

Wherever possible he omits material offensive to dissenters;[1] he leaves out the paragraph assuring De Pont that the French confiscation of Church lands 'has roused the people' in England to defend the property of their own Church;[2] and he excises Burke's long apology for monastic institutions.[3] The pattern here is obvious enough: S.J. had in mind a mass readership whose loyalty to the established Church and affection for religious tradition could not be counted on; writing which assumed such loyalties would defeat his purpose. Similarly, on the specifically political front, he is careful to withdraw Burke's heightened description of the humiliation of the French king;[4] he omits the claim that the French should have made votes 'proportioned to property' in their new electoral system;[5] Burke's protest that this system has removed power from the country gentlemen and placed it in the hands of the urban masses and monied men, and his adverse comment on voting by ballot also disappear.[6] In other words, though S.J. was powerless to change the essential features of Burke's thesis, the features of it which were unnecessarily offensive to even moderate opinion were removed.

This selection from the valuable evidence provided by S.J.'s edition confirms beyond doubt the extent to which the objectives Burke set out in his letter to Fitzwilliam, 5 June 1791, gave the character to his political theory and to his literary method:

> I do not conceive that any one can be much blamed for an endeavour to keep things in their old & safe course. On that ground, & on full deliberation, I wrote & published my late Reflexions. . . . I wished that Book to be, in the first instance, of service to the publick, in the second, to the party, as a valuable part of that publick. I believe the service of the party was only second in my thoughts: but perhaps it was the first. I am sure its Interests were important considerations with me in every step I have taken on this & on all occasions. . . . I was convinced to a certainty that whatever tended to unsettle the succession, & to disturb the recognised ranks & orders, & the fixed properties in the nation would be of all men the most fatal to your friends, I

[1] Cf. *Reflection*, in *Works*, II, 287 ll. 5–27.
[2] Ibid., II, 376 l. 39–377 l. 10.   [3] Ibid., II, 428 l. 10–434 l. 20.
[4] Ibid., II, 342 l. 37–343 l. 28.   [5] Ibid., II, 447 l. 41–448 l. 12.
[6] Ibid., II, 464 l. 20–466 l. 14; 476 l. 40–477 l. 4.

mean the Prince's friends, & the chiefs of your party, whether you are considered as politicians, or as private men of weight in your country.[1]

The aims set out here are obviously in harmony with the political faith proclaimed by the *Reflections*, but the kind of education, literary taste, aesthetic pre-suppositions, and the general temper of mind Burke assumed in Fitzwilliam and his associates as 'private men'—these features which are revealed by literary-critical analysis are also vitally important to a total assessment of the *Reflections*. Both political, cultural, and literary qualities become clearer when one examines S.J.'s valiant attempt to recast the book for an audience politically, educationally, and socially distinct from the recipient of the above letter.

And it is an assessment of the relationship between a writer, his ideas, and the public he addresses that should constantly exercise the minds of both the historian and the literary critic. E. H. Carr maintains that 'what the historian is called upon to investigate is what lies behind the act',[2] and it seems clear that part of that investigation must be in literary-critical terms. As soon as a political thinker commits himself to paper in an effort to communicate his ideas to people, the persuasive methods he adopts to convey and give vitality to those ideas become matters of critical importance. The one cannot be dissociated from the other—in a very real sense 'the phrase and the manner' give the character to 'the matter'. Paine's theory is organically related to his style, as is Burke's to his; Paine's theory in Burke's style would be a burlesque of both. The value and nature of each writer's philosophy must be established by theoretical analysis, but this task must not be thought adequately fulfilled unless analysis of his rhetoric is recognised as being part of it. It is a total assessment we should aim at in which the findings of the historian, political philosopher, and literary critic complete one another; to imagine that one is self-sufficient without the other two is a serious oversimplification.

[1] Fitzwilliam MSS. (Sheffield).   [2] *What is History?*, p. 46.

APPENDIX

CHRONOLOGICAL SURVEY OF THE CONTROVERSY CONCERNING BURKE'S *REFLECTIONS*, 1790–1793

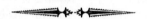

This survey is designed to show the development of the controversy and is based principally on evidence from contemporary newspapers and reviews. The newspapers used are *St. James's Chronicle* (*S.J.C.*) and the *London Chronicle* (*L.C.*), the reviews being the *Monthly Review* (*M.R.*) and the *Critical Review* (*C.R.*). Where a pamphlet was advertised in the Press—'This day was published'—over a period of several days, the date of the first announcement is assumed to have been the day of publication. Titles are shortened wherever possible; the titles of pamphlets (marked by an asterisk) which have been traced only in Press or review notices are given in full. In the case of anonymous pamphlets, where the author is known his name is given in square brackets.

Date of publication	Author	Title and Authority
1790		
1 Nov.	Edmund Burke	*Reflections*, 1790. (*S.J.C.*; *M.R.* Nov.–Dec. 1790.)
9 Nov.	Anon. [John Scott]	*Letter By a Member of the Revolution Society*, 1790. (*L.C.*; *M.R.* Jan. 1790.)
11 Nov.	Anon.	*Short Observations on Burke's Reflections*, 1790. (*L.C.*; *M.R.* Jan. 1791.)

Date of publication	Author	Title and Authority
15 Nov.	Edmund Burke	*Reflections*, 3rd edn., 1790. (*S.J.C.*)
17 Nov.	Anon. [David Williams]	*Lessons to a Young Prince*, 2nd edn., 1790. (*S.J.C.*; *M.R.* March 1791.)
23 Nov.	Richard Price	*A Discourse on the Love of our Country*, 4th edn., 1790. (*L.C.*)
27 Nov.	Anon.	*An Address to the National Assembly of France . . . By a Frenchman*, 1790. (*S.J.C.*; *M.R. Jan.* 1791.)
29 Nov.	Anon. [Mary Wollstonecraft]	*A Vindication of the Rights of Men*, 1790. (*S.J.C.*; *M.R.* Jan. 1791.)
29 Nov.	Anon. [Catherine M. Graham]	*Observations on the Reflections*, 1790. (*S.J.C.*; *M.R.* Jan. 1791.)
7 Dec.	Capel Lofft	*Remarks on the Letter of Burke*, 1790. (*L.C.*; *M.R.* March 1791.)
11 Dec.	Joseph Towers	*Thoughts on the Commencement of a New Parliament*, 1790. (*L.C.*; *M.R.* Feb. 1791.)
18 Dec.	Mary Wollstonecraft	*Vindication*, 2nd edn., 1790. (*S.J.C.*)
Dec. (?)	Anon. [George Rous]	*Thoughts on Government*, 1790. (*M.R.* Feb. 1791.)
Dec. (?)	Robert Woolsey	*Reflections upon Reflections*, 1790. (*C.R.* Jan. 1791.)
1791 12 Jan.	Anon.	*Temperate Comments on Intemperate Reflections*, 1791. (*S.J.C.*; *M.R.* April 1791.)
21 Jan.	Anon.	*Strictures on the Letter of Burke . . . By a Justice of the Peace*, 1791. (*S.J.C.*; *M.R.* April 1791.)
Jan. (?)	Joseph Priestley	*Letters to Burke*, 1791. (*S.J.C.*— mentioned in a letter, 25 Jan.; *M.R.* April 1791.)
Jan. (?)	Anon.	*A Comparison of the Opinions of Burke and Rousseau*, 1791. (*C.R.* Jan. 1791.)
3 Feb.	Sir Brooke Boothby	*A Letter to Burke*, 1791. (*S.J.C.*; *M.R.* May 1791.)
22 Feb.	Thomas Paine	*Rights of Man*, Pt. I, Printed for J. Johnson, 1791. (*S.J.C.*)

APPENDIX

Date of publication	Author	Title and Authority
Feb. (?)	John Butler	*Brief Reflections*, 1791. (*C.R.* Feb. 1791.)
Feb. (?)	Anon.	*A Vindication of Burke's Reflections*, 1791. (*C.R.* Feb. 1791.)
Feb. (?)	M. Rosibonne	*Letter to Burke*, 1791. (*C.R.* Feb. 1791.)
12 March	Thomas Paine	*Rights of Man*, Pt. I, Printed for J. S. Jordan, 1791. (*L.C.*; *M.R.* May 1791.)
15 March	Benjamin Bousfield	*Observations on Burke's Pamphlet*, 1791. (*L.C.*; *M.R.* May 1791.)
29 March	[ed. Thomas Percy?]	*An Abridgement of the Letter of Burke*, 1791; Price 6*d*. (*S.J.C.*)
1 April	Thomas Paine	*Rights of Man*, Pt. I, 3rd edn., 1791. (*S.J.C.*)
2 April	Samuel Cooper	*The First Principles of Civil and Ecclesiastical Government*, Pt. I, 1791. (*Diary of William Windham*, p. 221; *S.J.C.* 4 April; *M.R.* July 1791.)
18 April	Anon.	*Strictures on the Letter of Burke*, 1791. (*S.J.C.*; *M.R.* July 1791.)
19 April	Anon.	**The Wonderful Flights of Edmund the Rhapsodist into the Sublime and Beautiful regions of Fancy, Fiction, Extravagance, and Absurdity, exposed and laughed at*, 1791. (*S.J.C.*; *M.R.* June 1791.)
26 April	M. Capitaine	**Mr. Burke's Magical Squares reduced to their proper form; or, a New Map of France*, 1791. (*S.J.C.*)
27 April	Edward Tatham	*Letters to Burke on Politics*, 1791. (*S.J.C.*; *M.R.* Dec. 1791.)
7 May	James Mackintosh	*Vindiciae Gallicae*, 1791. (*L.C.*; *M.R.* June 1791.)
7 May	Thomas Christie	*Letters on the Revolution of France*, Pt. I, 1791. (*L.C.*; *M.R.* Aug. 1791.)
10 May	Edmund Burke	*Lettre de Mr. Burke à un membre de l'Assemblée nationale de France*, Paris, 1791. (*L.C.*)

S

267

APPENDIX

Date of publication	Author	Title and Authority
10 May	James E. Hamilton	*Reflections on the Revolution in France . . . considered*, 1791. (*L.C.*; *C.R.* May 1791.)
12 May	Anon.	*A Letter to Burke from a Dissenting Country Attorney*, 1791. (*S.J.C.*; *M.R.* June 1791.)
19 May	Edmund Burke	*Reflections*, 10th edn., 1791. (*L.C.*)
19 May	Edmund Burke	*A Letter to a Member of the National Assembly*, 1791. (*L.C.*; *M.R.* July 1791.)
28 May	Anon. [William Belsham]	*Historic Memoir on the French Revolution*,[1] 1791. (*L.C.*; *M.R.* Sept. 1791.)
31 May	Edmund Burke	*Two Letters from Burke, on the French Revolution: one to the translator of his Reflections . . . the other to Capt. W. on the same subject*, 1791. (*L.C.*; *M.R.* July 1791.)
May (?)	George Rous	*Thoughts on Government*, 4th edn., 1791. (*M.R.* May 1791.)
May (?)	Anon.	*A Short Letter to Burke . . . By a Member of Parliament*, 1791. (*Letter*, p. 25, dated 11 May 1791.)
7 June	Anon. [Henry Mackenzie]	*The Letters of Brutus to Celebrated Political Characters*, 1791. (*L.C.*; *M.R.* Aug. 1791.)
June (?)	M. Depont	*Answer to the Reflections of Burke*, 1791. (*M.R.* June 1791.)
2 July	James Mackintosh	*Vindiciae Gallicae*, 2nd edn., 1791. (*S.J.C.*)
July (?)	Anon.	**Lettre d'un Citoyen François à Edmond Burke*, 1791. (*C.R.* July 1791.)
2 Aug.	Anon. [Edmund Burke]	*An Appeal from the New to the Old Whigs*, 1791. (*L.C.*; *M.R.* Nov. 1791.)
27 Aug.	John Scott	*A Letter from Major Scott to Burke*, 1791 (*S.J.C.*)

[1] Extracts from the work with this title are included in the *Comparative Display of the Different Opinions . . . on the subject of the French Revolution*, 1793. In Belsham's *Essays Philosophical and Moral, Historical and Literary*, 1799 (II, 194–277), it is entitled 'Reflections on the French Revolution'.

Date of publication	Author	Title and Authority
20 Sept.	Anon. [Hon. F. Hervey]	*A New Friend on an Old Subject*, 1791. (*L.C.*; *M.R.* Jan. 1792.)
27 Sept.	Thomas Christie	* *The French Constitution* (Pt. I, Vol. II of *Letters on the Revolution of France*), 1791. (*L.C.*)
Sept. (?)	Anon.	*An Heroic Epistle to Burke*, 1791. (*C.R.* Sept. 1791.)
14 Oct.	A. de Calonne	*Considerations on the Present and Future State of France*, 1791. (*S.J.C.*)
Oct. (?)	Anon.	*A Rejoinder to Mr. Paine's Pamphlet . . . By an Englishman*, 1791. (*C.R.* Oct. 1791.)
Nov (?)	Charles Pigott	*Strictures on the new Political Tenets of Burke*, 1791. (*C.R.* Nov. 1791.)
1791	Anon.	*Parallel between the Conduct of Mr. Burke and that of Mr. Fox*, 1791.
1791	Anon.	*Essays on Political Subjects*, 1791.
1791	Edmund Burke	*Thoughts on French Affairs*, 1791.
1791	William L. Bowles	*A Poetical Address to Burke*, 1791.
1791(?)	Anon.	*Reflections on Reflections; or an obscure Author's Answer in prosaical Poetry, to a celebrated Author's Letter in poetical Prose*, n.d. (Ref. in l. 12 to Price who 'is just expiring'; he died 19 April 1791).
1792		
17 Jan.	Francis Stone	*An Examination of Burke's Reflections*, 1792. (*L.C.*; *M.R.* Feb. 1792.)
7 Feb.	Robert Applegarth	* *Rights for Man; or, Analytical Strictures on the Constitution of Great Britain and Ireland*, 1792. (*L.C.*; *C.R.* March 1792.)
16 Feb.	Thomas Paine	*Rights of Man*, Pt. II, 1792. (*L.C.*; *M.R.* March 1792.)
13 March	Anon.	* *The Owl, the Peacock, and the Dove. A Fable addressed to the Rev. Dr. Tatham and the Rt. Hon. Edmund Burke*, 1792. (*L.C.*; *C.R.* April 1792.)

Date of publication	*Author*	*Title and Authority*
March (?)	Anon.	*A Vindication of the Revolution Society against the Calumnies of Mr. Burke. By a Member of the Revolution Society*, 1792. (*C.R.* March 1792.)
19 April	Christopher Wyvill	*A Defence of Dr. Price and the Reformers of England*, 1792. (*L.C.*)
24 May	Arthur Young	*Travels, during the Years 1787, 1788, and 1789*, 1792. (*L.C.*; *M.R.* Jan.–March 1793.)
June (?)	Anon. [John Wolcot]	*Odes of Importance. By Peter Pindar*, 1792. (*M.R.* & *C.R.* June 1792.)
8 Sept.	Thomas Paine	*Rights of Man*, Pts. I & II, Printed for H. D. Symonds, 1792; Price 6*d*. (*L.C.*)
13 Sept.	Anon. [Charles Pigott]	*The Jockey Club*, Pt. III, 1792. (*L.C.*; *M.R.* Oct. 1792.)
4 Oct.	Joel Barlow	*Advice to the Privileged Orders*, Pt. I, 2nd edn., 1792. (*L.C.*)
4 Oct.	Joel Barlow	*The Conspiracy of Kings; A Poem*, 1792. (*L.C.*)
Nov. (?)	Samuel Parr	*A Sequel*, 2nd edn., 1792. (*M.R.* Nov. 1792.)
Nov. (?)	J. Sharpe	*A Rhapsody to E—— B—— Esq.*, 1792. (See above, p. 86.)
8 Dec.	ed. "S.J."	*Burke's Reflections*, Printed for J. Parsons, 1793; Price 1*s*. (*L.C.*)
11 Dec.	George L. Schoen	*Innovation. A Poem*, 1793. (*L.C.*; *M.R.* Jan. 1793.)
15 Dec.	Anon.	*A Comparative Display of the Different Opinions . . . on the subject of the French Revolution*, 1793. (*L.C.*; *M.R.* Feb. 1793.)
1792	Edmund Burke	*Heads for Consideration on the Present State of Affairs*, 1792.
1792 (?)	Anon.	*Paine and Burke contrasted*, n.d.
1793 26 Feb.	Arthur Young	*The Example of France, a Warning to Britain*, 1793. (*S.J.C.*; *M.R.* May 1793.)

Date of publication	Author	Title and Authority
March(?)	Anon. [John Courtenay]	*A Poetical and Philosophical Essay*, 1793. (*M.R.* March 1793.)
Aug. (?)	Robert Hall	*An Apology for the Freedom of the Press*, 1793. (*M.R.* Aug. 1793.)
29 Sept.(?)	Anon. [Daniel I. Eaton]	*Hog's Wash*, No. 1, 1793. (No. 1 dated 29 Sept. 1793.)
Oct. (?)	Anon. [James Parkinson]	*An Address to Burke from the Swinish Multitude. By Old Hubert*, 1793. (*M.R.* Oct. 1793.)
1793	Edmund Burke	*Reflections*, 12th edn., 1793.
1793	Friedrich von Gentz	*Betrachtungen über die französische Revolution*, Berlin, 1793.
1793(?)	Anon. [Thomas Spence?]	*Burke's Address to the Swinish Multitude*, n.d.
1793(?)	Anon. [James Parkinson]	*Pearls cast before Swine, By Edmund Burke, Scraped together by Old Hubert*, n.d.
1793–95	Anon. [Thomas Spence]	*Pig's Meat; or Lessons for the Swinish Multitude*, 1793–95. (Vol. I of 1st edn. entitled, *One Pennyworth of Pig's Meat*.)

INDEX

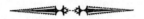

(Works of primary importance in this book are indexed under their titles; authors' names are given separately. For other works the name of the author only is included. Contents of footnotes are not distinguished from entries concerning the text.)

INDEX

Pares, R., 251, 253
Parkin, C., 102
Parkinson, J., 86, 260, 271
Parliamentary History of England, The, 77
Parnell, T., *The Hermit,* 175
Parr, S., 84, 270
Parallel between . . . Burke and Fox (Anon), 269
Passages in the Life of a Radical (Bamford), 260
Passages of a Working Life (Knight), 258
Pearls cast before Swine (Parkinson), 86, 260, 271
Percy, T., 261, 267
Peters, H., 118
Philosophy of Rhetoric, The (Campbell), 123
Pigott, C., 269, 270
Pigs' Meat (Spence), 87, 260, 271
Pitt, W., Earl of Chatham, 23
Pitt, W. (younger), 257
Plato, 126, 169
Poetical Address to Burke (Bowles), 95-6, 269
Poetical and Philosophical Essay, A (Courtenay), 96, 203–5, 271
Poor Man's Guardian, The, 260
Pope, A., 25, 31, 49, 50, 111, 252; Burke alludes to, 126; Courtenay alludes to, 204; *Dunciad,* 165; *Epilogue to the Satires,* 204; *Epistle to a Lady,* 204; *Epistle to Burlington,* 126; *Epistle to Dr. Arbuthnot,* 21; satiric purpose, 24
Portland, 3rd Duke of, 71
Price, R., 113, 165–6, 198, 201, 266; Burke on, 78, 116, 117, 118, 128, 129, 196; religio-political principles of, 90–2; sermon to Revolution Society, 76; use of *Nunc Dimittis,* 117, 128, 170
Priestley, J., 84, 118, 176, 185, 196, 266; confidence in reason, 192, 205, 206, 207; leading opponent of Burke, 90
Prior, J., 81

Proctor, Sir W., 28
Proverbs, Book of, 39
Public Advertiser, The, 17, 33, 46
Pursuits of Literature, The (Mathias), 138

Quincey, T. de, 214

Rambler, The, see Johnson, S.
Rasselas, see Johnson, S.
Reasons for Contentment (Paley), 256–7
Reflections on Reflections (Anon), 96, 200–2, 205, 269
Reflections on the Revolution in France, see Burke, E.
Reflections on the Revolution in France . . . considered (Hamilton), 268
Reflections upon Reflections (Woolsey), 187, 266
Regulations of the Society of the Friends of the People, 89
Rejoinder to Paine's Pamphlet, A (Anon), 269
Remarks on the Letter of Burke (Lofft), 84, 266; analysis of, 187–9, 190
Repository or Treasury of Politics and Literature, The, 18, 27
Revelation, Book of, 110
Review of A Free Enquiry, see Johnson, S.
Revolution Society, The, 76, 116, 189
Rhapsody to E— B— Esq., A (Sharpe), 86, 199–200, 270; illustrations to, 259
Richardson, S., 199
Richmond, 3rd Duke of, 71
Rickman, C., 88
Rights for Man (Applegarth), 269
Rights of Man, The, see Paine, T.
Rockingham, Marquess of, 23, 59–60, 66, 71; and the Wilkes affair, 12–15
Rosibonne, M., 267
Rous, G., 88, 257–8, 266, 268
Rousseau, J. J., 102, 183
Rowe, N., 201, 222
Rudé, G., 11

280

INDEX